W9-ATQ-319

# THE FUTURE OF US-CHINA RELATIONS

## UNA-USA POLICY STUDIES BOOK SERIES

The United Nations Association of the USA is a private, nonprofit organization dedicated to broadening public understanding of the activities of the United Nations and other multilateral institutions. Through its nationwide membership and network of affiliated national organizations, UNA-USA conducts a broad range of programs to inform and involve the public in foreign affairs issues.

The UNA-USA Policy Studies Program conducts projects involving research and analysis of a wide spectrum of policy issues of concern to the international community. The Program brings together panels of interested and knowledgeable Americans to study and make recommendations on specific problems of U.S. foreign policy and multilateral activities. As part of this process, a number of papers are commissioned from leading specialists.

The UNA-USA Policy Studies Book Series contains books based on rewritten and edited collections of some of these papers. UNA-USA is responsible for the choice of the subject areas and the decision to publish the volumes, but the responsibility for the content of the papers and for opinions expressed in them rests with the individual authors and editors.

**Already published:**
*Disaster Assistance: Appraisal, Reform and New Approaches,* edited by Lynn H. Stephens and Stephen J. Green.
*The New International Economic Order: A U.S. Response,* edited by David B. H. Denoon.
*The Politics of Human Rights* edited by Paula R. Newberg.

# THE FUTURE OF US-CHINA RELATIONS

**Edited by**
**JOHN BRYAN STARR**

New York University Press • New York *and* London

**Library of Congress Cataloging in Publication Data**
Main entry under title:

The Future of US-China relations.

(UNA-USA policy studies book series)
Includes index.
1. United States—Relations (general) with China—Addresses, essays, lectures. 2. China—Relations (general) with the United States—Addresses, essays, lectures. I. Starr, John Bryan. II. Series.
E183.8.C5F85 327.73051 81-9581
ISBN 0-8147-7818-6 AACR2

Manufactured in the United States of America

10 9 8 7 6 5 4 3 2

# CONTENTS

# CONTRIBUTORS

LYNN DIANE FEINTECH is Head of Political Analysis in Bank of America's Economics-Policy Research Department. She has written and lectured extensively on economic and political developments in the People's Republic of China and holds a Masters degree in Asian Studies from the University of California at Berkeley. In 1980, Ms. Feintech was a Visiting Fellow at the Overseas Development Council in Washington, DC.

ADMIRAL NOEL GAYLER, USN (Retired), airman and mariner, served as an experimental test pilot, as Assistant Chief of Naval Operations for Research and Development, as Deputy Director, Strategic Target Planning, Joint Chiefs of Staff, as Director, National Security Agency, and as Commander-in-Chief of all US Pacific Forces (CINCPAC). Since his retirement from active duty he has formed associations in space, intelligence, atomic energy, air transport, international affairs and creative leadership. He is a lifelong student of history and foreign politics.

BERNARD K. GORDON is Professor of Political Science, University of New Hampshire. He holds a Ford grant for work on Southeast Asia, which he visited again (including Vietnam) in 1980. He is the author of *Toward Disengagement in Asia, The Dimensions of Conflict in Southeast Asia,* and of recent articles in *Orbis* and *Foreign Affairs*.

DONALD C. HELLMANN is Professor of Political Science and Asian Studies at the University of Washington. He is a specialist in Japanese politics and the international relations of East Asia, and is a frequent consultant to government and private institutions concerned with public issues. His publications include *Japanese Domestic Politics and Foreign Policy* (1969), and *Japan and East Asia* (1972).

WILLIAM A. HEWITT is currently Chairman and Chief Executive Officer of Deere and Company. He is a Director of American Telephone and Telegraph Company, Baxter Travenol Laboratories, Inc., Continental Illinois Corporation, Continental Illinois National Bank and Trust Company of Chicago, and Conoco Inc. He is a member of the Asia Society, Atlantic Institute for International Affairs, the Business Council, Business Committee for the Arts, the Business Roundtable, the Chase Manhattan Bank International Advisory Committee, the Council on Foreign Relations Inc., and Emergency Committee for American Trade. He was Chairman of the National Council for US-China Trade from 1975 through 1978.

JOYCE K. KALLGREN teaches in the Department of Political Science at the University of California, Davis. For some time she served as Vice Chairman of the Center for Chinese Studies at Berkeley. She has travelled to China on numerous occasions, including trips in 1978, 1979 and 1980. Much of the research for her contribution was carried out during the academic year 1978–79, when she was a Research Associate at the Fairbank East Asian Research Center, Harvard University. In 1980 she became Editor of the *Journal of Asian Studies*.

CHONG-SIK LEE is Professor of Political Science at the University of Pennsylvania. His publications include *The Politics of Korean Nationalism* (1963), *Communism in Korea* (1973, co-authored with Robert A. Scalapino), and *The Korean Workers' Party: A Short History* (1978).

STEVEN I. LEVINE teaches East Asian politics and international relations at the School of International Service, the American University in Washington, DC. He has written extensively on Sino-Soviet and Sino-American relations and is completing a book on *World Politics and Revolutionary Power in Manchuria, 1945–1949*.

VICTOR H. LI is President of the East-West Center at the University of Hawaii. He was formerly a member of the faculty at Stanford Law School. Trained at Columbia and Harvard Law Schools, he is a member of the New York Bar. His research interests center on political-legal work in the PRC, including control of deviancy, dispute resolution, regulation of the economy and foreign trade practices. He is also a specialist on public international law, particularly problems involving US-China relations. His publications include *Law and Politics in China's Foreign Trade, Law without Lawyers: A Comparative View of Law in China and the United States, De-recognizing Taiwan: The Legal Problems,* and *The Future of Taiwan.*

CHRISTOPHER H. PHILLIPS is President of the National Council for US-China Trade. Ambassador Phillips served from 1948–53 as a state senator in Massachusetts. After service in the State Department and the Civil Service Commission, he went to the United Nations as US Representative to the Economic and Social Council. Following a period of work with Chase Manhattan Bank and the US Council of the International Chamber of Commerce, he returned to the US Mission to the UN, serving as deputy US representative from 1970–73.

ROBERT A. SCALAPINO is Robson Research Professor of Government, Director of the Institute of East Asian Studies, and Editor of *Asian Survey* at the University of California at Berkeley. He is the author of numerous books and articles on Asia and US foreign policy. Among his recent books are *Elites in the People's Republic of China* (University of Washington Press, 1972), *Asia and the Road Ahead* (University of California Press, 1975), and *The Foreign Policy of Modern Japan* (University of California Press, 1976).

GLENN T. SEABORG, Nobel Prize winner, University Professor of Chemistry and Associate Director of the Lawrence Berkeley Laboratory at the University of California, played a key role in the discovery and development of major sources of nuclear energy. He is the co-discoverer of ten transuranium elements, and served as Chairman of the US Atomic Energy Commission for ten years under three Presidents, beginning with President Kennedy in 1961. He also served in advisory positions to President Eisenhower and President Truman. He was president of the 120,000-member American Chemical Society in 1976.

JOHN BRYAN STARR is Executive Director of the Yale-China Association, an international education and cultural exchange organization based in New Haven. He also serves as Lecturer in the Department of Political Science at Yale University and as Director of East Asian Projects at the United Nations Association of the USA in New York. In this latter capacity, he directs the UNA-USA National Policy Panel to Study US-China Relations, from whose work this book is derived. He has written extensively on contemporary Chinese politics and political thought. His most recent book is *Continuing the Revolution: The Political Thought of Mao* (Princeton University Press, 1979).

# PREFACE

In September 1978 I was asked by the United Nations Association of the USA to chair a newly formed National Policy Panel to Study US-China Relations. The Association had conducted a similar project some twelve years earlier, the product of which was a pair of reports dealing with China's potential role in the world community. I agreed with the Association's assessment that the time was right for a new look at the state of America's relationship with China and the implications of the evolution of that relationship for our position vis-à-vis the other major powers in East Asia.

Progress toward normalization of diplomatic relations between the United States and China had been stalled during the mid-1970s, largely as a result of domestic political considerations in both countries. By the fall of 1978, however, it appeared that progress toward the establishment of diplomatic ties was again possible, despite major unresolved questions, the most important of which was the way in which American relations with the government on Taiwan would be affected by strengthening our ties with Peking.

The panel, as it was finally constituted, was made up of leaders in a range of areas in American public life—the corporate world, academia, the media, and private public affairs organizations concerned with world affairs. Panel members brought to their work on this project considerable familiarity with China and the problems of Sino-American relations as well as a range of views on the problems requiring resolution as our relationship to China developed. The panel held its first meeting in Washington in late October 1979 and mapped out its work for the ensuing eight months. Subpanels were formed to focus on specific aspects of US-China relations: economic considerations; legal problems; strategic implications; and the problems attendant on the establishment of cultural, scientific, and technological exchanges between the two countries.

As the work of these subpanels was getting under way, the announcement was made, on 15 December, that full diplomatic relations between the two countries would be established effective 1 January 1979. At this point the focus of the project shifted somewhat. Although conceived from the outset as dealing with the evolution of the relationship following the establishment of full diplomatic ties, the project had also concerned itself with the way in which this step would be taken. This latter question having been resolved by the action of the Carter administration, the panel turned its attention to the development of all aspects of the new relationship beyond normalization.

In March 1979 the panel traveled to East Asia, visiting Tokyo, Peking, and Taipei and conducting discussions with political and economic policymakers in the three capitals. The delegation visit to China took place immediately following the announcement that Chinese troops were being withdrawn from Vietnam and in the midst of the reassessment, by party and government leaders in China, of the program of economic development known as the Four Modernizations. It was the first nongovernmental group concerned with US-China relations to visit both Peking and Taipei on the same itinerary. Based on its conversations and impressions during this trip, and on extensive discussions among the panel members, a report was formulated containing a number of policy recommendations regarding the evolution of US relations with China. The report was released in July 1979 and was widely distributed to administration officials, members of Congress, the media, and opinion leaders throughout the country.[1] A delegation from the panel met with Cyrus Vance, then secretary of state, and discussed the panel's recommendations with him.

During the course of its work the panel commissioned a number of studies from experts in the various fields with which it was concerned. It is these works, revised and updated, that are presented here. Taken together they provide, I believe, a detailed exploration of the problems that lie ahead as we develop this critically important relationship with a quarter of the world's population after a hiatus of nearly thirty years.

William A. Hewitt
Chairman of the Board, Deere and Company

## NOTE

1. *Beyond Normalization: Report of the UNA-USA National Policy Panel to Study US-China Relations* (New York: UNA-USA, 1979).

# INTRODUCTION

**John Bryan Starr**

Executive Director
Yale-China Association

The eighteen months following the establishment of full diplomatic relations between the United States and China were remarkable because of the speed with which the new relationship was fleshed out. The nearly thirty-year break in contact between Washington and Peking had resulted in the almost complete absence of the legal and institutional framework through which normal political, economic, and cultural interactions between nations are customarily conducted. Although the process of constructing this framework was begun in a modest way following the signing of the Shanghai Communiqué by Richard Nixon and Zhou Enlai in February 1972, both governments moved slowly in their pursuit of this goal because of domestic political and legal constraints.

So stalled had this process become that by 1978 many American observers were convinced that it would not prove possible for the Carter administration to take the major steps required to complete the process of normalization prior to the onset of the 1980 presidential campaign and that the development of US-China relations would remain impeded for another two years. Thus, the simultaneous announcement by President Carter and Chinese Premier Hua Guofeng on 15 December 1979 that full diplomatic relations would be established two weeks later was as startling for most China watchers as it was for the American public as a whole. Public statements at the time suggest that the US State Department had similarly been caught somewhat off guard by the timing of the move, particularly as that move affected US relations with Taiwan.

The process of constructing the framework for a full relationship between the two countries began in earnest with Vice Premier Deng Xiaoping's visit to this country in January 1979. In addition to conducting talks with Carter, Deng and his colleagues signed a number of important agreements during their stay in Washington. The president and the vice premier signed an agreement on science and technology and a cultural agreement. Additional agreements and letters of understanding dealing with cooperation between the United States and China in education, agriculture, space, and high-energy physics were also drafted and signed. Finally, an agreement was concluded on the establishment of consular relations and on the opening of consulates general in the two countries.

Vice Premier Deng's visit was only the first of what became an unparalleled exchange of high-level governmental delegations that took place during the course of 1979. On the Chinese side, Vice Premier Kang Shien and the ministers of petroleum, metallurgy, finance, and foreign trade visited Washington. On the American side, four cabinet-level delegations visited Peking, including the secretaries of Agriculture; Health, Education, and Welfare; the Treasury; and Commerce. During the course of the latter two visits a Trade Agreement between the two countries was drafted and signed, and an agreement was reached concerning the settlement of claims against assets of the two countries that had been frozen when the US trade embargo against the PRC was imposed at the outset of the Korean War.

In August, Vice President Mondale visited China and, in an important speech at Peking University, outlined the administration's plans for the expansion of economic and cultural ties with China. During the vice president's trip an agreement implementing cultural exchanges in 1980–81 was concluded, as was a protocol on cooperation in hydroelectric power and water resource management. The vice president extended an invitation on behalf of Carter to Premier Hua Guofeng to visit the United States in 1980 and, in turn, received an invitation for a return visit by Carter.

In January 1980 Secretary of Defense Harold Brown visited China. Taking place immediately following the Soviet invasion of Afghanistan, Brown's visit added a new dimension to the emerging relationship—that of possible military cooperation. While the administration had hewed closely to its policy of an evenhanded treatment of the Soviet Union and China following normalization, events in Afghanistan caused a marked shift from the earlier position. Brown's visit was reciprocated four months later by the visit to Washington of a Chinese military delegation headed by Geng Biao, vice chairman of the Military Affairs Commission of the Chinese Communist Party. Visits to the United States by the Chinese ministers of health and education also took place in 1980.

Two consulates general were established by the United States in China—one in Guangzhou and one in Shanghai. Chinese consulates general were simultaneously opened in Houston and San Francisco. Exchanges between local-level governments were also developed; delegations were exchanged; and "sister" relationships were established between Chinese and American states, provinces, and cities. Finally, the Trade Agreement concluded in 1979 was approved by Congress in January and took effect on 1 February 1980. Included in the provisions of this agreement was the granting by the United States of most-favored-nation (MFN) treatment for China.

Private exchanges between the two countries burgeoned during the first eighteen months after normalization. Numerous commercial contacts were established, and Chinese and American businessmen exchanged visits, studied each other's industrial strengths and needs, and in some instances concluded contracts. In 1979 two-way trade between the United States and China was double that in 1978. More than 40,000 American tourists visited China in 1979, and the projections for 1980 were even higher. Some 2,500 Chinese visited this country in 1979, the majority as members of the many governmental and institutional delegations sent to the United States by China. The first group of thirty American scholars to participate in the Committee on Scholarly Communication with the PRC program of academic exchanges traveled to China for research and language work. Meanwhile, institution-to-institution academic exchanges proliferated, provided the facilities for numerous Chinese and American scholars to visit one another's countries for research and training programs.

As a result of this quite remarkable spate of visits, discussions, and agreements during 1979 and 1980, much of the framework requisite to the conduct of a normal relationship has been put in place and many of the most critical problems in that relationship have been at least tentatively resolved. As a result, it seems likely that the pace of the development of US-China ties in the months ahead will be more measured. The inauguration of a new administration in this country has also served to reduce the possibility of the rapid undertaking of major new initiatives.

Similarly, on the Chinese side, there are factors that are likely to result in a somewhat less frenetic pace in developing ties with the United States in the coming months. It is a period during which Deng Xiaoping is attempting to consolidate his approach to political and economic development as he prepares for his future retirement. In the political sphere he has recently accomplished a series of major appointments to positions of party and state authority of relatively younger men with broad practical experience and with views parallel to his own. In the economic sphere, it is the second year of a three-year-long reassessment and readjustment of the goals and policies of the Four Modernizations program, designed to develop China's agriculture, industry, defense establishment, and scientific and technological capability.

In the articles presented in this volume, various viewpoints and opinions are brought to bear on the problems and prospects for the development of US-China relations in the 1980s. The development of economic ties is clearly among the most important aspects of the relationship. Lynn Feintech discusses the effect China's internal economic readjustment will have on the growing interaction between the Chinese economy and the world economy. She sets forth the major steps that have been taken in the United States and in China to permit effective economic interaction and provides a sound basis for an assessment of the future of US-China trade.

At the outset of the process of normalization, our relations with China tended to be conceived of in something of a vacuum: China was treated as a special case in American foreign policy. Subsequently, the development of ties with Peking were often treated exclusively on the basis of the effect it would have on our relations with Moscow. To provide a corrective view, the treatment of the other critical aspects of US-China relations—the political and strategic—a symposium is presented, in which experts in Soviet, Korean, Japanese, and Southeast Asian politics discuss the emergent relationship between the United States and China from the viewpoint of Moscow, Seoul, Pyongyang, Tokyo, and the capitals of the Southeast Asian states. Steven Levine discusses the ways in which the Soviet Union feels itself threatened by the developing ties between Peking and Washington, noting that Soviet leaders were thwarted in their expectations that Mao's death would result in an improvement in Sino-Soviet relations. Chong-sik Lee describes the reaction in Seoul and Pyongyang to the tentative resolution of the Taiwan question by the US government and discusses the effect of US-China relations on the possibilities for future resolution of the division of Korea. Donald Hellmann describes how the development of Sino-Japanese ties served to pave the way for normalization of US-China relations, depicts Japanese reluctance to being drawn into a tripartite alliance with the United States and China aimed against the Soviet Union, and argues for closer consultation between Washington and Tokyo on issues of mutual concern in East Asia as Chinese power and influence in the region grow. Bernard Gordon argues that the timing of the normalization of relations between the United States and China can best be understood in the context of a series of events involving the Soviet Union, Vietnam, China, Japan, and the United States; he also explains the relatively cautious position taken by the Association of Southeast Asian Nations (ASEAN) with regard to the development of ties between China and the United States. Finally, Robert Scalapino weighs the policy options available to the United States in its interaction with the Asian-Pacific nations and argues forcefully for what he calls an "equilibrium" policy that avoids a significant tilt in the direction of either Moscow or Peking. He also advocates the maintenance and strengthening of our existing alliances in East Asia.

The development of scientific, technological, and cultural relations between the United States and China is discussed by Joyce Kallgren in a chapter that constitutes the first overview of the history of the development of these ties and the organizations responsible for their conduct on both sides. She points to the problems that are likely to arise from the lack of parallelism between Chinese and American sponsoring organizations as well as from the growing tendency for exchanges to be carried out on an institution-to-institution basis rather than under American governmental supervision.

In these three parts, Christopher Phillips, Noel Gayler, and Glenn Seaborg, members of the UNA-USA National Policy Panel to Study US-China Relations who served as subpanel chairmen, offer their views on the essays that contributed to the conclusions reached by their respective subpanels and that were incorporated in the panel's report and recommendations.

The question of Taiwan, while temporarily resolved in such a way as to permit the establishment of diplomatic relations between the United States and China, remains a potential problem for the future development of relations between Washington and Peking. Victor Li discusses the legal implications of the formulas devised by the US government to permit a continuing relationship with Taiwan following normalization of relations with the PRC. He goes on to suggest the ways in which the Taiwan question may once again reinsert itself as a problem for the United States in the future.

Finally, in the Conclusion, I suggest the importance of a realistic approach by both China and the United States in the building of the new relationship as a means for avoiding the pendulum swings between love and hate that have characterized that relationship during the last century and more.

Taken as a whole, then, the collection of papers that follows suggests that, while the prospect for the development of US-China relations is generally favorable, the problems that have beset the relationship in the past have by no means all been finally settled. It further suggests that we are far from having achieved unanimity in this country with regard to how those problems are to be resolved in the future. We now have sufficient experience, however, to have gained some perspective on our new ties with China. Moreover, a new administration has recently taken office in Washinton. It is thus a particularly appropriate time to reconsider, with the aid of the material presented here, the problems and prospects for US-China relations beyond normalization.

# I. ECONOMIC ASPECTS OF THE FUTURE OF US-CHINA RELATIONS

## Chapter 1

# MODERNIZATION IN THE PRC: WHAT DOES IT MEAN FOR US-CHINA RELATIONS?

**LYNN D. FEINTECH**

Head of Political Analysis
Economics-Policy Research Department, Bank of America

### INTRODUCTION

In 1978 China began a massive campaign to modernize the economy by the year 2000. The campaign was undertaken with the same fervor and enthusiasm that had characterized past political movements in China, for the modernization effort was not only an economic program—it was a political campaign and an ideological struggle. The campaign marked a turn away from the policy of economic self-reliance, relegating self-reliance to an end goal instead of a means of achieving development.

Integral to the modernization drive was an "opening to the West," in both a commercial and a philosophical sense. China began to study the advanced industrial countries, particularly Japan, as role models for rapid economic development. Moreover, Yugoslavia and Hungary were scrutinized for the adaptations they had made in their socialist economies. Most important, China showed a new openness to questions of economic development and began to emphasize local experimentation within the economy in order to find the policies that would best serve the entire country.

There were two rationales behind the emphasis on economic development. First, China needed to strengthen the economy in order to stand up to the potential threat posed by the Soviet Union. China's industrial sector was too weak to provide the inputs for both defense and civilian needs. The opening to the West was an extension of a policy that identified the Soviet Union, and not the United States, as the major enemy. The second motivation for the policy shift was the low standard of living within China. The ten years of the Cultural Revolution and the "Gang of Four" had disrupted the industrial and transport sectors of the economy, severely affecting output. Moreover, the Cultural Revolution's stress on ideology and continuous revolution had displaced managers and officials who based their authority on technical competence with cadres who had political credentials.

Since the introduction of the plan, there have been a number of major readjustments to the plan's initial targets. The role for imports of equipment and technical expertise had been narrowed. The original emphasis on heavy industry had been reduced, with agriculture and light industry now accorded the first and second priority, respectively. The readjustments have continued throughout 1980, and further reductions in the pace and scope of the modernization effort should be anticipated. However, it is significant to note that the direction of the overall policy remains constant, two and one-half years after the plan was first introduced.

To keep support among the people for the emphasis on economic development, former Vice Premier Deng Xiaoping and other leaders are moving at a rapid pace to try to obtain a visible improvement in the standard of living. Officials are hoping to increase the grain ration and the availability of consumer goods in order to insure continued support for their policies. If tangible results are not seen, however, those officials who support the concept of self-reliance and of a more insular China will find support for their belief that any dependence on foreign countries in the modernization effort is too great a compromise for China to make. Along those lines, if China's foreign debt were to increase to the point where foreign exchange obligations were a burden on the economy, a backlash might also be felt. It is for these reasons that Deng and others have been insistent that exports be promoted and export capacity be increased. In addition, China has made clear to its trading partners in the industrialized countries that their markets must remain open to Chinese goods if China's imports from the industrial countries are to be increased. Such demands will not be easily met if there is continued slow growth among the industrial countries and increased protectionism.

The effect of China's modernization plan on US-China relations has been dramatic. China's move away from ideological campaigns and away from self-reliance sparked the attention of all governments of the industrialized countries. Once again the potential of the "China market" was held out to the international business community, and concern arose in the United States that US economic interests would suffer in the absence of diplomatic relations. More important, however, was a belief among many officials in the US government that the new pragmatic leadership of the PRC presented the opportunity for a new working relationship to be built between the two countries.

The move to open relations with the PRC was not without opposition in the United States. Concerns were voiced that the United States was sacrificing an ally—Taiwan—for the commercial prospects held out by a rapidly developing China. With the shift of recognition to the PRC, US-Taiwan relations were handled by a US corporation created by the Congress and staffed by US government employees on leave. Economic relations between the United States and Taiwan continued to grow, and informal governmental ties remained strong. While the Mutual Defense Treaty between Taiwan and the United States ended in 1980, the United States reserved the authority to sell defensive weapons to Taiwan. Relations with Taiwan have not proved to be a significant issue between the United

States and China, although the possibility of closer US-Taiwan ties was raised by Ronald Reagan in the 1980 presidential campaign.

The rate at which the US-China relationship has developed has outpaced most expectations. Spurred in part by the Soviet invasion of Afghanistan, relations moved forward to the point that by the summer of 1980 the United States had agreed to sell China technology with military applications, short of actual weapons. Technical, commercial, and educational exchanges rapidly increased, and numerous protocols in these areas were signed by the two countries. These exchanges and protocols provided a means for the two countries to build a relationship quickly, overcoming the diplomatic break that had existed for almost thirty years.

The US-China commercial relationship has developed slowly, mirroring China's cautious approach in increasing levels of trade and foreign debt. Unexpectedly, the short-term commercial benefits of the US-China relationship have been overshadowed by confluence of the two countries' political concern. This confluence largely centers on the anti-Soviet policies of each country; however, it has spread to other areas as well. Although an alliance between the two countries does not exist, it should no longer be ruled out as a long-term possibility.

The developments in the US-China relationship since 1978 are not without risk. The United States has abandoned, at least temporarily, its evenhanded approach to relations with the Soviet Union and China. A Trade Agreement has been signed with China, extending to the PRC "most-favored-nation" tariff treatment and the facilities of the US Export-Import Bank. Reimbursable aid has been approved for China, and export controls have been eased. Yet China is still advocating an economic and political system that is at odds with that of the United States. The East-West aspects of the relationship could resurface quickly, particularly if China and the United States found themselves on opposing sides in a regional conflict. Moreover, there are North-South issues to be considered. China is becoming increasingly active in international political and financial institutions. As a developing country, China is likely to side with other LDCs in pushing for economic and financial reforms that have as their goal a transfer of resources from the developed to the developing world.

Thus, the road ahead is not without its pitfalls. The US-China relationship is bound to be strained, as the interests of the two countries diverge. At present the United States and China are linked by a common concern—the Soviet Union. What remains unclear is whether the domestic situation in each country and the international environment will foster a long-term relationship, built on common goals rather than on common concerns.

## CHINA'S MODERNIZATION EFFORT

The introduction of a development plan by Premier and Party Chairman Hua Guofeng in March 1978 signaled a shift in the priorities of the Chinese leadership. The emphasis was to be on rapid economic development, with a major role in such development to be played by the foreign business community. The plan, as originally outlined, was clearly a political document. Many of the goals were unattainable within the seven-year time frame (1978–85) initially specified. However, the importance of the plan rested in its symbolic representation of the new leadership's intent to focus the energies of the nation on rapid modernization (see Table 1).

The plan embodied an emphasis on the Four Modernizations, first introduced by the late Premier Zhou Enlai. Industry, agriculture, defense, and science and technology were all to be modernized. However, the four sectors were not to be treated equally. Although lip service was paid to agriculture as the first priority, the program's main emphasis was on the development of industry.

The use of the catch phrase "Four Modernizations" proved to be a useful political tool. It gave some continuity to the leadership's approach by harking back to previous government policies. Even more important, however, the Four Modernizations represented a link to the late Zhou Enlai, a man who had strong support among the Chinese people. While the plan

Table 1. China's Ten-Year Development Plan 1976–85 (as introduced, March 1978)

| |
|---|
| Build 120 Large-Scale Projects, Including: |
| 10 Iron and steel complexes |
| 10 Oil and gas fields |
| 9 Nonferrous metal complexes |
| 8 Coal mines |
| 30 Power stations |
| 6 Railway trunk lines |
| 5 Major harbors |
| The Key Targets to Be Met by 1985: |
| Steel production to more than double to 60 million metric tons |
| Grain production to increase from 295 to 400 million metric tons |

*Source:* Author.

has been significantly readjusted since its introduction in 1978, this tie to Zhou's policies had not been downplayed.

In looking at the readjustments that have taken place since the plan's introduction, each has led to a successively slower pace of development and to a lower priority for heavy industry. As policy now stands, agriculture is to be emphasized, followed by light industry, and finally by heavy industry. Heavy industry is further broken down into specific sectors, only a few of which are to be targeted for substantial investment. The plan itself has also been downplayed and has been replaced by an emphasis on a policy of economic modernization. A new Ten-Year Plan is due to be introduced for the period 1981–90.

## THE TEN-YEAR DEVELOPMENT PLAN IS INTRODUCED: MARCH 1978

The plan, as initially introduced, outlined 120 large industrial projects, scheduled for completion by 1985. Many of the projects called for imports of whole plants, equipment, and foreign expertise. Along with these major industrial projects, China was to continue to rely on small- and medium-sized industrial facilities in almost all sectors of the economy. These smaller projects were to serve to alleviate transport bottlenecks as well as to reduce capital expenditures required by the central government. In most cases funds for these small- and medium-sized projects were to be generated locally.

With the readjustments, the number of major projects scheduled for construction has been reduced. Nevertheless, an overview of the original plan will provide a means of summarizing the problems facing China in various industrial sectors. In addition, although the scope of the plan has been reduced in the short run, similar types of projects will ultimately be essential if China is to modernize successfully.

*Ten Iron and Steel Complexes.* Iron and steel account for China's largest single import category, and reductions of these imports would be an important step for China. The PRC has the necessary natural resources. Reserves of both coal and iron ore are extensive, although much of the iron ore is of poor quality. Ten new complexes were planned as a means of more than doubling China's output of steel over the life of the plan to a figure of 60 million metric tons. However, insufficient transport facilities and shortages of electric power have proved too great a constraint to allow for such rapid development of this industrial sector. In addition, lack of quality control in steel fabrication must be overcome if the steel produced is to be up to industrial standards. In the revisions of the plan, iron and steel had been dramatically downgraded, and only one major steel complex (Baoshan, outside Shanghai) is still scheduled for construction with foreign participation.

*Ten Oil and Gas Fields.* The new oil and gas fields envisioned by the plan were to be comparable in size to Daqing, which in 1979 accounted for 40 percent of China's crude oil output. Readjustments have scaled back these plans, and development of new fields will be less rapid. Medium-term potential for new fields is greatest in the North China Basin, near Peking, where both onshore and offshore reserves can be tapped. Offshore reserves in the South China Sea provide another, slightly less accessible area for development, although exploration may be complicated by boundary disputes among the countries in the area. Proven natural gas reserves are to be found, in large part, in the province of Sichuan. In the long term, reserves of both gas and oil are thought to be plentiful in the thinly population and relatively inaccessible northwest region of China. The Chinese leadership has been candid in admitting that the scope of onshore and offshore resources remain unknown. When questioned in March 1979 by the United Nations Association Panel on the scope of China's oil reserves, Vice Premier Li Xiannian responded, "I myself can get no satisfactory results from the study of the question. Oil will be important, but finding out how much we have is a problem. George Bush cited [reserve] figures to us. I asked him how he knew."[1] A partial answer to this question will be forthcoming in 1981. Analysis of seismic studies conducted by major international oil companies should be complete, giving the first extensive data on China's offshore potential. Onshore reserves will remain an area of supposition.

Crude oil figures significantly in China's export plans and will be an important source of foreign exchange earnings. Unfortunately, in 1978 and 1979 there were only minimal increases in China's crude oil output. Production expanded at a rate of approximately 2 percent each year. As a result, in late 1979 the government invited foreign companies to engage in onshore exploration, a shift from the initial Chinese position limiting them to offshore areas. Moreover, the government agreed to consider production-sharing arrangements, whereby foreign companies could take oil in repayment for their investment. Such arrangements would allow China to acquire foreign technology and expertise without any outlay of foreign currency.

Petrochemical exports will increase significantly during the 1980s. Between 1981 and 1985 four imported ethylene plants, each with a capacity of 300,000 metric tons, will begin prodution. This increased capacity is significant when compared with 1979's output of 435,000 metric tons. Development of polyester fibers will add to domestic textile supplies as well as exports.

*Nine Nonferrous Metal Complexes.* While the Chinese are uncertain as to the quantity and accessibility of their petroleum reserves, proven reserves do exist for many of the nonferrous metals. Copper, antimony, tin, tungsten, and bauxite are but a few of the metals that are both abundant in supply and relatively accessible. The quality of copper deposits is not yet known, although feasibility studies now under way should soon make clear China's potential in this area. In the past many of these metals were not exported in large quantities, although policies to foster export expansion should alter this situation. In the near term, China considers production-sharing arrangements to be an important means of attracting foreign participation in exploration and extraction efforts. However, development of new mines will be hampered by inadequate roads, rails, and power supplies.

*Eight Coal Mines.* The plan set a goal of doubling coal production over a ten-year period from the 1977 level of 500 million metric tons. China's reserves of coal, outstanding in quantity and for the most part in quality, are located primarily in the north of the country. At present, coal supplies more than 70 percent of China's energy needs, and this situation must continue if China is to expand crude oil exports. Unfortunately, developments in this sector are being held back by inadequate transport links. It is possible that technology such as mine-mouth thermal plants, which produce power at the minesite, could alleviate the need for rails to move bulk coal. However, transmission links to carry the electric power to the needed areas would then have to be built—a situation that underscores the drag on various sectors caused by inadequate infrastructure.

*Thirty Power Stations.* The readjustments to the plan have served to increase the emphasis to be placed on expansion of China's electric power output. Mine-mouth thermal plants and hydroelectric power are two major areas from which China hopes to draw increased capacity. Success in increasing electric power is crucial to China's drive for modernization. Yet, at present, this sector is the "weak link" in the economy; hydroelectric power accounts for approximately 2 percent of China's energy needs, even though China has the world's largest hydroelectric potential. Simultaneous development of large, medium, and small hydroelectric projects was envisioned by the initial plan as a means of rapid expansion of this sector, with maximum reliance on locally generated funds. Subsequent readjustments have increased the emphasis on large hydroelectric projects, particularly along the Yangzi River. However, the capital outlays required for such projects will slow the timetable for their construction. Nuclear energy remains an option only for the long term. Expansion in this area would require imports of entire nuclear plants, an approach China is currently rethinking in light of its finite foreign exchange reserves.

*Six Railway Trunk Lines.* The transport sectors, along with the power sector, are holding back growth in other industrial sectors of the economy. At present, 70 percent of China's freight is transported by rail, and raw material shortages have often been the result of inadequate rail transport rather than of shortages in domestic supplies. Lack of adequate transport has also led to a policy of importing grain to feed the coastal urban areas, in order to avoid dependence upon transport from the inland rural areas. In the rail sector, existing lines are to be modernized and, in certain cases, double-tracked. Along with construction of new lines, some automation is to be accomplished, relying in part on imports of both equipment and expertise.

*Five Major Harbors.* Port capacity is a major constraint in any increase in China's foreign trade and therefore a major constraint in meeting the goals of the modernization drive. China suffers both from insufficient depth in its ports and from a lack of modern container facilities, although efficient use of containers is also hampered by the inadequate rail system. While port expansion must remain a priority, foreign participation in this sector is now limited to feasibility studies and selected equipment imports.

*Agriculture.* A broad-ranging agricultural investment program called for expanded mechanization as well as for improved inputs to agriculture. Improvements in inputs to agriculture were necessary if the plan's target of a 4 to 5 percent annual growth in grain output was to be achieved. The specific target set for 1985 was 400 million metric tons of grain, compared with 1978 production of 300 million metric tons. Eighty-five percent mechanization in all major processes of farm work was to be achieved by 1985. By the end of the plan there was to be a major chemical fertilizer plant in each of the thirty-one provinces. In 1978, thirteen were already completed or under construction. Seed breeding was to be improved, a burden that would fall primarily on China's own scientists. This was because China's stress on multiple cropping made it necessary to develop seeds suited to China's agricultural conditions.

With the readjustments to the plan, the emphasis on agriculture has increased, although the goals for mechanization have been put aside. Policies have been instituted that rely on material incentives to increase agricultural output. In 1979 the government increased by 20 percent the price paid to peasants for compulsory amounts of grain sold to the state. For grain sold to the state beyond the required amount, the purchase price was increased by 50 percent. At the same time, prices for inputs to agriculture were lowered. Farm machinery, chemical fertilizer, insecticides, and other goods manufactured for farm use were made available at a reduced price, even though supply rather than price was often the limiting factor. The government indicated its intention to gradually increase the purchase price for cotton, edible oil, sugar, animal by-products, and aquatic and fresh products. In addition, rural free markets were reintroduced after an absence of ten years.

The impact of the renewed emphasis on agriculture was reflected in the 1979 production statistics. Grain output increased 9 percent, reaching 332 million metric tons.[2] Per capita grain supplies, which had been lower in 1977 than they had been in 1957, surpassed their previous peak.[3]

Further pricing increases in November 1979 affected eight nonstaple food items: pork, beef, mutton, poultry, fish, eggs, milk, and vegetables. Moreover, that same month price controls were lifted on more than 10,000 farm and manufactured goods, following twenty-three years of essentially stable prices. Special supplements of 5 yuan ($3.30) per month were paid to urban workers to offset these price increases.

The increases in government procurement prices, along with the November 1979 measures, should continue to contribute to further production gains in 1980. However, the pace of these price changes has been too rapid, and future policy shifts are likely to be more gradual. Deng Xiaoping admitted this in January 1980, commenting that while the increase in procurement prices was correct, the price changes should have been phased in.[4]

*Light Industry.* The light industry is now the second priority for development. Production is being expanded to provide goods both for the domestic market and for exports. While investment in the sector is rising, light industry suffers from the constraints of China's inadequate infrastructure. Supplies of raw materials for processing and distribution of finished products are hampered by weak transportation links. Plants have been unable to run at full capacity because of insufficient electric power. As a result, in the near term new factories are likely to be located in the better-developed coastal urban areas. Moreover, many of the new factories producing goods for export will be located near Guangzhou (Canton) in order to make use of the improving transport links to Hong Kong.

## THE FIRST READJUSTMENT: DECEMBER 1978

The Communiqué of the Third Plenary Session of the Eleventh Central Committee of the Chinese Communist Party (CCP) served to give official notification of a shift in China's approach to modernization. "The session thoroughly discussed questions in agriculture and held that the whole Party should concentrate its main energy and efforts on advancing agriculture as fast as possible. . . . The rapid development of the national economy as a whole and the steady improvement in the living standards of the whole country depends on the vigorous restoration and speeding up of farm production.''[5]

The shift in focus to accord agriculture the highest priority reinforced concerns voiced by Hu Qiaomu, president of the Chinese Academy of Social Sciences, who had addressed the State Council in July 1978. In November 1978 a summary of his speech was published. Hu noted the disparity in the standard of living between the urban and rural areas and indicated further work was necessary to raise the living standards of the peasants. Agriculture was to be the key to China's socialist development, for, as Hu bluntly stated, ''One cannot expect to build a modern, prosperous socialist China on the basis of a poverty-stricken, backward countryside; this is quite obvious.''[6]

Both the Communiqué of the Third Plenum and Hu's speech to the State Council addressed certain policy changes that would be necessary if modernization were to succeed. Two major areas discussed were the need to rely on economic laws and economic management and the need for more decentralization in decision making.

As with his points on agriculture, Hu stated the problem quite directly: ''there are still quite a number of cadres directing economic work in industry and agriculture who either do not recognize the objective nature of economic laws and who refuse to take economic laws as such into account. . . . These comrades have forgotten that . . . over and above the economic laws and in objective existence, politics itself cannot create other laws and impose them on the economy.''[7] The Communiqué of the Third Plenum took this concept one step further by citing to China's need for political stability: ''It has been shown in practice that whenever we maintain the society's necessary political stability and work according to objective economic law, our national economy advances steadily and at a high speed; otherwise our national economy develops slowly or even stagnates and falls back.''[8] Integral to this reliance on economic principles was a focus on the law of value: "the value of every commodity is determined by the socially necessary labor time required to produce it."[9] To rely on the law of value, "we must see to it that all enterprises (including the defense industry) make strict economical use of time, constantly strive for the best possible ratio between the expenditure of labor and material (materialized labor) and economic results, practice strict business accounting, strive to lower the unit cost of production, and raise labor productivity and the rate of profit on funds invested. . . . No enterprise and no worker should be allowed to waste time, not even a single minute, and both should be held responsible for losses caused by the waste of time."[10]

Decentralization of planning and decision making was another key decision taken by the Third Plenum. The balance between centralization and decentralization has been a longstanding debate within the Chinese Communist Party, and various shifts in that balance have been favored during the past thirty years. The Communiqué of the Plenum states that "one of the serious shortcomings in the structure of economic management in our country is the overconcentration of authority, and it is necessary boldly to shift it under guidance from the leadership to lower levels so that the local authorities and industrial and agricultural enterprises will have greater power of decision in management under the guidance of unified state planning."[11] This policy of decentralization has had a particularly marked effect on the foreign trade sector of the economy. Foreigners are now dealing directly either with local branches of the foreign trade corporations or with individual factories and communes that are the actual end users or producers of a product.

The first major readjustment to the development plan was significant in that it not only reordered priorities but also gave a more concrete direction to the policies that would underlie the entire modernization process. The Communiqué of the Third Plenum marked a public return to support for the importance of economic management and economic principles in China's road to socialism. This shift was underscored by the appointment of veteran economic planner Chen Yun as a vice chairman of the Communist Party, as well as head of the party's new disciplinary commission. Out of favor since 1958, Chen had been on record as supporting a gradual, balanced approach to economic development.

## THE SECOND READJUSTMENT: FEBRUARY 1979

News of the second readjustment came, not from internal documents of the Chinese Communist Party, but from the Japanese firms trading with China. In late February eight Japanese trading companies were informed by cable that several plant and machinery contracts had been frozen, owing to questions of financing. Included among contracts so frozen was the Nippon Steel construction of the Baoshan steelworks, outside Shanghai. The Baoshan contract was considered signed by most outside observers. However, it soon became known that a condition of the contract had been approval within a sixty-day period by each party's government. When that sixty-day period ran out, Chinese government approval had not been given.

The freezing of the Japanese contracts led to concerns within the foreign business community as to China's commitment to significantly increase imports of plant and equipment. In retrospect, the freeze was indicative of two problems. First, too many contracts were under simultaneous negotiation, without sufficient coordination among the various Chinese organizations involved. Second, the Bank of China determined that although China had not yet run out of hard currency, contract signings at the rapid pace that had been set would soon exhaust foreign exchange reserves.

As a result of both of these situations, a need for more coordination and planning in the foreign trade sector became clear. However, this need for coordination was bound to bring with it increased centralization of decision making at the very time that decentralization was being stressed. With these contradictions in mind, decisions were taken both to tighten control over foreign exchange and to elevate the importance of the external sector of the economy, while more local automony was granted in contract negotiations.

In April the Bank of China, the foreign exchange arm of the People's Bank of China (PBC), was moved out from under the PBC and put directly under the State Council. At the same time, a new group was created to monitor China's foreign exchange situation. Called the General Administration of Exchange Control (GAEC), this group was given the responsibility of drafting decrees to unify China's foreign exchange control and of examining and supervising the commercial and noncommercial foreign exchange balance of payments.[12] The Bank of China would then be able to concentrate on "the international clearance of all commercial and noncommercial exchange, the organization of foreign funds in a planned way, and the handling of import and export credits and loans."[13]

At the same time that these organizational changes were instituted, a marked slowdown in the pace of import contract negotiations occurred. As an outgrowth of the December readjustment, heavy industrial import negotiations became more selective. An emphasis was also placed on investigating the potential for certain inputs to light industry, to increase production for both the domestic and foreign markets.

### THE THIRD READJUSTMENT: JUNE 1979

The Second Session of the Fifth National People's Congress (NPC) gave official approval to the readjustments in the modernization plan that had occurred since its introduction at the 1978 session of the Fifth NPC. The speeches and communiqués of the congress made clear China's continued commitment to modernization, but at a slower pace and with greater selectivity among projects. A high priority was assigned to monitoring and expanding the external sector of the economy. Foreign participation in China's development was encouraged through the joint-venture law approved by the congress. Finally, more efficient economic management was stressed, at both the level of the government and the level of the individual enterprise.

Hua Guofeng's speech to the congress reflected the increased priority given to agriculture and light industry, as well as the selectivity in heavy industrial projects: "The main problem now facing us is that our agricultural expansion cannot yet keep up with the demands of a growing population. Many important products of the light and textile industries are insufficient in quantity, poor in quality and limited in variety, so there are not enough marketable goods. Although the coal, petroleum and power industries and the transport and communication services have grown at a relatively swift pace, they still lag behind what is required by our expanding economy. . . . In capital construction, far too many projects are being undertaken at the same time and many will not contribute to our production capacity for years."[14]

Hua's speech, along with other documents from the congress, indicated that the government had come to terms with the need for a more modest modernization program over the years 1979–81. Described as the "three years of readjustment," they were to be followed by a Sixth Five-Year Plan for the period 1981–85. Thus, the entire concept of a ten-year modernization plan for the period through 1985 had been dropped. The economic goals set out for the period 1979–81 were much less specific than the goals in the initial plan, and there were no precise output targets. Instead, a series of "major aims" was set forth by Hua, including:

- relative correspondence between the growth of grain production and other sideline production on the one hand and that of population and industry on the other
- growth in light and textile industries at a rate equal to or slightly greater than that of heavy industry; output in light and textile industries to increase in line with the rise in domestic purchasing power, as well as in line with expanded export targets
- increased production, as well as conservation, in the fuel and power industries and the transport and communication services; increased production, along with better quality and more variety, in metallurgical, machine-building, chemical, and other heavy industries
- a narrower scope of capital construction, allowing for a

concentration on major projects; attention to reduced costs, and shortened construction periods for such projects
- increased average income of all peasants from the collectives and in the average wage of all nonagricultural workers and staff[15]

Continued reliance on foreign participation in the modernization process was reinforced both in statements made during the congress and by the approval of the joint-venture law. Hua indicated in his speech that the government would continue to carry out the policy of "actively importing advanced technology and making use of funds from abroad."[16]

The joint-venture law, which went into effect on 8 July 1979, marked a new phase in China's treatment of foreign businesses: foreigners were to be given the right to own Chinese resources. The role of law was elevated—in sharp contrast to its position during the previous thirteen years, a change that affected not only the foreign business community but, more significantly, the people of China. The congress passed a total of seven laws—six of which solely addressed China's citizens. These included a criminal law and a law of criminal procedure.

The Fifth Congress reinforced the shift toward economic management that had been apparent during the previous eight months. Hua stated: "We should ensure a system of clearly defined job responsibility for everyone from the top down in every enterprise, so that there is a person responsible for each link in the production process, and production and operation will be organized along rational, efficient, and civilized lines."[17] In line with the shift toward assessment of an individual's performance was a clarification of how the state was to deal with the performance of individual enterprises: "Badly managed enterprises which have shown deficits over a long period should reverse the situation and turn from deficits to profit within a year or must stop operation and undergo a shake-up; they will get no subsidies from the government or credits from the bank."[18] This renewed role for banks, a role that was abrogated during the Cultural Revolution, had been advocated earlier by Hu Qiaomu.[19] Hua Guofeng himself had stated to the 1978 session of the NPC that "We must fully utilize finance, banking and credit in promoting and supervising economic undertakings."[20] This return to the use of the banking system to monitor the efficiency and profitability of enterprises was to insure a reliance on more objective economic law in the planning process.

Finally, the congress named Chen Yun vice premier and head of the State Finance and Economic Commission under the Standing Committee of the NPC. These appointments, along with Chen's party position as vice chairman, elevated his role to that of senior official for China's economic and financial policies.

## FURTHER READJUSTMENTS AND PROSPECTS

The June 1979 National People's Congress formally ended the concept of the 1978–85 modernization plan; however, China's emphasis remains on economic development. Shifts in China's approach to development continued throughout 1979 and 1980 and should not be expected to abate. The PRC faces problems with inadequate data and a weak cadre of economic planners. Thus, new situations are continually coming to light that necessitate new policy shifts. In addition, political factors will dictate changes in China's economic policies, as the leadership is forced to deal with contending factions within the Communist Party. As of September 1980, however, it is clear that the main reason to forecast further policy shifts is the broad scope of economic experimentation taking place within selected factories and communes within China. These experiments affect the organization of enterprises, the role of efficiency and profits, the pricing system, and the role of banks in promoting economic efficiency in investments. Equally crucial are discussions on the appropriate role of the state budget and the extent to which state enterprises might successfully be taken out of the central government's economic plan.

At the same time that these experiments are under way, changes are taking place within China's leadership. Many personnel changes reflect the October 1979 reversal on the official party line regarding the Cultural Revolution. It was admitted that the Cultural Revolution had been a disaster to the country, and in 1980 Liu Shaoqi, the highest-ranking victim of the Cultural Revolution, was posthumously rehabilitated. Discussions on Mao's record at the party's highest levels have begun in earnest, with an aim of criticizing Mao's policies without destroying his role as a unifying symbol for the Chinese people.

With the September 1980 session of the National People's Congress, Hua Guofeng stepped down as premier. Zhao Ziyang, who replaced him, is known for his work in reviving Siquan's economy in the wake of the Cultural Revolution. Thus, Zhao is a symbol of the country's shift to a group of leaders who stressed economic development over ideology. In addition to Hua, Deng Xiaoping and five other vice premiers resigned their government posts in favor of younger leaders; however, all retained their party positions. Although these officials may remain in the background, their influence on policy will remain significant.

Looking ahead, further policy changes should be anticipated. Certain factors will be important determinants in whether these policy shifts continue to underscore an emphasis on economic growth or move China back toward concerns of ideology:

- An increasing emphasis on efficient management techniques, profits, free market prices, and decentralization in planning has already been observed. Integrating these concepts into a socialist economic system will not be easy, however. Policy shifts in this area could be extremely erratic, particularly if a number of these experiments prove to be unsuccessful.
- China's military and civilian sectors are competing for scarce resources, in terms of funds for both domestic investment and foreign exchange. Renewed conflict along the Sino-Soviet border or in Indochina could lead to a shift in investment and import priorities, away from the current emphasis on the civilian sectors. At present, military imports are being kept at a minimum and few armaments have been contracted for. In 1979 total domestic investment in

the military sector increased 20 percent, owing to the conflict in Vietnam. However, in 1980 spending for the military was cut to offset the high level of spending in 1979. Such a move reinforces the current leadership's determination to hold down military expenditures; however, a response from the military should be anticipated, as senior officers work to increase the military's role in the Four Modernizations.

- China is now working to strengthen the basic structure of the economy. As long as the transport and energy sectors remain weak, China's absorptive capacity will be limited. However, while the physical constraint on China's ability to absorb is an important one, there is also a human constraint. China lacks the skilled workers, technicians, and scientists integral to any country's modernization. The Cultural Revolution decimated the educational system and did away with any role for the technical specialist. Such a situation will take years to repair.
- Political support for the modernization program is likely to remain strong at the central government level as long as economic growth remains strong. The ability of Zhao Ziyang to lead the country is unknown, however. While he will not operate independently from Deng and the senior leaders, his appointment represents a significant change. His reputation grows out of his economic initiatives and his willingness to experiment. Yet, some of these experiments have been extreme. The population policies he instituted in Sichuan were effective in dramatically reducing the birthrate, but they included harsh economic penalties for couples who had more than two children. The approach he will take on a national level is not yet clear.
- The return to power of a radical faction is not anticipated unless there are major economic setbacks within China or major upheavals in the international environment. However, major instability is not the only threat to success in China's modernization effort. Simple intransigence on the part of China's bureaucracy will be sufficient to cause disruptions in the economy. If this were to occur, senior leaders might moderate their support for economic development

as a means of offsetting the rise to power of a competing political faction.

## FOREIGN TRADE POLICIES

China's current approach to modernization has expanded the role to be played by foreign trade, a sector traditionally looked down upon in China. Policy changes have also been instituted to allow a more flexible approach to increasing imports. Foreign debt, compensation trade, and joint ventures are all acceptable methods of accelerating the pace of China's modernization effort. An overview of these policies is crucial, as they will in large part determine the role to be played by the United States and others in China's economic effort.

The role of foreign trade is tied to the issue of "self-reliance," an issue that has been debated in China for more than a century. There is a philosophical debate that centers on whether China can import and integrate foreign technology and methods into the economy without sacrificing China's cultural and philosophical spirit. There is also the pragmatic debate about whether China should allow foreigners to play a crucial role in China's development, allowing the foreigners a greater degree of leverage with China than they might otherwise have. This latter concern has been voiced at intervals since the founding of the PRC. Until 1978, large imports of capital goods were an important component in China's economic plans only at two points in the PRC's development—once in the 1950s and once again in the early 1970s. In both instances those who opposed reliance on foreign imports found justification for their stands.

In the 1950s China relied on the Soviet Union for technology and technical expertise. One of the largest technology transfers in history was under way when in 1960 the USSR recalled its technicians from China—a move tied to the deepening Sino-Soviet dispute. Without Soviet assistance, China faced major setbacks on numerous heavy industrial projects. The effects of this disruption were magnified by severe setbacks in agriculture, resulting both from the policies of the Great Leap

Forward and from extremely poor weather conditions. China was able to recover by the mid-1960s and to repay the Soviets for their aid; a severe strain was placed on the economy, however. Owing to the barter arrangement the Soviet Union had with China, repayment meant not in currency but in goods. China relied heavily on increased textile exports to the USSR to clear its debt.

In the early 1970s China again turned to imports of capital goods on a large scale, this time from the industrialized countries (see Table 2). Given that these imports were to be paid for with hard currency, China planned to increase its exports to earn the necessary foreign exchange. To ease China's payment requirements, the suppliers of plant and equipment exports to China allowed the PRC to pay for the goods over a three- to seven-year period, arranging financing with their commercial banks. Because the supplier had arranged the financing and because the interest payments were built into the price of the goods, as that price was presented to the Chinese, the PRC continued to claim that it was free of foreign debt and that it paid no interest to the foreign banks.

Even with this use of supplier credits to stretch out payments, China faced problems in earning sufficient foreign exchange to pay for its projected imports. In 1973 the OPEC (Organization of Petroleum Exporting Countries) oil crisis hit, followed by a recession that dampened demand for Chinese exports. As a result, in 1974 China's balance of trade went into deficit. The government's response was to cancel some of the planned plant and equipment contracts and to sharply reduce other discretionary imports. In doing so, China was able to avoid any direct borrowings in foreign currency, and by 1976 the balance of trade once gain showed a substantial surplus.

The experience of the 1950s exemplified for China the danger of dependence on a single country. The experience of the 1970s exemplified the risks of integrating China into the world economy. It is in the context of China's past record with foreign imports that the modernization's role for foreign trade is all the more significant. Even with the readjustments leading to more selective growth in heavy industry, foreign trade remains

Table 2. China's World Trade, 1970–79 (billions of US dollars)

| | *1970* | *1971* | *1972* | *1973* | *1974* | *1975* | *1976* | *1977* | *1978* | *1979* | *1980*[2] |
|---|---|---|---|---|---|---|---|---|---|---|---|
| PRC exports[1] | 2.16 | 2.53 | 3.22 | 5.10 | 6.73 | 7.13 | 7.26 | 8.11 | 10.05 | 13.75 | 17.90 |
| PRC imports[1] | 2.04 | 2.14 | 2.58 | 4.63 | 6.81 | 6.83 | 5.57 | 6.60 | 10.30 | 14.53 | 18.00 |
| Balance | 0.12 | 0.39 | 0.64 | 0.47 | −0.08 | 0.30 | 1.69 | 1.51 | −0.25 | −0.78 | −0.10 |
| Total trade | 4.20 | 4.67 | 5.80 | 9.73 | 13.54 | 13.96 | 12.83 | 14.71 | 20.35 | 28.28 | 35.90 |

*Source:* National Foreign Assessment Center, Central Intelligence Agency, *China: International Trade Quarterly Review*, First Quarter, 1980, ER CIT 80-004, (Washington, D.C., September, 1980).

[1] f.o.b.

[2] estimate

important. China's foreign trade rapidly increased upon the introduction of the 1978 plan. Imports grew 55 percent in 1978 and 44 percent in 1979. Exports grew 23 percent and 35 percent during the same period. However, with the narrowing of the scope of the plan and the slowing of the modernization effort, the expansion of foreign trade began to slow in 1980.

The main reason for the slowdown in the increase in foreign trade was the sharp cut in major plant and equipment purchases. While this drop is a direct result of the lower priority for heavy industry, it is also a result of China's decision to move more slowly and keep the country's current account in a near balance. (The current account includes not only trade in merchandise and services but also aid, earnings from tourism, and remittances from overseas Chinese.) China's growth in exports is subject to constraints posed by China's trading partners, particularly in the area of light industrial goods. Textile exports cannot increase at the rate China desires, owing to bilateral agreements and quotas to which China must adhere. In the natural resource area, exports are constrained by China's inadequate transport systems and insufficient electric power generation that prevent mining and extraction of many of the deposits in the interior.

If China is unwilling to run large trade deficits, there will be a trade-off between agricultural and industrial imports. China's increased emphasis on improving living standards has led to large purchases of grain to feed the population in the urban coastal areas. The weak transportation system throughout the country insures that large purchases will continue, probably through the 1980s. Even with good harvests, China's grain purchases will continue to account for as much as 10 percent of the country's imports in the early 1980s, with the percentage declining in the latter part of the decade.

If China is willing to run large deficits, it does have the access to foreign currency it would need. One of the most significant departures of the 1978 modernization plan was the announcement of the government's willingness to take on direct foreign debt. This announcement made clear to the foreign business community that China was considering an increased role for imports—although the role has proved to be smaller than was initially perceived. Since that policy announcement, more than $25 billion in foreign credits have been extended to China. More than two thirds of those credits are from the various export-import banks of the industrial countries (see Table 3). The credits are available to China only for the purchase of goods from the country extending the credit. Most carry an annual interest rate of 7.25 to 7.5 percent, depending upon the duration of the credit. Such rates are in line with an agreement set by the members of the OECD (the Organization of Economic Cooperation and Development), an organization of industrial countries, which has set a minimum floor for export credits. Only the credit from Japan's Export-Import Bank is lower, at 6.25 percent. The Japanese position is that all their funds are tied to China's purchase of equipment and expertise to develop oil and coal; thus, the funds are aid for resource development rather than general export credits. The other exception to the OECD guidelines is the United States, which has rates significantly above the other export credit facilities, with an annual interest rate of 8.75 percent.

The extension of such massive credits to the PRC reflects a number of factors. First, the PRC has maintained a reputation for tight fiscal control. Imports and exports have been closely monitored, and foreign exchange reserves have been for the most part well managed. Moreover, the actual level of China's foreign debt at the onset of the plan (the debt being in the form of obligations due to suppliers of equipment rather than to the banks) was relatively low, approximately $1.5 billion at the end of 1977. Finally, the PRC is a new market to penetrate—one of the few new markets to be found. Thus, both foreign governments and foreign commerical banks have been anxious to give the foreign business community as much support as possible to allow them to increase their exports to China.

Most of the credits to China were put in place during 1979 and early 1980. Yet by late 1979 it was clear that Chinese officials were uncomfortable with the notion of increasing debt at even a moderate pace. Instead, they preferred to rely on counter trade and joint ventures to increase trade without in-

Table 3. Major Government-subsidized Credit Facilities Available to China

| *Country* | *Amount* | *Terms* |
|---|---|---|
| United Kingdom (December 1978) | $1.2 billion | Consortium of UK banks provide Eurodollar funds, with Britain's Export Credit Guarantee Department (ECGD) providing the guarantees and subsidizing the interest rate. Credit is extended for export contracts drawn by March 1985, with interest rates of 7.25% to 7.5% for periods of up to 10 years. |
| France (May 1979) | FF 30 billion (approx. $6.8 billion) | Consortium of 18 French banks, guaranteed by COFACE (France's official guarantee organization). Financing covers 85% of the purchase price. Final maturity of ten years with pricing of 7.25% for the first 7 years and 7.5% for the remaining years. |
| Japan (May 1979) | Y 420 billion (approx. $2 billion) | Japan's Export-Import Bank loan, classified as resource aid. Interest rate of 6.25% with a 10-year repayment period. |
| Italy (May 1979) | $1.2 billion | Consortium of special financial institutions. Credit to be extended in four equal stages with an interest rate of 7.5% and repayment over a period of 8.5 years. |
| Canada (May 1979) | $2 billion | Extended by Canada's Export Development Corporation for a period of 5 years. |
| Sweden | $350 million | Unknown. |

*Source:* Author.

curring debt. It is these policies that will be crucial in determining the rate at which China will increase imports throughout the 1980s.

Countertrade includes barter trade and compensation trade. China has used barter only minimally with the industrial countries. Compensation trade, however, has proved more attractive. In compensation trade, the foreign firm supplies technology and is repaid with the goods produced by that technology. Several additional forms of compensation or buy-back have been developed, particularly for light industrial products, calling for a range of inputs to be supplied by the foreigner. In one type of arrangement, the foreign firm supplies the raw materials, parts, and even the packing materials for production. The Chinese then process and assemble the item for a set fee. In a second type of contract, the foreign firm supplies some of the parts and raw materials, for which the Chinese supply the remaining materials and labor. The first type of arrangement may or may not add to China's stock of technology—it may serve only to expand China's light industrial export capacity. The second type of arrangement and other compensation agreements in the heavy industrial areas, however, are an actual exchange of technology for products. Such contracts have three advantages for China. First, technology is acquired with little or no output of capital. Second, personnel are trained in the use of that technology. Third, the foreign firm, by accepting products to amortize its investment, takes the marketing burden from the Chinese. Problems with distribution or with protectionism are then borne by the foreigner.

Joint ventures have been less widespread than compensation trade arrangements. This is primarily due to the general nature of China's joint-venture law and the slow pace at which the government has issued the implementing regulations. The law was put into effect in July 1979, following its adoption by the National People's Congress in June. The law marked a new phase in China's treatment of foreign businesses. Foreigners were given the right to own Chinese resources—to hold an equity position in a venture with the Chinese.

China's State Planning Commission has the authority to decide which major joint ventures are to have priority. All such agreements must be approved by the Foreign Investment Commission, headed by Vice Premier Gu Mu. The China International Trust and Investment Corporation (CITIC) has been established to assist foreigners in identifying Chinese partners for joint ventures and to help Chinese enterprises make initial contacts with foreigners.

The joint-venture law calls for the formation of limited liability companies.[21] The minimum proportion of foreign investment is set at 25 percent; no maximum is stated. In order to insure that outmoded equipment is not put up as the foreign contribution to the joint venture, Article 5 of the law states that the "technology or equipment contributed by the foreign participant as investment shall be truly advanced and appropriate to China's needs. In cases of losses caused by deception through the intentional provision of outdated equipment or technology, compensation shall be paid for the losses." Discussions have arisen as to the liability of a foreign investor who contributes technology that is not "state of the art" because such equipment would be too advanced for China's level of development. Thus far this question must be addressed on a case-by-case basis.

Profits are subject to a joint-venture income tax. Profits that are remitted are subject to foreign exchange regulations. In September 1980 China announced that the tax rate on the joint venture would be 35 percent. In addition, foreign employees of the venture working in China would be subject to a personal income tax. Beyond these two tax actions, supplemental regulations on the administration of the joint venture have yet to be issued. As a result, each contract must set out all operational aspects of the venture. For this reason, joint ventures have been slow to develop, and as of mid-1980 only three had been announced as signed.

China has made a number of moves to decentralize foreign trade transactions, and these should serve to increase the rate at which countertrade agreements and, to a lesser extent, joint ventures are signed. Three cities (Peking, Shanghai, and Tianjin) and two provinces (Guangdong and Fujian) have been given a large degree of autonomy in setting their own foreign trade practices. Each is able to sign compensation trade agreements and joint ventures up to $1 million in value without prior approval from the central authorities. Each is able to negotiate extensively with foreigners and offer special incentives for investment. Guangdong and Fujian have set up special export zones, where foreign trade and investment policies are more liberal than those for the rest of the country. These moves have been successful in attracting increasing foreign participation, particularly in compensation arrangements in the light industrial area. However, it is still too early to assess the impact of such liberalization on the trade policies for the rest of the country.

## ECONOMIC RELATIONS BETWEEN THE UNITED STATES AND CHINA

When the PRC introduced the modernization program in March 1978, the US and China still lacked diplomatic relations. Throughout 1978 it became increasingly clear that China was committed to a new emphasis on economic development, based upon an environment of political stability. It also became clear that the foreign business community would play a role in China's development and that without diplomatic relations US companies were at a disadvantage. Thus, when US President Jimmy Carter announced the establishment of relations between the two countries, effective 1 January 1979, there was a great deal of optimism about the future for US-China commercial relations.

That optimism was reinforced by the announcement of US-China trade totals for 1978: total trade increased from a level of $374 million in 1977 to $1.15 billion in 1978—an increase of more than 200 percent. Yet, closer examination of the components of trade showed that the increase in US exports was due almost exclusively to sales of agricultural commodities rather than to industrial exports. Thus, US firms were not yet reaping the benefits of China's increased plant and equipment imports.

While diplomatic relations had been normalized in 1979, economic relations remained incomplete. Full economic and commercial ties could not come about until such problems as frozen assets and blocked claims, most-favored-nation tariff treatment (MFN) and Export-Import Bank (Exim Bank) credits were negotiated. Such issues called for agreement not only between the United States and China but also between the executive branch and the Congress within the United States.

### FROZEN ASSETS—BLOCKED CLAIMS

The first barrier to full commercial relations fell with the signing of an agreement on frozen assets and blocked claims. Arising from confiscation actions taken by the United States and China during the Korean War, this problem had prevented direct banking and shipping relations up through the time of normalization. The agreement called for the United States to unblock by 1 October 1979 all PRC-related assets that remained in blocked bank accounts as of 2 March 1979. However, the United States took the stand that in unblocking the assets it was making no determination as to their rightful ownership. The PRC agreed to go to the US courts in the case of any dispute over the rightful ownership of the assets in those accounts, a procedure likely to diminish the funds ultimately remitted to China. The PRC, for its part, agreed to pay a lump sum of $80.5 million to the US government. The US government in turn distributed the funds to US claimants, with a settlement of approximately 40 cents on the dollar (based upon the value of US claims at the time of confiscation).

The frozen assets–blocked claims issue was somewhat technical in nature. Yet until it was settled, Chinese exhibitions could not come to the US, nor could PRC funds be deposited in US banks, for fear of attachment by US claimants. With its settlement, the issue of private claims between the countries was resolved.

### BILATERAL TRADE AGREEMENT: MOST-FAVORED-NATION TARIFF TREATMENT AND EXPORT-IMPORT BANK FACILITIES

On 7 July 1979 a bilateral Trade Agreement was signed by the United States and China. Approved by the Congress in

January 1980, the agreement serves as the core of the US-China commercial relationship. The congressional action marked an important shift in US-China relations. Until late 1979 the US government officially pursued an evenhanded policy toward China and the USSR. A shift to strengthen the relationship with China ran the risk of damaging US-Soviet relations. However, with the Soviet invasion of Afghanistan there was a clear move by the US government to speed the pace at which the US-China relationship was developing.

The US-China Trade Agreement conforms to the requirements of the Trade Act of 1974 (Public Law 93-618), which stipulates that trade agreements between the United States and a nonmarket economy must have the approval of Congress and can run for no more than three years. After three years, the agreement must again be submitted to the Congress. It is renewable only if: (1) a satisfactory balance of concessions in trade and services had been maintained during the life of the agreement, and (2) the president determines that actual or foreseeable reductions in US tariffs and nontariff barriers to trade resulting from multilateral trade negotiations are satisfactorily reciprocated by the other party of the bilateral agreement.

Congressional approval of the bilateral Trade Agreement between the United States and China hinged on the requirements of the Jackson-Vanik Amendment (Section 402 of the Trade Act of 1974). This section of the Trade Act mandates that before MFN or Exim Bank facilities can be extended to any nonmarket economy the president must report that the country in question (1) does not deny its citizens the right or opportunity to emigrate, (2) does not impose more than a nominal tax on emigration, or (3) does not impose more than a nominal tax on any citizen as a consequence of this desire to emigrate. Following receipt of the president's report, either the House or the Senate may still pass a resolution of disapproval to deny extension of MFN and Exim facilities. The president does have the authority temporarily to waive this restriction on free emigration, but only if he has received assurances from the country involved that such a waiver will promote free emigration. Carter used this authority, and the

US-China Trade Agreement was passed by Congress on 24 January 1980. It took effect on 1 February 1980.

While the bilateral Trade Agreement has a myriad of provisions to expand commercial ties between the United States and China, the extension of MFN and Exim Bank facilities are the core of the agreement. MFN is available to China only through such a bilateral Trade Agreement. Prior to receiving MFN status, Chinese exports to the United States were subject to the high tariff rates of the 1930 Hawley-Smoot Act. Numerous studies have been undertaken to determine the effects extension of MFN will have on the volume and pattern of the Chinese export to the United States.[22] Although there are differing conclusions, the central issue is that from the standpoint of the PRC lack of MFN was synonymous with economic discrimination. The Chinese argued that MFN would be necessary if they were going to be able to compete on an even footing with other countries exporting to the United States. Such a viewpoint is probably valid, in that the few countries that have not been extended MFN by the United States may actually be considered as having "least-favored-nation" tariff treatment. Under the provisions of the Trade Act of 1974, Congress must give approval each year to renew MFN for China, and that approval must be based upon China's satisfactory compliance with the emigration requirements of the Jackson-Vanik Amendment. In August 1980, hearings for the first renewal of MFN for China were held, and renewal is expected for 1981. At present, Chinese emigration to the United States is not limited by PRC policies but by the US annual immigration quota of 20,000 for Chinese-born people from all countries.

Availability of U.S. Exim Bank programs for the PRC was somewhat more complex than the extension of MFN. While Exim facilities are subject to the same Jackson-Vanik restrictions, there was an additional obstacle of defaulted loans from the pre-1949 government. It was and continues to be the position of the PRC that these pre-1947 debts are the responsibility of the Guomindang (pre-1949) government. In the spring of 1980, John Moore, president of the Exim Bank, temporarily set aside this issue of the loans. His move followed President Carter's "presidential determination" that Exim facilities for China was in the national interest—an action required by the Trade Act of 1974. As with MFN, annual congressional confirmation that the PRC is meeting the emigration requirements of Jackson-Vanik is necessary to keep Exim facilities available for US exports to China.

Although Exim programs are desired by the Chinese, their primary advantage is to the US exporter who is trying to compete with businesses in other industrial countries that have access to government-subsidized export credit facilities. The US Exim Bank offers financing for medium- and long-term projects at 8.75 percent and will cover up to 65 percent of the value of the exports. Such interest rates are significantly below market rates of interest. However, the terms still do not compare favorably with the facilities offered by other industrial countries. Other Exim banks offer rates as low as 7.25 percent, although US officials claim that once fees are added in, such terms are .5 to .75 percent lower than those offered by the United States. More significant than the rate differential is the fact that other Exim banks cover as much as 85 percent of the value of the project. US officials do not expect any improvement in Exim coverage in the foreseeable future, as funds are insufficient to cover the projects US exporters need financed. This lower proportion of coverage is viewed as the most equitable way of stretching the coverage of these insufficient funds. The PRC was told by Vice President Walter Mondale that the United States would be willing to extend $2 billion in Exim credits for exports to China through 1985. However, this target figure may not be reached, in light of China's slowdown of plant and equipment imports. Exim does not finance agricultural exports, although the Commodity Credit Corporation has been given authority by the Congress to finance US agricultural exports to China at concessionary rates.

The PRC leadership has indicated to the Exim Bank that its counterpart within China will be the Bank of China (BOC). The BOC will be the obligor and guarantor for exports financed by the US Exim Bank, as it is for the Exim programs of the other industrial countries. While US exporters may approach the Exim Bank with requests to finance exports to China, it is up to the Bank of China to indicate to the Exim Bank which projects it wishes to be financed. Thus, the BOC will communicate China's priorities and indicate when a contract has progressed to the stage where it needs to be financed. As of September 1980 only one US project had received a preliminary commitment from the Exim Bank. Wean United, of Pittsburgh, is to supply a portion of the equipment for a cold rolling mill at the Baoshan steel complex, and its share of the project will total approximately $80 million.

### OPIC

In July 1980 the US Congress passed legislation to allow the Overseas Private Investment Corporation (OPIC) to support US businesses investing in China. OPIC, a US government corporation, provides long-term political risk insurance, as well as loan guarantees and various financial programs for small businesses. OPIC must still sign an operating agreement with a Chinese agency before it can extend coverage to US projects in China; however, applications for coverage are already being accepted.

The availability of political risk insurance from OPIC or from private insurance companies may be crucial for certain companies considering joint ventures in China. OPIC's insurance is available for a maximum period of twenty years and covers inconvertibility of currency, expropriation, or losses caused by war, revolution, or insurrection. China is the third communist country to be voted eligible for OPIC programs. In 1971, OPIC was made available to U.S. investments in Rumania and Yugoslavia.

### EXPORT CONTROLS

Further liberalization of US policies toward China occurred in the area of export controls. In January 1980 US Secretary of Defense Harold Brown led a delegation to China, a delegation whose importance was increased in the wake of the Soviet Union's invasion of Afghanistan. Following the trip,

Brown announced that the United States would sell China technology to upgrade its military equipment, supplying basic support equipment, communications gear, and early-warning radar. The United States would not sell China weapons; however, it would not prevent other NATO members from doing so. In March 1980 the State Department announced that the US government would consider, on a case-by-case basis, license applications for export to the PRC of certain items and technology covered by six categories of the US Munitions List. This was the first time the United States had specifically set out the categories of military support equipment available to China.[23]

By August 1980 the United States had developed a policy to allow China to purchase technology with military applications. China would be able to purchase computers that were more sophisticated than those sold to any other communist country except Yugoslavia. In addition, the United States would no longer automatically refuse to grant an export licence because the purchaser was a PRC military organization.

### PROTECTIONISM: TEXTILES AND GENERAL IMPORT RESTRICTIONS

While barriers to certain US exports to China are diminishing, the area of US import restrictions could hold future problems. The area of textiles is a particularly sensitive one for China and the United States. For the Chinese, textiles represent one of the best areas for a short-term increase in production. Textiles and apparel are also an area where the Chinese have a strong competitive advantage in the price of their goods for export. For the United States, however, textiles represent an area where domestic enterprises are losing their ability to compete on both the home and the world market.

The United States and China reached an accord in principle on a bilateral textile agreement in July 1980. This agreement is expected to increase by 50 percent certain levels of Chinese textile exports that had been allowed under unilateral quotas set by the United States in June 1979. The quotas applied to the bulk of China's apparel exports to the United States and had been initiated to offset congressional opposition to the US-

China bilateral Trade Agreement. Without specific limits on Chinese textile exports, special-interest groups might have successfully lobbied before the Congress and prevented approval of the agreement.

China is the fifth largest supplier of textiles and clothing to the United States and may soon surpass Japan to take over fourth place. Yet this situation must be put in perspective. The PRC continues to purchase more cotton from the United States than it sells in textiles. Moreover, China consistently runs a trade deficit with the United States. Extension of MFN should help to reduce this deficit. China will be able to diversify its exports to the United States into areas that were not price competitive, owing to the high tariff structure. However, MFN will not solve China's problems in the textile area. All textile trade is regulated by agreements between the major producing and consuming nations. Other developing countries have already carved out sections of the market under these multilateral and bilateral treaties. With China entering the US (and other markets) late in the game, it will be hard pressed to overcome this disadvantage.

Aside from the area of textile trade, the United States has a system of sanctions that can be brought against goods of any origin to curb the growth of imports. These sanctions include antidumping measures and countervailing duties. There are additional market disruption provisions that are geared specifically to goods from nonmarket economies. The availability of these sanctions to US producers contributes to a mood of uncertainty for both the PRC and the US importers purchasing goods from China.

Antidumping procedures penalize imports that are priced at "less than fair market value." Fair market value is defined as the selling price or export price in a market economy or the constructed value of the product in a market economy. If "dumping" is found to have occurred and an investigation by the US International Trade Commision (ITC) shows that US producers are being injured by unfair competition, duties may be imposed on the imports.

Countervailing duties may be levied against products entering the United States that have benefited from subsidies or grants in the producing or exporting country. No proof of injury to the US producers need be proved.

For China, the most important sanction is the market disruption provision of the Trade Act of 1974. If an import from the PRC is found to be a significant cause of injury to a US producer, or poses the threat of injury, quotas on that import may be imposed. Two cases have been adjudicated under this provision, the first involving cotton work gloves from China and the second involving wooden clothespins. In the first case the ITC ruled there was no injury to the domestic industry. However, soon afterward the United States imposed quotas on cotton work gloves from China as part of the larger action to set textile quotas. In the second case the ITC ruled there was injury; however, President Carter made a determination that quotas against the PRC were not in the national interest. The final outcome of the case involved an imposition of a three-year quota on imported clothespins from all sources, in a separate action brought before the ITC.

Thus far, the import sanctions have not posed any major problems. However, with the 1980 extension of MFN, a wider range of goods from the PRC will be entering the United States. This will be an important area to monitor, particularly in the first half of 1980s when patterns in US-China trades will become more clear.

## COMMERCIAL BANK RELATIONS

A final area to summarize in the US-China commercial relationship is banking. There is a restriction facing all US banks involved in lending to the PRC that may curtail their activities with China: the "legal lending limit." This limit, which exists for all financial institutions (although the exact figure differs for state-chartered and nationally chartered banks), sets a cap on the percent of a bank's capital that may be lent to a single borrower. For national banks this limit is 10 percent. This cap on loans is a restriction that is not faced by foreign banks competing in the China market.

The limit applies only to an individual borrower. In market economies, this limit proves to be no problem, as individual enterprises can be evaluated as to their own economic viability. For a nonmarket economy, the situation differs. It is more difficult to evaluate the financial independence of any one entity. At present, all loans to China are classifed as "sovereign risk." That is, all loans are considered to be loans to the government rather than to the specific enterprise involved. Once US banks can identify borrowers in the PRC who are financially independent of the central government, the 10 percent limit will not apply.

The comptroller of the currency has set out for national banks a "means-and-purpose test" that is to be applied once an initial decision has been made that a potential borrower does have some separate and independent existence apart from the central government. Both the means and the purpose test must be successfully met in order to avoid treating all loans to China as sovereign risk. The "means test" states that the borrower must have resources or revenues of its own sufficient over time to service its debt obligations. The "purpose test" states that the loan must be obtained for a purpose consistent with the borrower's general business. US banks differ in their evaluation as to whether the Bank of China meets these tests and should be considered a borrower that is independent from the central government. However, perhaps more important, with the new autonomy available to provinces and municipalities, certain local entities may meet the criteria set out by the comptroller. In particular, joint ventures are likely to be viewed as independent economic units, a development that will become increasingly important as the number of these ventures expands.

## OUTLOOK FOR US-CHINA TRADE

The normalization of US-China commercial and economic relations has placed the United States on a more equal footing with China's other trading partners. Through the 1980s, price, quality of products, financing, and marketing expertise will determine the pace at which US-China trade expands. The United States is likely to remain one of the top four trading partners for China. From the standpoint of the overall US balance of trade, the PRC will continue as only a minor trading partner; however, the PRC will remain a major purchaser of US agricultural commodities.

In 1979 the United States became China's third largest trading partner, following Japan and Hong Kong (see Table 4).

Table 4. China's Five Major Trading Partners, 1976–79

| *1976*[1] | *1977*[2] | *1978* | *1979* |
|---|---|---|---|
| Japan | Japan | Japan | Japan |
| Hong Kong | Hong Kong | Hong Kong | Hong Kong |
| West Germany | West Germany | West Germany | United States |
| France | Australia | United States | West Germany |
| Rumania | Rumania | Canada | United Kingdom |

*Source:* Author.
[1] US ranked eighth.
[2] US ranked seventh.

Japan was the source of 25 percent of China's imports and purchased 21 percent of China's exports. The United States, in comparison, was the source of 12 percent of China's imports and purchased only 4 percent of China's exports (see Table 5). The imbalance in US-China trade, heavily weighted in favor of the United States, is likely to constrain the rate of growth of US-China trade in the first half of the 1980s. Japan is able to keep a better balance (and to generate higher values of trade) because of the mix of products exchanged by the two countries. Japan exports iron and steel, capital goods, and high-technology items to China. In return, China exports raw materials, primarily petroleum and coal. Increased Chinese exports of crude oil and refined products would have a significant impact on the US-China commercial relationship, as such products would bring the trade into closer balance. Yet, China's commitments to Japan and other Asian countries make it unlikely that China will have excess export capacity in this area until

Table 5. Sino-US Trade, 1971–80 (millions of US dollars)

| | *1971* | *1972* | *1973* | *1974* | *1975* | *1976* | *1977* | *1978* | *1979* | *1980* |
|---|---|---|---|---|---|---|---|---|---|---|
| PRC exports[1] | 5 | 32 | 65 | 115 | 158 | 201 | 203 | 324 | 592 | 1058 |
| PRC imports[2] | 0 | 63 | 740 | 819 | 304 | 135 | 171 | 824 | 1716 | 3748 |
| Balance | 5 | −31 | −675 | −704 | −146 | 66 | 32 | −500 | −1124 | −2690 |
| Total | 5 | 95 | 805 | 934 | 462 | 336 | 374 | 1148 | 2308 | 4806 |

*Source:* 1971–79: National Council for U.S.-China Trade, *Sino-US Trade Statistics, 1979* (June 1980) 1980: U.S. Department of Commerce, *US Trade Status with Communist Countries* (6 March 1981).

[1] 1971–79 f.o.b.; 1980 customs value.

[2] f.a.s.

the latter half of the decade when new production capacity is developed.

### PRC PRODUCTS

US sales of agricultural commodities will continue to dominate US exports to China in the first half of the 1980s. In 1979 wheat, corn, soybeans, soybean oil, and cotton constituted almost two thirds of US exports to the PRC. Agriculture has dominated US-China trade in other years, except for the period 1975–77 when problems with smut infestation led the Chinese to cut off grain imports from the United States.

Given China's emphasis on increasing consumption, high levels of grain imports should be anticipated. In addition, the emphasis on production of consumer goods will keep PRC imports of cotton high. At present, the PRC is the main purchaser of raw cotton from the United States. If China is able to increase domestic production, cotton imports may decline by the mid-1980s.

In addition to agricultural commodities, US exports of inputs to agriculture should increase. Fertilizer, feed concentrates for livestock production, chemicals, herbicides, pesticides, and farm equipment are growing areas of export. Technical expertise in agriculture is also being sought by the PRC, and such expertise can form the basis of the US contribution to compensation agreements in areas such as dairy farming and poultry. Food processing is another priority area for compensation arrangements.

Aerospace equipment is an area where the United States holds a competitive edge. In the early 1970s the PRC made major purchases from Boeing, and in 1978 Boeing received a contract for three 747-SP planes. Further purchases of aviation equipment tied to tourism is likely. However, for aerospace equipment with military capability, competition will be strong from other NATO suppliers—particularly France and the United Kingdom.

Petroleum may hold the largest opportunity for US firms in terms of the aggregate dollar amount of business to be transacted. The United States has held a strong position in sales of petroleum-related equipment to the PRC. In the 1980s, however, production-sharing agreements will be the focus of foreign participation in this sector of the economy. A number of major US oil firms engaged in seismic studies in China's offshore areas. Participation in the studies, however, does not insure a role in the actual extraction of the oil. It will be 1981 before a clearer picture of China's offshore oil potential will be available.

Power generation is a sector where the United States faces strong competition. Hydroelectric projects will use both Japanese and US technology, although contracts for major projects have yet to be signed. The Japanese government has offered China aid to develop selected infrastructure projects, including a hydroelectric facility. The aid, which provides funds at an interest rate of 3 percent per year, should give Japanese firms an important advantage, although the Japanese government will allow foreign firms to bid to supply equipment to tap these low-interest funds.

Mining equipment exports will rely heavily on compensation arrangements. The PRC puts a high priority on the export of raw materials; yet the realities of the weak transport and power sectors will slow development. Thus, US sales in this area will grow in importance only after China tackles the basic weaknesses in the economy. The exception to this assessment will be exports for the few major projects, such as the Baoshan steel complex, which are under construction in spite of the readjustments.

High-technology items will be a growing area for US exports as long as the political relationship between the United States and China remains stable. Export controls at present allow license applications for items such as sophisticated computers, communications satellites, lasers, and advanced physics equipment. Given China's emphasis on science and technology, this area will be a significant one for increased purchases.

Exports of plant and equipment to increase capacity in light industrial production provide broad opportunities for the US firms. Contracts in this area are likely to take the form of compensation agreements however. US companies have yet to widely accept such agreements, and with the structure of US import protection some hesitancy should be anticipated in this product area.

## PRC EXPORTS

US-China trade will continue to suffer in the early 1980s from the PRC's concentration in light industrial exports to the United States. Textiles will remain a major export category. In addition, pottery and china, feathers and down, antiques, specialty foods, and baskets will be significant export items. Extension of MFN should lead to a wider range of PRC exports, a change that will first show up in the 1980 trade statistics.

PRC exports of raw materials hold the largest potential for increased trade in the 1980s. China has indicated its willingness to sell to the United States scarce metals such as titanium, vanadium, and tantalum. China is believed to have substantial reserves of these lightweight, heat-resistant metals, all of which are in low supply in the United States.

In 1979 crude oil and gasoline accounted for 16 percent of China's exports to the United States. China's shipments of crude oil were valued at $72 million. In 1980 crude oil exports will be less significant, although exports of refined products will increase. Petroleum will become an important area in US-China trade in the latter half of the 1980s, when new onshore and offshore deposits come onstream. Until then, the United States will remain a residual export market for these products.

# Appendix I

# People's Republic of China Law on Joint Ventures

(Released 8 July 1979)

Article 1. With a view to expanding international economic cooperation and technological exchange, the People's Republic of China permits foreign companies, enterprises, other economic entities or individuals (hereinafter referred to as foreign participants) to incorporate themselves within the territory of the People's Republic of China, into joint ventures with Chinese companies, enterprises or other economic entities (hereinafter referred to as Chinese participants) on the principle of equality and mutual benefit and subject to authorization by the Chinese Government.

Article 2. The Chinese Government protects, by the legislation in force, the resources invested by a foreign participant in a joint venture and the profits due him pursuant to the agreement, contracts and Articles of Association authorized by the Chinese Government as well as his other lawful rights and interests.

All the activities of a joint venture shall be governed by the laws, decrees and pertinent rules and regulations of the People's Republic of China.

Article 3. A joint venture shall apply to the Foreign Investment Commission of the People's Republic of China for authorization of the agreements and contracts concluded between the parties to the venture and the Articles of Association of the ventures formulated by them and the Commission shall authorize or reject these documents within three months. When authorized, the joint venture shall register with the General Administration for Industry and Commerce of the People's Republic of China and start operations under license.

ARTICLE 4. A joint venture shall take the form of a limited liability company.

In the registered capital of a joint venture, the proportion of the investment contributed by the foreign participant(s) shall in general not be less than 25 percent.

The profits, risks, and losses of a joint venture shall be shared by the parties to the venture in proportion to their contributions to the registered capital.

The transfer of one party's share in the registered capital shall be affected only with the consent of the other parties to the venture.

ARTICLE 5. Each party to a joint venture may contribute cash, capital goods, industrial property rights, etc., as its investment in the venture.

The technology or equipment contributed by any foreign participant as investment shall be truly advanced and appropriate to China's needs. In cases of losses caused by deception through the intentional provision of outdated equipment or technology, compensation shall be paid for the losses.

The investment contributed by a Chinese participant may include the right to the use of a site provided for the joint venture during the period of its operation. In case such a contribution does not constitute a part of the investment from the Chinese participant, the joint venture shall pay the Chinese Government for its use.

The various contributions referred to in the present Article shall be specified in the contracts concerning the joint venture or in its Articles of Association, and the value of each contribution (including that of the site) shall be ascertained by the parties to the venture through joint assessment.

ARTICLE 6. A joint venture shall have a Board of Directors with a composition stipulated in the contracts and Articles of Association after consultation between the parties to the venture; and each Director shall be appointed or removed by his own side. The Board of Directors shall have a chairman appointed by the Chinese participant and one or two vice-chairmen appointed by the foreign participant(s). In handling an important problem, the Board of Directors shall reach decision through consultation by the participants on the principles of equality and mutual benefit.

The Board of Directors is empowered to discuss and take action on, pursuant to the provisions of the Articles of Association of the joint venture, all fundamental issues concerning the venture; namely, expansion projects, production and business programs, the budget, distribution of profits, plans concerning manpower and pay scales, the termination of business, the appointment or hiring of the president, the vice-president, the chief engineer, the treasurer and the auditors, as well as their functions and their remuneration, etc. The president and vice-president(s) (or the general manager and assistant general manager(s) in a factory) shall be chosen from the various parties to the joint venture.

Procedures covering the employment and discharge of the workers and staff members of a joint venture shall be stipulated according to law in the agreement or contract concluded between the parties to the venture.

ARTICLE 7. The net profit of a joint venture shall be distributed between the parties to the venture in proportion to their respective shares in the registered capital after the payment of a joint venture income tax on its gross profit pursuant to the tax laws of the People's Republic of China and after the deductions therefrom as stipulated in the Articles of Association of the venture for the reserve funds, the bonus and welfare funds for the workers and staff members and the expansion funds of the venture.

A joint venture equipped with up-to-date technology by world standards may apply for a reduction of or exemption from income tax for the first two to three profit-making years.

A foreign participant who reinvests any part of its share of the net profit within Chinese territory may apply for the restitution of a part of the income taxes paid.

ARTICLE 8. A joint venture shall open an account with the Bank of China or a bank approved by the Bank of China.

A joint venture shall conduct its foreign exchange transactions in accordance with the Foreign Exchange Regulations of the People's Republic of China.

A joint venture may, in its business operations, obtain funds from foreign banks directly.

The insurance appropriate to a joint venture shall be furnished by Chinese insurance companies.

ARTICLE 9. The production and business programs of a joint venture shall be filed with the authorities concerned and shall be implemented through business contracts.

In its purchase of required raw and semi-processed materials, fuels, auxiliary equipment, etc., a joint venture should give first priority to Chinese sources. It may also acquire them directly from the world market with its own foreign exchange funds.

A joint venture is encouraged to market its products outside China. It may distribute its export products to foreign markets through direct channels or its associated agencies or China's foreign trade establishments. Its products may also be distributed on the Chinese market.

Wherever necessary, a joint venture may set up affiliated agencies outside China.

ARTICLE 10. The net profit which foreign participant receives as his share after executing his obligations under the pertinent laws and agreements and contracts, the funds he receives at the time when the joint venture terminates or winds up its operations, and his other funds may be remitted abroad through the Bank of China in accordance with the foreign exchange regulations and in the currency or currencies specified in the contracts concerning the joint venture.

A foreign participant shall receive encouragements for depositing in the Bank of China any part of the foreign exchange which he is entitled to remit abroad.

ARTICLE 11. The wages, salaries or other legitimate income earned by a foreign worker or staff member of a joint venture, after payment of the personal income tax under the tax laws of the People's Republic of China, may be remitted abroad through the Bank of China in accordance with the Foreign Exchange Regulations.

ARTICLE 12. The contract period of a joint venture may be agreed upon between the parties to the venture according to its particular line of business and circumstances. The period may be extended upon expiration through agreement between the parties, subject to authorization by the Foreign Investment Commission of the People's Republic of China. Any application for such extension shall be made six months before the expiration of the contract.

ARTICLE 13. In cases of heavy losses, the failure of any party to a joint venture to execute its obligations under the contracts or the Articles of Association of the venture, force majeure, etc., prior to the expiration by consultation and agreement between the parties and through authorization by the Foreign Investment Commission of the People's Republic of China and registration with the General Administration for Industry and Commerce. In cases of losses caused by breach of the contracts by a party to the venture, the financial responsibility shall be borne by the paid party.

ARTICLE 14. Disputes arising between the parties to a joint venture which the Board of Directors fails to settle through consultations may be settled through conciliation or arbitration by an arbitral body of China or through arbitration by an arbitral body agreed upon by the parties.

ARTICLE 15. The present law comes into force on the date of its promulgation. The power of amendment is vested in the National People's Congress.

# Appendix II

# Agreement on Trade Relations Between The United States of America and The People's Republic of China

The Government of the United States of America and the Government of the People's Republic of China;

Acting in the spirit of the Joint Communiqué on the Establishment of Diplomatic Relations between the United States of America and the People's Republic of China;

Desiring to enhance friendship between both parties;

Wishing to develop further economic and trade relations between both countries on the basis of the principles of equality and mutual benefit as well as nondiscriminatory treatment;

Have agreed as follows:

## Article I

1. The Contracting Parties undertake to adopt all appropriate measures to create the most favorable conditions for strengthening, in all aspects, economic and trade relations between the two countries so as to promote the continuous, long-term development of trade between the two countries.

2. In order to strive for a balance in their economic interests, the Contracting Parties shall make every effort to foster the mutual expansion of their reciprocal trade and to contribute,

each by its own means, to attaining the harmonious development of such trade.

3. Commercial transactions will be effected on the basis of contracts between firms, companies and corporations, and trading organizations of the two countries. They will be concluded on the basis of customary international trade practice and commercial considerations such as price, quality, delivery and terms of payment.

### Article II

1. With a view to establishing their trade relations on a non-discriminatory basis, The Contracting Parties shall accord each other most-favored-nation treatment with respect to products originating in or destined for the other Contracting Party, i.e., any advantage, favor, privilege, or immunity they grant to like products originating in or destined for any other country or region, in all matters regarding:

(A) Customs duties and charges of all kinds applied to the import, export, re-export or transit of products, including the rules, formalities and procedures for collection of such duties and charges;

(B) Rules, formalities and procedures concerning customs clearance, transit, warehousing and transshipment of imported and exported products;

(C) Taxes and other internal charges levied directly or indirectly on imported or exported products or service;

(D) All laws, regulations and requirements affecting all aspects of internal sale, purchase, transportation, distribution or use of imported products; and

(E) Administrative formalities for the issuance of import and export licenses.

2. In the event either Contracting Party applies quantitative restrictions to certain product originating in or exported to any third country or region, it shall afford to all like products originating in or exported to the other country treatment which is equitable to that afforded to such third country or region.

3. The Contracting Parties note, and shall take into consideration in the handling of their bilateral trade regulations, that, at its current state of economic development, China is a developing country.

4. The principles of Paragraph 1 of the Article will be applied by the Contracting Parties in the same way as they are applied under similar circumstances under any multilateral trade agreement to which either Contracting Party is a party on the date of entry into force of this Agreement.

5. The Contracting Parties agree to reciprocate satisfactorily concessions with regard to trade and services, particularly tariff and non-tariff barriers to trade, during the term of this Agreement.

ARTICLE III

For the purpose of promoting economic and trade relations between their two countries, the Contracting Parties agree to:

A. Accord firms, companies and corporations, and trading organizations of the other Party treatment no less favorable than is afforded to any third country or region;

B. Promote visits by personnel, groups and delegations from economic, trade and industrial circles; encourage commercial exchanges and contacts; and support the holding of fairs, exhibitions and technical seminars in each other's country;

C. Permit and facilitate, subject to their respective laws and regulations and in accordance with physical possibilities, the stationing of representatives, or the establishment of business offices, by firms, companies and corporations, and trading organizations of the other Party in its own territory; and

D. Subject to their respective laws and regulations and physical possibilities, further support trade promotions and improve all conveniences, facilities and related services for the favorable conduct of business activities by firms, companies and corporations, and trading organizations of the two countries, including various facilities in respect of office space and residential housing, telecommunications, visa issuance, internal business travel, customs formalities for entry and re-export of personal effects, office articles and commercial samples, and observance of contracts.

### Article IV

The Contracting Parties affirm that government trade offices contribute importantly to the development of their trade and economic relations. They agree to encourage and support the trade promotion activities of these offices. Each Party undertakes to provide facilities as favorable as possible for the operation of these offices in accordance with their respective physical possibilities.

### Article V

1. Payments for transactions between the United States of America and the People's Republic of China shall either be effected in freely convertible currencies mutually accepted by firms, companies and corporations, and trading organizations of the two countries, or made otherwise in accordance with agreements signed by and between the two parties to the transaction. Neither Contracting Party may impose restrictions on such payments except in time of declared national emergency.

2. The Contracting Parties agree, in accordance with their respective laws, regulations and procedures, to facilitate the availability of official export credits on the most favorable terms appropriate under the circumstances for transactions in support of economic and technological projects and products between firms, companies and corporations, and trading organizations of the two countries. Such credits will be the subject of separate arrangements by the concerned authorities of the two Contracting Parties.

3. Each Contracting Party shall provide, on the basis of most-favored-nation treatment, and subject to its respective laws and regulations, all necessary facilities for financial, currency and banking transactions by nationals, firms, companies and corporations, and trading organizations of the other Contracting Party on terms as favorable as possible. Such facilities shall include all required authorizations for international payments, remittances and transfers, and uniform application of rates of exchange.

4. Each Contracting Party will look with favor towards participation by financial institutions of the other country in appropriate aspects of banking services related to international trade and financial relations. Each Contracting Party will permit those financial institutions of the other country established in its territory to provide such services on a basis no less favorable than that accorded to financial institutions of other countries.

## Article VI

1. Both Contracting Parties in their trade relations recognize the importance of effective protection of patents, trademarks and copyrights.

2. Both Contracting Parties agree that on the basis of reciprocity legal or natural persons of either Party may apply for

registration of trademarks and acquire exclusive rights thereto in the territory of the other Party in accordance with its laws and regulations.

3. Both Contracting Parties agrée that each Party shall seek, under its laws and with due regard to international practice, to ensure to legal or natural persons of the other Party protection or patents and trademarks equivalent to the patent and trademark protection correspondingly accorded by the other Party.

4. Both Contracting Parties shall permit and facilitate enforcement of provisions concerning protection of industrial property in contracts between firms, companies and corporations, and trading organizations of their respective countries, and shall provide means, in accordance with their respective laws, to restrict unfair competition involving unauthorized use of such rights.

5. Both Contracting Parties agree that each Party shall take appropriate measures, under its laws and regulations and with due regard to international practice, to ensure to legal or natural persons of the other Party protection of copyrights equivalent to the copyright protection correspondingly accorded by the other Party.

### Article VII

1. The Contracting Parties shall exchange information on any problems that may arise from their bilateral trade, and shall promptly hold friendly consultations to seek mutually satisfactory solutions to such problems. No action shall be taken by either Contracting Party before such consultations are held.

2. However, if consultations do not result in a mutually satisfactory solution within a reasonable period of time, either Contracting Party may take such measures as it deems appropriate. In an exceptional case where a situation does not admit any delay, either Contracting Party may take preventive or

remedial action provisionally, on the condition that consultation shall be effected immediately after taking such action.

3. When either Contracting Party takes measures under this Article, it shall ensure that the general objectives of this Agreement are not prejudiced.

### ARTICLE VIII

1. The Contracting Parties encourage the prompt and equitable settlement of any disputes arising from or in relation to contracts between their respective firms, companies and corporations, and trading organizations, through friendly consultations, conciliation or other mutually acceptable means.

2. If such disputes cannot be settled promptly by any one of the above-mentioned means, the parties to the dispute may have recourse to arbitration for settlement in accordance with provisions specified in their contracts or other agreements to submit to arbitration. Such arbitration may be conducted by an arbitration institution in the People's Republic of China, the United States of America, or a third country. The arbitration rules of procedure of the relevant arbitration institution are applicable, and the arbitration rules of the United Nations Commission on International Trade Law recommended by the United Nations, or other international arbitration rules, may also be used where acceptable to the parties to the dispute and to the arbitration institution.

3. Each Contracting Party shall seek to ensure that arbitration awards are recognized and enforced by their competent authorities where enforcement is sought, in accordance with applicable laws and regulations.

### ARTICLE IX

The provisions of this Agreement shall not limit the right of either Contracting Party to take any action for the protection of its security interests.

### Article X

1. This Agreement shall come into force on the date on which the Contracting Parties have exchanged notifications that each has completed the legal procedures necessary for this purpose, and shall remain in force for three years.

2. This Agreement shall be extended for successive terms of three years if neither Contracting Party notifies the other of its intent to terminate this Agreement at least 30 days before the end of a term.

3. If either Contracting Party does not have domestic legal authority to carry out its obligations under this Agreement, either Contracting Party may suspend application of this Agreement, or, with the agreement of the other Contracting Party, any part of this Agreement. In that event, the Parties will seek, to the fullest extent practicable in accordance with domestic law, to minimize unfavorable effects on existing trade relations between the two countries.

4. The Contracting Parties agree to consult at the request of either Contracting Party to review the operation of this Agreement and other relevant aspects of the relations between the two Parties.

In witness whereof, the authorized representatives of the Contracting Parties have signed this Agreement.

Done at Peking in two original copies this 7th day of July, 1979, in English and Chinese, both texts being equally authentic.

| Leonard Woodcock | Li Qiang |
|---|---|
| For the United States of America | For the People's Republic of China |

## NOTES

1. UNA-USA National Policy Panel to Study US-China Relations Delegation meeting with Vice Premier Li Xianian, 10 March 1979, Peking.

2. New China News Agency news release, 30 April 1980.

3. Lardy, Nicholas R., *China's Economic Readjustment: Recovery or Paralysis,* (Washington, D.C., The Asia Society, March 1980), p. 6.

4. Deng Xiaoping, "Report on the Current Situation and Tasks," translated in *Foreign Broadcast Information Service* (FBIS), 11 March 1980, Supplement 1-27.

5. "Communiqué of the Third Plenary Session of the Eleventh Central Committee of the Communist Party of China," *Peking Review* (PR) 21:52 (29 December 1978) 12.

6. Hu Qiaomu, "Observe Economic Laws, Speed Up the Four Modernizations," PR 21:47 (24 November 1978) 19.

7. Ibid.,,PR 21:45 (10 November 1978) 8.

8. "Communiqué of the Third Plenary Session . . . ," op. cit., 11.

9. Hu, op. cit., PR 21:46 (19 November 1978) 18.

10. Ibid.

11. "Communiqué of the Third Plenary Session . . . ," op. cit., 12.

12. New China News Agency news release, 11 April 1979.

13. Ibid.

14. Hua Guofeng, "Report on the Work of the Government," *Beijing Review* (BR) 22:27 (6 July 1979) 11.

15. Ibid., 12.

16. Ibid., 13.

17. Ibid., 11.

18. Loc. cit.

19. Hu, op. cit., PR 21:47 (24 November 1978) 16.

20. Hua Guofeng, "Report on the Work of the Government," PR 21:10. (10 March 1978) 25.

21. See Appendix I, above.

22. United States International Trade Commission, "Special Report to the Congress and the East-West Trade Board on Implications for US Trade of Granting Most-Favored-Nation Treatment to the People's Republic of China," USITC Publication 816, May 1977. See also Philip T. Lincoln and James A. Kilpatrick, "The Impact of Most-Favored-Nation Tariff Treatment on P.R.C. Exports," in Joint Economic Committee, Congress of the U.S., *Chinese Economy Post-Mao* (Washington, 9 November 1978).

23. U.S. Department of State, *Munitions Control Newsletter* No. 81 (March 1980).

# US-CHINA TRADE IN LONG-RUN PERSPECTIVE

## A Comment on the Chapter by Lynn Feintech

**CHRISTOPHER H. PHILLIPS**

President
The National Council for US-China Trade

The most significant policy change in recent years, which Lynn Feintech carefully chronicles, is China's gradual abandonment since the Fifth National People's Congress in February 1978 of Maoist economic precepts that shackled economic planning for thirty years. Among these was the spurious doctrine that economic development was really only a problem of increasing output. Turning away from this dogma, the government has recently begun to confront the need for better management and higher-quality standards.

Ms. Feintech's discussion of US-China trade relations is equally thorough. Not only are the main obstacles that stood in the way of improved trade relations between the United States and China enumerated—such as the lack of a trade agreement and most-favored-nation tariff treatment for China—but less well known hindrances to improved trade relations are also discussed. These include the "legal lending limit" established in May 1979 by the US comptroller of the currency, which places a ceiling on the size of loans to China if the rules are strictly interpreted. They include as well problems with letters of credit used to finance China's imports that do not conform with the Uniform Customs and Practices for Documentary Credits of the International Chamber of Commerce. This latter problem could become a serious impediment to US-

China trade when China starts paying for its imports with time letters of credit. As the maturity of these payment documents lengthens, businessmen will be less likely to accept the risks involved unless the legal language of these documents is in complete conformity with standard international practices.

I agree fully with Ms. Feintech's view that the significance of these trade obstacles must be understood in their political context. The concept of reciprocity is the key to an enduring and successful trade relationship with the PRC. When trade barriers between China and Western nations have been removed in the past in order to achieve reciprocity, trade has usually far surpassed the levels one would have predicted simply on the basis of lower trade barriers.

China keenly felt the lack of reciprocity that was represented by the absence of most-favored-nation treatment for its goods in the US marketplace. Chinese trade delegations to the United States in 1979 indicated that US-China trade would not achieve its full potentiality without MFN. The private message of Chinese leaders was even more pointed, emphasizing that the lack of MFN was the main reason US banks (with one exception) did not participate in China's recent signing of approximately $23 billion in foreign credits. Ironically, these loans were mainly denominated in US dollars, the currency China desires most.

China's sensitivity to the MFN issue derived in part from the fact that US-China trade is heavily balanced in favor of the United States. Consequently, a portion of the costly loans China has signed with European and Japanese bankers at high interest rates will have to be used to bridge China's growing trade gap with the United States. The trade imbalance was 1 to 4 in our favor throughout 1978 and during the first half of 1979.

China has indicated a willingness to live with the situation of a long-term trade imbalance with the United States, but only under the condition that the trade gap is the result of the free interplay of economic forces and it not caused by artificial impediments of a political nature.

It is noteworthy that China sought MFN despite the fact that with MFN US-China trade will probably turn even more sharply in America's favor. The reason for this, first of all, is that the present lopsidedness in US-China trade is the consequence of underlying economic factors that MFN will not alter in the short term. China's exports to the United States consist mainly of tin, textiles, footwear, specialty foods, and carpets. With the exception of petroleum products, which entered the trade statistics for the first time in 1979, demand for Chinese products is not expected to increase fast enough, even under the reduced MFN tariff schedule, to pay for China's enormous demand for American technology and food grains.

Second, the extension of MFN to China has set the stage for US Export-Import Bank credits to China. Such credits will help US exporters match the concessionary terms of overseas rivals, most of whom have enjoyed government-subsidized credits for many years.

Vice President Mondale indicated, in his 27 August 1979 Peking University speech, that $2 billion in US Exim Bank credits would be earmarked for China through 1984, once three additional statutory requirements were met: the Jackson-Vanik emigration provision of the 1974 Trade Act was either waived or amended; the president determined that such credits are in the national interest; and settlement was reached on $26 million in Exim Bank claims against China dating from 1946–47. At this writing, the first two requirements have been met, and it appears that the third will be resolved without difficulty.

The one area to which Ms. Feintech might well have given greater emphasis is that of joint ventures and compensation trade arrangements with China, although there are obvious difficulties in obtaining information about this new area of activity. At the present time some twenty to thirty US corporations are actively engaged in negotiating joint-venture protocols or contract agreements. Some of the terms under discussion involve joint management for as long as thirty years, a closely monitored transfer of technology under license, and marketing arrangements both inside and outside China.

These new trade relationships now being formalized between US corporations; and national, provincial, and local Chinese entities will severely test the ingenuity and cooperative spirit of both parties. But they hold out the promise of a far more mutually advantageous long-term commercial relationship between the United States and China than has ever been known before.

# II. STRATEGIC CONSEQUENCES OF THE EVOLUTION OF US-CHINA RELATIONS

# Chapter 2

# US-CHINA RELATIONS AS VIEWED BY THE MAJOR INTERNATIONAL ACTORS IN THE EAST ASIAN REGION: A SYMPOSIUM

# A. THE SOVIET PERSPECTIVE

**STEVEN I. LEVINE**

Associate Professor of International Service
The American University, Washington, D.C.

No one has observed the course of Chinese-American relations more closely in recent years than the leaders of the Soviet Union. American policymakers in turn have taken a keen interest in the Kremlin's reaction to developments in the Washington-Peking relationship. Some in Washington, playing on Soviet anxieties, have sought to prod the Russians into agreements or concessions they might otherwise decline. Others have worried that flaunting the so-called China card might so antagonize the Russians as to jeopardize the prospects for further agreements with Moscow on arms control and other issues, impair the procedures for maintaining a tenuous peace in the nuclear age, and encourage the Russians to play their own "China card" when the game permits.

In this section I will examine Soviet perspectives on Sino-American relations in order to contribute to an intelligent resolution of the complex policy issues imbedded in the relations between Washington, Moscow, and Peking. It surveys Soviet reactions to the establishment of full Sino-American relations in 1979 and Soviet views of the prospects for US-China relations in the coming years.

## SOVIET PERSPECTIVES ON US-CHINA RELATIONS PRIOR TO NORMALIZATION

At a time when many Western observers point apprehensively to the growing Soviet military presence in Asia as an indication of Moscow's dangerous global posture, Soviet political observers, for their part, perceive the outlines of a hostile anti-Soviet coalition taking shape in East Asia where major Soviet interests are present. The maximum Soviet concern is that such a hostile coalition, comprising the United States, China, and Japan, could metamorphose into a formal or informal military alliance directed against the USSR. Such a development might negate a decade and a half of intensive military and diplomatic efforts to improve the Soviet Union's strategic and political position in Asia, give substance rather quickly to what is now seen as a long-term Chinese threat, limit the USSR's economic intercourse with the region, and deny Moscow the regional political influence its global power would seem to confer.

Soviet leaders face the task of communicating their concern to Washington, Tokyo, and Peking in such a way as to avoid encouraging the formation of the very combination they fear while continuing to augment their military strength against this same contingency. Given the undistinguished record of the USSR's diplomacy in East Asia and the inherent delicacy of the task, one might be inclined to minimize the chances for success. In fact, however, for a variety of reasons, none of the putative partners in this hostile coalition is likely to pursue the maximum goal that Moscow finds abhorrent.

The source of Soviet anxieties about the possible future course of Sino-American relations is not difficult to fathom. In the decade since the bloody border conflicts of 1969, the Soviet government has sought to reduce the level of tension with China and to improve state-to-state relations by offering a number of proposals, including a nonaggression treaty, a mutual undertaking to renounce the use of force, the restoration of cultural exchanges, stepped-up trade, and so forth.[1] Peking rejected or ignored all of these overtures, and the meetings of Soviet and Chinese deputy foreign ministers that have occurred intermittently since 1969 have failed to yield any agreements. During this same period, a steady drumfire of Chinese criticism directed against Soviet domestic and foreign policies accompanied Peking's seemingly abrupt turn toward the West and the United States in particular.[2]

The death of Mao Zedong in September 1976 quickened pulses in Moscow because for many years China specialists there had been inclined to impute a major share of the anti-Soviet direction of Peking's foreign policy to Mao's evil genius. His alleged pursuit of great power chauvinist objectives was said to be responsible for the Sino-Soviet split and Peking's drift into the enemy camp. Mao was viewed as an aberrant figure whose death would remove both a major cause of conflict and an obstacle to reconciliation.

When this somewhat wishful scenario failed to accord with reality (at least in the short run), the concerns of Soviet analysts intensified. In their perspective the coup of October 1976 against the Cultural Revolution radicals had not led to a fundamental transformation of the Maoist regime but had merely removed political incompetents such as Jiang Qing and Wang Hongwen and brought to the fore experienced old guard Maoists such as Deng Xiaoping, Li Xiannian, Geng Biao, and others. The new leaders, committed to the restoration of internal order in place of the turbulence that had characterized the last decade of Mao's life, were much more dangerous enemies because they were more likely to achieve the basic objectives Mao had bequeathed. As an authoritative Soviet journal noted in a symposium entitled "Maoism without Mao":

> It is the principal aim of the Chinese leaders today to buttress the regime, toughen the military-bureaucratic dictatorship and create economic conditions for a military buildup in order to implement their Great Power policy.[3]

A notable feature of China's foreign policy under the new leadership, it was asserted, was a further turn toward the right manifested in an effort to consolidate relations with the United States and reactionary, anti-Soviet forces in Europe and elsewhere.[4] Another leading scholar noted:

> Rapprochement with the US will open the way to utilizing America's industrial, financial and scientific-technical potential in order to accelerate modernization of the Chinese

economy and furnish China's armed forces with new weapons, both American and, through the assistance of the US, with West European arms too.[5]

Prior to 15 December 1978, Soviet observers were able to derive some satisfaction even from this gloomy prospect because of the seeming inability of Washington and Peking to take the final steps toward normalized relations. As widely noted, domestic political instability in both the United States and China and the initial reluctance of the Carter administration to tackle the Taiwan problem contributed to the impression that Sino-American relations had reached a plateau from which further ascent was too difficult and hazardous.[6] A Soviet commentary published in February 1978 observed that "If we tried to represent American-Chinese relations in the last year and a half on a graph, the curved line would slope down rather than up."[7] Noting a conflict in Washington between "reasonable people" (i.e., those opposing a bloc with Peking) and "ultrareactionary circles who are trying to use China as an instrument to achieve their global aims," the Soviet journal concluded that "the question of which tendencies will prevail in the Carter administration's China policy has obviously not yet been resolved."[8] Any Soviet complacency must have been shattered by National Security Advisor Zbigniew Brzezinski's trip to Peking in May 1978 and the subsequent indicators (clear at least in retrospect) that the White House had taken China policy out of the hands of a cautious State Department and was determined at long last to secure the elusive normalization agreement.

## THE SOVIET RESPONSE TO NORMALIZATION

Well before the dramatic announcement of normalization on 15 December 1978 the Kremlin had made clear that, whereas it had no objections to normalization per se, it was the motives and consequences of normalization for the behavior of its two main adversaries that most concerned it. In this connection, Moscow could hardly ignore the inclusion in the normalization agreement of a clause pledging Chinese and American opposition to any third-party attempt to establish hegemony in the Asia-Pacific region or anywhere else. This was an unmistakable reference to the PRC refrain that the Soviet Union is seeking such hegemony—something Moscow heatedly denies. To be sure, in presenting the agreement to the public, President Carter asserted that "We do not undertake this important step for transient tactical or expedient reasons" (clearly an attempt to reassure the Soviets), and Brzezinski stated that "We see no fundamental incompatibility between a better relationship with China and a better relationship with the Soviet Union."[9] But when the president publicly conveyed the misleading impression that Brezhnev had endorsed the normalization agreement, the Soviet news agency Tass was quick to supply what Carter had omitted—Brezhnev's objection to the "antihegemony" clause and his blunt observation that "the Soviet Union will most closely follow what the development of American-Chinese relations will be in practice and from this will draw appropriate conclusions for Soviet policy."[10]

It is clear even from open Soviet sources that there was disagreement about how to assess the impact of US-China ties on Soviet interests. The Soviet army newspaper *Red Star*, for example, warned of the impending creation of a NATO for Asia, an "alliance of US imperialists, Japanese revanchists and Chinese great power chauvinists who viewed the Soviet Union as their common enemy."[11] Another hard-line assessment suggested that normalization "is designed to encourage the Chinese nationalists' hegemonic aspirations and strengthen the positions of imperialism in the struggle against world socialism."[12] But a senior commentator in *Pravda* was more optimistic.

> On the strategic level, the American leaders understand that a deterioration of Soviet-American relations would create difficulties and problems for the US that could not be overridden or compensated for by an improvement in Chinese-American relations. I find it hard to believe that the United States will enter into a broad coalition with

> China aimed against the USSR. But on the tactical level there is no doubt that the Americans regard the normalization of their relations with the PRC as a lever for exerting pressure on the Soviet Union.[13]

Soviet analyses of the negotiations leading up to normalization suggested that while Brzezinski's May 1978 visit to Peking had gotten things moving, it was the Chinese who had basically set the pace and controlled the negotiating process. The agreement itself, it was recognized, embodying mutual concessions, in particular on the vexed issue of Taiwan, represented an alleged victory in the United States of conservative forces opposed to the improvement of Soviet-American relations.[14]

In sum, the same two Soviet analytic tendencies that were discernible prior to normalization continued to exist thereafter. The pessimists place the darkest interpretation on Sino-American ties; the optimists stress the limits imposed upon Washington's dalliance with Peking by American recognition of the primacy of Soviet-American relations. The long-drawn-out character of the process of normalization may have partly blunted the Soviet reaction, because both the incentives and constraints operating within the Washington-Peking relationship had become well known in advance of the announcement of 15 December.

The visit of Chinese Deputy Premier Deng Xiaoping to the United States (29 January–5 February 1979) tested the interpretation of the Soviet optimists. Deng's persistent attacks on the dangers of Soviet expansionism evoked the displeasure of the Soviet press, which asked the United States to clarify its position once again on the issues of arms control, détente, East-West relations, and the like.[15] Soviet Premier Kosygin pointedly told a high-ranking American delegation that the Carter administration should have refuted Deng's anti-Soviet remarks, while *Pravda* observed: "It appears that anti-Sovietism is the basis for the 'common interests' and 'similar points of view' mentioned in the American-Chinese [joint press] communiqué."[16] Yet the continuing divergence in Soviet interpretation was shown by another commentator's view that "Deng's actions met with more concern than approval in the [US] press," and that despite normalization, Washington's policy was still "characterized by vacillation . . . a competition between belligerent tendencies and more moderate ones."[17] Such a competition was not merely a figment of Soviet imagination, of course, but reflected the reality of China policy politics in Washington. Moscow's concern was that Chinese diplomatic forays such as that by Deng Xiaoping and the increasing interaction of Chinese and US officials might exert an influence upon American public opinion and policy sufficient to produce anti-Soviet outcomes.

## SOVIET REACTION TO CHINA'S INVASION OF VIETNAM

In this context, China's "punitive" invasion of Vietnam a scant two weeks after Deng's departure from Washington seemed both to validate the pessimists' view of Sino-American collusion and to stand as a confirmation to the United States of Soviet warnings that Peking is inherently bellicose and an unsuitable ally. One senior analyst of Sino-American relations suggested that a primary purpose of Deng Xiaoping's visit to Washington had been to ascertain that Washington's inevitable pro forma condemnation of China's action in Vietnam would not affect the substance of Sino-American relations.[18] *Pravda*'s pseudonymous I. Aleksandrov, who speaks for the CPSU Central Committee on Chinese Affairs, commented that "the US government's reaction to the Chinese aggression most nearly resembles, if not approval, then at least indirect encouragement. . . . The position taken by US ruling circles in the face of the Chinese leadership's open threats against Vietnam [during Deng's visit] was ambiguous, to say the least, and *in essence it was a contributory factor in Peking's open embarkation on a path of war*."[19] Despite the accusation, this was a relatively mild formulation of supposed American complicity in China's aggression against Vietnam. Aleksandrov and others preferred to underline the therapeutic warning to the West that

Peking's action contained. "Those who now hope to warm themselves with those flames [of war] rashly risk becoming the next victims of the aggressor and its adventurist policy."[20] A senior *Pravda* commentator claimed that "the Americans are now beginning to realize that their new 'ally' may be dragging them to the brink of a dangerous abyss . . . the US is coming to realize that this game is very, very dangerous and that the maintenance of normal relations with the USSR is a vital necessity."[21] The Soviet analyst drew a pointed contrast between Peking's desire to provoke an American-Soviet conflict and Moscow's supposed statesmanlike response to the attack on its Vietnamese ally.

Moscow's claim that the Chinese attack had failed to secure its major objectives is not very far off the mark. Even though the Soviets refrained from an immediate military response to China's invasion of Vietnam, it is reasonable to suppose that Moscow's blunt warning to Peking of the possible consequences of its action as well as the Soviet airlift and sealift of military supplies to Vietnam, troop movements along the Sino-Soviet border, and stepped-up air and naval activity in the Tonkin Gulf were factors Peking carefully calculated in limiting its strike.[22]

Looking toward the long-term significance of the Sino-Vietnamese war, we may point to two rather contradictory consequences with potentially far-reaching implications for Chinese-American relations. The first is the further militarization of power relations in East and Southeast Asia in the wake of China's attack. The Russians have been given a more plausible excuse as well as a greater opportunity for extending their military power into Southeast Asia, and the Soviet navy and air force have already moved toward acquiring permanent bases in southern Vietnam at Cam Ranh Bay and Danang. This complements the prior Soviet decision to establish new bases in the North Pacific on the islands of Kunashiri and Etorofu, which Japan claims as part of its *terra irredenta*. In general, one may suppose that military considerations in the formulation of Soviet foreign policy have been boosted by the perceived need to deter further Chinese adventures in Vietnam and to counterbalance the continued American presence as well as by Japan's reemerging interest in strengthening its armed forces. While Peking's American connection to some extent eased Chinese anxieties about an immediate Soviet military response to the invasion of Vietnam, Moscow seems determined to deploy its military power so that the Chinese will realize the longer-term folly of such calculation. Soviet military power can more than match the Chinese on the southern flank without substantially weakening the powerful air and armored forces deployed directly along the Sino-Soviet border in the north. Moscow's message to the Chinese, in other words, is that the Sino-American relationship may do little if anything to enhance Chinese foreign policy options, in this respect at least.

A second potential consequence may be suggested more diffidently, namely that in a peculiar fashion the Sino-Vietnamese war may have been the harbinger of a new, if brief period of reduced tension in the Sino-Soviet relationship. The recalcitrance of the Vietnamese backed by their Soviet allies, the heavy costs of the war itself, the weaknesses revealed in the Chinese military machine, and the knowledge of how expensive and lengthy a process it will be to remedy them, along with the concomitant reevaluation of Peking's ambitious economic development plans, may have combined to convince China's leaders that the time had arrived to explore Sino-Soviet détente through new negotiations. Further, it may be suggested that even if (as Moscow charged) Sino-American normalization encouraged China's attack against Vietnam, its more important long-term consequence may have been to enable the Chinese to proceed to the last remaining item on their current foreign policy agenda—limited Sino-Soviet détente. Peking's offer in April 1979 of negotiations with Moscow without prior conditions in order to resolve outstanding issues and improve relations eclipsed the means through which the offer was transmitted—an official notification that China would not renew the 1950 Treaty of Friendship, Alliance, and Mutual Assistance.[23] As a new series of Sino-Soviet talks began to appear probable in mid-1979, Deng Xiaoping cautioned against expecting too much in the way of improving relations with Moscow.[24] But a sometimes more candid Hong Kong communist journal suggested not only that a Sino-Soviet détente "would be a good thing" but also that "improving relations between China and the Soviet Union is a difficult, but not impossible task."[25] Of course, although the potential benefits to both sides of a reduction in Sino-Soviet tension have long been evident, one cannot preclude the possibility that China's offer had a purely tactical significance designed to engage the Soviets in further rounds of inconclusive talks and slow down Moscow's diplomatic and military drive into Asia. However, the Soviets, for their part, treated the Chinese offer seriously and seemed more than willing to test whether negotiations might not produce a new basis for Sino-Soviet relations. If nothing else, by playing its own "China card" Moscow attempted to raise anxieties in Washington about the strategic and political utility of its links with the PRC. Whether or not these were the motivations for China's reopening talks with the Soviet Union, the talks themselves proved fruitless and were suspended at Chinese initiative following the Soviet invasion of Afghanistan in December 1979. However, it would be unfortunate, to say the least, if the United States perceived any future reduction in Sino-Soviet tension primarily as a threat to American interests rather than as an opportunity for pursuing solutions to regional and global problems.

## THE SOVIET POSITION IN ASIA

The ambivalence of the Soviet response to the development of Sino-American relations—the leitmotif of our analysis up to this point—derives in part from the contradiction between Soviet political and military positions in Asia. On the one hand are the tangible signs of the growth of Soviet armed forces in Asia. This not only allays Soviet concerns about their own security, of course, but also increases their penchant for playing an important role in the regional politics of East, South, and Southeast Asia. While it is true that an accelerated rate of Japanese rearmament coupled with massive Western transfers of military technology to the PRC could theoretically reverse the favorable military trend, the political rather than the military realm is a more likely focus of Soviet concern.

Despite a great deal of diplomatic effort, and notwithstanding the American defeat in Indochina, the Soviets' political position in Asia compared with that of the United States and the PRC has, if anything, deteriorated in recent years. The US-Japanese security relationship remains in good shape; neutralism has declined as an option for Japanese foreign policy; and a more favorable climate exists in Japan for the planned growth of Japanese military power. Crude Soviet threats failed to avert the signing of the Sino-Japanese Treaty of Peace and Friendship in August 1978 with its "antihegemony" clause, and successive Japanese governments have put Moscow on notice that the issue of the northern territories will not fade away. The Association of Southeast Asian Nations (ASEAN) continues to view the USSR as a potential adversary and a nonlegitimate actor in its region. China's relationship with Moscow has already been sketched. Against this may be weighed Moscow's close ties with Hanoi, the ouster of the pro-Chinese Pol Pot regime in Kampuchea in early 1979; and the Soviet Union's tenuous occupation of Afghanistan. Taken together, these hardly cancel out the negative indicators of Moscow's relative political impotence in the area. In general, as Professor Robert Scalapino notes, Moscow has had relatively few successes in Asia and seems unlikely to derive substantial political benefits from its increasing military power at least in the foreseeable future (see page 152).[26] It is in this context that we must view Soviet concerns about the possible emergence of a hostile Washington-Tokyo-Peking coalition directed against the expansion of Soviet influence and power.

## FUTURE SOURCES OF CONCERN FOR THE SOVIET UNION

How much substance is there, then, to the nominal Soviet concern about such a tripartite united front? While a US-Japan-PRC military alliance is a theoretical policy option, it is unlikely to become a reality, as the more analytical of the Soviet commentators themselves realize. That Washington, even when piqued at provocative Soviet behavior, will jeopardize the central Soviet-American relationship by entering into a formal military partnership with Peking seems improbable. However, the Soviet invasion of Afghanistan undoubtedly accelerated the development of US-Chinese security ties symbolized by the exchange of visits by the US and Chinese defense ministers in the first half of 1980. Tokyo, too, notwithstanding its current interest in the Chinese economy and the burgeoning contacts with the PRC, will want to retain at least some semblance of its theoretically equidistant policy toward Moscow and Peking and may be expected to reject Chinese suggestions for a doubling of its defense expenditures. The issue of Taiwan may return to haunt the relations among the United States, China, and Japan. If, as seems very likely, Peking's united front approach toward Taiwan, combining inducements and reassurance, fails to break the resolve of Taiwan's leaders to maintain their de facto independence, PRC leaders may then resort to a more overtly threatening posture even at the risk of US and Japanese displeasure. Moreover, there can be no guarantee that disputes over trade, investment, cultural and educational exchanges, human rights, and international political and economic issues will not arise to complicate the US-PRC relationship.

Strangely enough, in some respects the Soviets may even stand to gain from the new Sino-American relationship. In the area of trade, for example, the proposal to grant MFN status to China was initially linked with its extension to the USSR at the same time. This linkage was broken by congressional resistance to SALT II and by the response to Soviet action in Afghanistan. However, the extension of MFN benefits to China in late 1979 nonetheless may serve as a precedent for similar largesse toward Moscow when US-Soviet relations improve. In fact, as one Soviet commentator pointed out, such economic issues are among "those practical questions that can be used as a test of whether or not the American assertions that they do not intend to put an anti-Soviet filling in the American-Chinese pie correspond to the truth."[27] US policy on export licensing for advanced technology may also be such a test, although Washington is likely to feel justified in perpetuating a favorable and growing China differential in view of the disparity of Soviet and Chinese technology as well as the political relationship concerned. (There is some question, in any case, as to how effective these controls are in practice.)[28]

The Soviet Union has by no means been a passive observer of the Washington-Peking entente. Although obviously reluctant to take new initiatives toward Peking after its earlier proposals were spurned, Soviet leaders including Brezhnev have indicated that these proposals are still open for discussion. As already noted, Moscow responded cautiously but affirmatively to the PRC's unexpected offer of new talks in the spring of 1979, in the expectation of at least deriving some marginal pressure against the United States. Even after the collapse of these talks in January 1980 Moscow has not totally abandoned the hope of ameliorating relations with its difficult neighbor.

While exploring the possibilities of a settlement with the PRC, Soviet leaders are apparently just a bit more sanguine that the United States and its allies will heed Soviet warnings against the folly of forging too close a relationship with China. Soviet commentators and leaders alike have frequently reiterated their opposition to a Sino-American relationship based on anti-Soviet sentiment, particularly one that took the form of close cooperation in security matters such as American supply of advanced military technology to the PRC. However, Moscow has not retaliated against the United States for normalizing relations with China—for example, by raising new issues in arms control negotiations. But a senior Soviet official warned even before normalization that a Sino-Soviet military alliance was not compatible with détente and would provoke Soviet countermeasures.[29] Not satisfied with Washington's disavowal of any intention to provide China with arms, Moscow has tried, so far in vain, to seal the valve before the flow of West European technology to China commences in earnest with American blessing. It seems not unlikely that the Soviets will prove even more difficult a negotiating partner in any further arms control talks with the United States, particularly those involving intermediate-range and "gray-area" weapons, if the United States and West Europe contribute significantly to the acceleration of China's military modernization. However, there is little if any evidence that the issue of Sino-American relations had a significant impact upon SALT II.

In the absence of a limited Sino-Soviet rapprochement, the most important impact of the new Sino-American relationship on Soviet behavior is likely to be its acceleration of Moscow's existing efforts to achieve positions of military strength in Asia. This in turn will fuel the familiar arms race spiral involving the United States, Japan, and China as well. The prospects for negotiated agreements on regional arms limitation measures, the Korean question, the neutralization of Southeast Asia, and so forth will further recede.

This is not the place to draw out the policy implications of our analysis. In any case, Professor Scalapino cogently argues the case for a policy of equilibrium rather than of a united front with China against the USSR (see page 151). Here it may be enough to note that Soviet concerns about the motives and objectives of the new Sino-American relationship are grounded in reality, however distorted Moscow's perceptions of that reality may be. Although the script of Sino-American relations contains numerous clauses of reassurance to the USSR that the Washington-Peking link is not directed against the Soviet Union, the subliminal message of an anti-Soviet combination is a sufficient goad to Moscow's suspicions. This is certainly not to argue that American foreign policy must be immobilized from fear of injuring Soviet sensibilities but simply to suggest that restrained and responsible statesmanship will recognize the wisdom of distinguishing between Chinese and American interests. Even as we intensify our interaction with the Chinese we must not jeopardize the equally important goal of bringing under control our continuing destructive competition with the USSR.

## NOTES

1. These offers are detailed and analyzed in Kenneth G. Lieberthal, *Sino-Soviet Conflict in the 1970s: Its Evolution and Implications for the Strategic Triangle* (Santa Monica: The Rand Corporation, 1978), R-2342-NA.

2. Actually, as Thomas M. Gottlieb demonstrates, the American option was raised in Peking as early as 1966. See his *Chinese Foreign Policy Factionalism and the Origins of the Strategic Triangle* (Santa Monica: The Rand Corporation, 1977), R-1902-NA.

3. *Far Eastern Affairs* (Moscow) No. 3 (1978) 14.

4. "Peking's Home and Foreign Policies," *Far Eastern Affairs* No. 2 (1979) 22–27.

5. B. N. Zanegin, "Demokraticheskaya administratsiya i diplomaticheskoe priznanie KNR" (The Democratic Administration and the Recognition of the PRC), *SShA* (USA) No. 3 (1979) (111) (March 1979) 53.

6. See the author's "China Policy in Carter's Year One," *Asian Survey* 18:5 (May 1978) 437–447.

7. *SShA* No. 2, 1978 (98) (February 1978) 31.

8. Ibid., 39, 38.

9. *Los Angeles Times*, 18 December 1978, I, 13.

10. *New York Times*, 22 December 1978, A7.

11. *Los Angeles Times*, 18 December 1978, I, 13.

12. *Far Eastern Affairs* No. 2 (1979) 26.

13. A. Bovin, "New Aspects of Relationships," *Izvestia*, 14 January 1979, 5; in *Current Digest of the Soviet Press* (CDSP) 31:2 (7 February 1979) 6.

14. Zanegin, "Demokraticheskaya administratsiya," op. cit., 54f.; A. Ivkov, "USA: Playing the 'Chinese Card' in Asia," *Far Eastern Affairs* No. 2 (1979) 77f.

15. "On the American-Chinese Meeting," *Pravda*, 2 February 1979, 5; in CDSP 31:5 (28 February 1979) 2; also *Christian Science Monitor*, 5 February 1979, 1.

16. *New York Times*, 10 February 1979, 4; *Pravda*, 4 February 1979, 4; in CDSP 31:5 (28 February 1979) 3.

17. S. Kondrashov, "Sower of Distrust and Hostility," *Pravda*, 8 February 1979, 5; in CDSP 31:5 (28 February 1979) 4.

18. B. N. Zanegin, "Vashington i Pekinskaya agressiya protiv SRV" (Washington and Peking's Aggression Against the SRV), *SShA* No. 5, 1979 (113) (May 1979) 78.

19. "Give Peking's Aggression a Resolute Rebuff," *Pravda*, 28 February 1979, 4; in CDSP 31:9 (28 March 1979) 7. (Emphasis added.)

20. Loc. cit.

21. Yury Zhukov, "The King of the Monkeys and the Two Tigers," *Pravda*, 5 March 1979, 4; in CDSP 31:9 (28 March 1979) 9.

22. A. Bovin, "Defeat," *Izvestia*, 21 March 1979, 5; in CDSP 31:12 (18 April 1979) 1ff.; *Christian Science Monitor*, 6 March 1979, 3.

23. Xinhua in English, 3 April 1979, in Foreign Broadcast Information Service Daily Report—The People's Republic of China (hereafter FBIS—PRC) 3 April 1979, C1.

24. Kyodo in English, in FBIS—PRC, 17 May 1979, D1.

25. Cheng Liu, "Sino-Soviet Relations Should Be Thawed," *Zhengming* (Hong Kong) 19 (1 May 1979) 64; in FBIS—PRC, 17 May 1979, U1.

26. See also Donald S. Zagoria, "The Soviet Quandary in Asia," *Foreign Affairs* 56:2 (January 1978) 306–323.

27. A. Bovin, "New Aspects of Relations," op. cit., 6.

28. See *New York Times*, 2 June 1979, A2.

29. Interview with G. Arbatov in *The Observer* (London), 21 November 1978, 15–17.

# B. NORMALIZATION OF SINO-AMERICAN RELATIONS AND THE KOREAN PENINSULA

**CHONG-SIK LEE**

Professor of Political Science
University of Pennsylvania

One of the ironies involved in the normalization of relations between China and the United States is that the two major powers came to terms in spite of the fact that the turbulent situation on the Korean peninsula has not been resolved. This is an irony, in that the Korean War was one of the principal causes of the delay in the establishment of diplomatic relations between the two countries. Had there not been the Korean War, and had the Chinese "volunteers" not intervened in that war, the United States might have recognized the People's Republic of China (PRC) in the 1950s. Korea is the only place in the world where troops of the United States and China have engaged in battle. Today, Korea is the only divided nation where the United States and the PRC maintain security treaties, respectively, with the opposing sides. The Republic of Korea (ROK) in the South signed a security treaty with the United States in 1954. The Democratic People's Republic of Korea (DPRK) in the North signed defense treaties with the PRC and the Soviet Union in 1961.

The normalization of relations between the two principal allies of North and South Korea therefore gave rise to the hope that the Sino-American accord would significantly change the course of events on the Korean peninsula and that as a result an atmosphere of peace would be ushered in. It appears, however, that whatever spillover effect there may be on the Korean peninsula will emerge only gradually and measuredly. In spite of the frequent mention of the Korean issue by Chinese and American leaders, and in spite of an attempt by UN Secretary General Kurt Waldheim to establish a bridge between the two Koreas, the confrontation in Korea remains as intractable as ever. In fact, the situation in Korea appears to have hardened even more after China and the United States signed their accord. Why has this been the case? Why is it that the two major nations with such magnitude of power have not been able to reduce tension in Korea? What are the future prospects?

## BACKGROUND TO NORMALIZATION: DIFFERING PERSPECTIVES OF THE TWO KOREAN STATES

The primary reason, of course, is the wide gap in goals and priorities between North and South Korea. The principal goal for North Korea has been the attainment of unification. Toward this end, the North Korean army invaded the South in 1950, and it had all but succeeded in defeating the South Korean forces when US forces intervened. Since then, the removal of foreign troops from the Korean soil has been one of North Korea's major aims or, indeed, credos. Since 1960 North Korean leaders have repeatedly advocated the removal of US troops, the establishment of a confederation, a reduction of armed forces on both sides, and an eventual unification. North Korea flatly rejects peaceful coexistence between the two Koreas as a plot of the "splitists" to perpetuate the division of Korea. The North Koreans repeatedly argued that the "German formula" is not applicable to Korea because Korea was not an aggressor defeated by the allies. The South Korean side, on the other hand, sees no alternative but to peacefully coexist for the time being, until such time as the two sides can interact without fear and distrust. The South Koreans regard the US troops in South Korea as the major deterrent against another invasion from the North in spite of the repeated disclaimer by North Korean leaders that they had not initiated the war in 1950 and that they have no intention of ever launching an invasion. While the South Koreans ardently hope for unification, it is a goal for the long term rather than for the immediate future.

Although the environment of détente created by President Nixon's historic visit to China in February 1972 did bring the representatives of North and South Korea together in May of that year, resulting in the issuing of a historic joint communiqué on 4 July, they nonetheless found the gap between their respective positions to be totally unbridgeable. When the North Korean side determined that South Korean authorities were willing neither to have the US forces withdrawn from South Korea nor to engage in talks to reduce armaments, the talks were abruptly terminated. The South Korean insistence on first dealing with the less sensitive and less difficult issues—such as trade and exchange of personnel—in order to build trust was interpreted as South Korea's unwillingness to resolve the central problem. The DPRK, instead, attempted to persuade world public opinion and particularly that in the United States of the validity of its stand, but its efforts were only partially successful. The DPRK spurned all the numerous calls from the ROK for resumption of bilateral talks.

When President Carter was inaugurated in 1977, North Korean leaders had reasons to be elated, particularly because he had advanced the withdrawal of US troops from Korea as one of the planks in his campaign platform. The North Koreans, therefore, toned down their hostile rhetoric against "American imperialism" and made a number of overtures for direct negotiations between the DPRK and the United States. But by March 1978 the North Korean leaders abandoned all hopes of President Carter's fulfilling his pledge. The 28 March issue of the party organ, *Nodong Sinmun* (Labor News), published an editorial entitled "The Beastly Nature of Imperialism Will Not Change" and launched the most vitriolic attack ever directed against the United States. President Carter was personally attacked as a man "more cunning than all the presidents before him," and his government was charged for "pushing through the aggressive policy toward Korea in the most wily and unscrupulous manner." The editorial further declared that "We shall firmly uphold our basic stand of fighting against American imperialism as before, and hoist the banner of anti-American struggle ever higher." The editorial also reaffirmed North Korea's stance against "the splitists in and out of Korea who attempt to create 'two Koreas' and perpetuate the division of the nation."[1]

President Carter's visit to South Korea in July 1979 and the call for tripartite talks among the two Koreas and the United States was met by outright hostility and scorn. The DPRK's Foreign Ministry's spokesman declared that "Carter's recent South Korean trip was not a 'peace' trip as he claimed, but a powder-reeking trip of a hypocrite agitating for aggression and war." The United States and South Korea were alleged to have "revealed once again their insidious schemes to perpetuate the division of Korea into 'two Koreas' by coming out with the theory of 'simultaneous admission of the north and the south of Korea into the UN' and the theory of their 'cross recognition.'" The three-way talks were rejected because they "are utterly infeasible and do not stand to reason . . . [i]t is a confused proposal."[2] The DPRK insisted that only it and the United States should discuss the question of withdrawing the US troops from South Korea and replacing the Korean Armistice Agreement with a peace treaty, and that the two Koreas should confine themselves to discussion of solutions for the reunification of Korea. Under this formula, the ROK in the South would have no right to interject itself even on matters dealing with a peace treaty in Korea, because only the United States and the DPRK were "actual parties to the armistice agreement." In 1954 President Syngman Rhee had refused to sign the armistice agreement, and Gen. Mark Clark alone had signed it for the allies in his capacity as the commanding general of the UN forces.

## REACTIONS TO NORMALIZATION

The manner with which the United States and the PRC "resolved" the Taiwan issue in conjunction with the normalization of relations with the PRC presented cause neither for joy nor for the relaxation of tension on the part of Pyongyang as well as that of Seoul. In fact, the formula adopted by the United States and China was the worst that could have been expected as far as the two governments in Korea were concerned. Both the DPRK and the ROK have attached major symbolic value to the treatment of Taiwan by the respective allies. Thus, in 1976, when Premier Hua Guofeng assumed his new office as the chairman of the Chinese Communist Party, President Kim Il-sŏng of the DPRK had seen fit to urge the new chairman to "build [his] country into a powerful socialist state, liberate Taiwan and unify the whole of China."[3] It is highly likely that the North Korean leadership regarded the handling of the Taiwan issue as an important yardstick in measuring the Chinese leaders' commitment to anti-imperialist revolution. This was particularly so because Peking's handling of the Taiwan issue had a direct bearing upon the Chinese attitude toward the unification of the Korean peninsula. A Chinese regime that was willing to compromise on the Taiwan issue could scarcely be relied upon to provide active support to North Korea's effort to unify Korea by "any possible means." As it happened, of course, the government of Premier Hua Guofeng was more concerned with the Soviet threat and the need to modernize China than with liberating Taiwan. This obviously gave no cause for the North Korean leaders to celebrate the Sino-American rapprochement.

The Taiwan formula was no less repulsive to the South Korean leaders. In January 1973, soon after the normalization of relations between China and Japan—a move that involved the Japanese abrogation of its treaty with the Republic of China in Taiwan (ROC)—President Park Chung Hee decried the "great blow" inflicted on the ROC. He saw a lesson there:

> Here we arrive at a conclusion that the small powers are urgently required to be armed with discreet judgment and behavior in pursuing their own survival, independence, and peace, and in shaping their own destiny amidst the whirlpool of international developments.[4]

While no similar statement was issued in the wake of the Sino-American normalization, President Park stated in his press conference of 19 January 1979: "In international politics, there is no perpetual friend nor a permanent enemy. Only national interest exists permanently."[5]

The third reason for the limited impact of the Sino-American rapprochement on the Korean peninsula is the hardening of the Soviet attitude toward the new triangular entente among China, Japan, and the United States. In 1971, when Sino-American détente began to take shape, some American strategists evidently assumed that the détente would usher in a new and peaceful environment in East Asia that would inevitably reduce the bellicosity of the North and South Korean regimes. This would, in turn, enable the United States to withdraw its ground troops in South Korea. Soviet-American relations appeared to be amicable, and the Soviet Union was not expected to react violently to the new turn of events, at least not to the extent that it would upset the balance of power in the region in favor of the United States.

These assumptions and expectations, however, proved to be illusory. The Soviet Union not only continued its program of reinforcing its military and naval strength in the Far East but also concluded a Treaty of Friendship and Cooperation with Vietnam in November 1978, causing alarm in Japan and the United States.[6] In December, Vietnam invaded Cambodia, and in February 1979 the Chinese invaded Vietnam.[7] The Sino-American détente may have reduced tension between China and the United States and improved the environment for Japan to engage in wide-ranging political and economic contacts with China, but it stiffened the Sino-Soviet and Soviet-American relations.

The US decision to withdraw its ground troops from Korea also resulted in heightening of tension on the Korean peninsula rather than the reverse. The initial decision to withdraw US troops was accompanied by a crash program of modernizing the South Korean military forces, which were inferior in armaments to those of North Korea. Either in response to this development or because the North Korean leaders had other motives, North Korea also engaged in a significant military buildup, in spite of its economic difficulties and the unwillingness of the Soviet Union to supply more sophisticated modern weapons. This escalation of the arms race was hardly conducive to the reduction of tension.

It was also clearly manifested that the North Korean allies lacked both the ability and the incentive to affect North Korean behavior. There are two factors that severely constrain the ability of both China and the Soviet Union. The first is that the DPRK leadership holds its strategy on unification to be sacrosanct and brooks no interference from any outside power, friend or foe. The second is the geographic location and political position of the DPRK between China and the Soviet Union. We shall return to these points presently.

These several factors prevented Sino-American détente from affecting the continuing confrontation between the two Koreas. The two Korean governments had already tested each other at negotiating tables in 1972 after the United States and China announced their decision to engage in talks and found the other side totally intractable.[8] Differences in *Weltanschauung*, differences on how the unification of Korea should be brought about, and differences regarding the respective priorities of the two sides were too great to be bridged merely by a change in the international environment.

The two governments on the Korean peninsula, therefore, reacted toward the news of Sino-American agreement of December 1978 with little emotion. The only public statement from the North appeared in the form of an editorial of the party organ, *Nogong Sinmun*, dated 23 December 1978. In it the North Koreans perfunctorily welcomed the normalization as a reflection of "an irresistible trend of our times" but sought to link the Sino-American accord to the Korean situation. It noted "with interest" that the United States declared not to pursue hegemony. "If the United States does not want to pursue hegemony in Asia," the editorial argued, it should withdraw all of its forces from the Korean peninsula. Other than this demand, the long editorial refrained from using pejorative terms against the United States. The mild tone of the editorial contrasted sharply with the vitriolic tone of the 28 March editorial.

Having accepted the Sino-American accord as a fait accompli, the North Korean leaders evidently decided to approach Washington to pursue the goal of having the US forces removed from Korea. The attitude of the DPRK toward the United States in subsequent months can be characterized as conciliatory. Thus, President Kim refrained from even mentioning the United States in welcoming Secretary General of the United Nations Kurt Waldheim on 3 May 1979. In welcoming Prince Norodom Sihanouk of Cambodia on 20 May, Kim praised his guest's struggles against "imperialism," but again, no mention was made of the United States.[9] On the occasion of hosting the world table tennis championship meet between April and May, some two dozen Western correspondents and some US residents of South Korean origin were invited to Pyongyang and given the standard welcome accorded to foreign visitors. Some of these reporters were given lengthy interviews with Kim Yŏng-nam, head of the International Program of the Korean Workers' Party, who has been quoted as having given the pledge that North Korea will "guarantee not to touch or harm" American interests in South Korea once the United States has withdrawn its troops from the South and helped to achieve Korean reunification through a confederation formula. He further pledged that North Korea would engage in talks with South Korea once the United States and the DPRK agreed on an agenda for future bilateral talks.[10]

These subtle moves by the DPRK, along with reports by visitors to Peking in April and May, indicated that North Korea was making a concerted effort to approach the United States and that it was willing to moderate its stance toward South Korea to a considerable extent in order to establish official contacts with the United States. Senator Jacob Javits of New York, who visited Peking in April, reported, for instance, that the Chinese were supportive of a tripartite meeting on Korea involving both North and South Korea and the United States.[11] Secretary Waldheim also reported on 1 May from Peking that the Chinese leaders expected the United States to play a role in facilitating Korean talks.[12] These "straws in the wind" were reciprocated by the United States. "Carter Administration sources" were quoted as having said in May that the United

States was "prepared to improve relations with North Korea if one of the two North Korean principal allies, China or the Soviet Union, takes the same action toward South Korea."[13] In June, DPRK diplomats at the UN were permitted to join a three-day seminar held in Washington, participants of which toured the White House and attended briefings by Pentagon and National Security Council officials.[14] Also in June, a Japanese newspaper, *Yomiuri Shimbun*, reported that the Japanese government was advised by the US government of its intention to permit North Korean travel in the United States for cultural activities and athletic events.[15]

This "diplomacy by gestures," however, came to an abrupt end in July, when the DPRK rebuffed a joint proposal by Presidents Carter and Park to hold tripartite talks. In the statement denouncing the proposal, as noted earlier, the DPRK made it clear that it was interested solely in bilateral talks with the United States, primarily to accomplish the withdrawal of US troops rather than to broaden the scope of discussions to the overall problems on the Korean peninsula. It is highly likely, of course, that the North Koreans were piqued by President Carter's announcement of 21 June in Japan that US troops would not be withdrawn until relations between the two Koreas improved.

North Korea was not alone in testing the new waters after the Sino-American accord was announced. President Park of the ROK announced on 19 January 1979 that he was ready to have South Korean officials meet with North Korean authorities anytime, anywhere, at whatever level, and without any conditions. He declared further that if North Korea accepted his proposal, the talks would deal with any subject that might be raised by either side.[16] This proposal led to a meeting of delegates from both sides at Panmunjom on 17 February, but the talks were moribund even before that meeting. The North Korean side chose to utilize the Central Committee of the Democratic Front for the Unification of the Fatherland, one of North Korea's front organizations, as a vehicle for negotiations, rather than the North-South Coordinating Committee that had been created in 1972 to deal with North-South relations. On 23 January the North Korean side issued a "new proposal" calling for a Pan-National Conference consisting of representatives of political parties and mass organizations from North and South Korea. It should be noted that the call for the Pan-National Conference had been made previously by President Kim Il-sŏng on 23 June 1973 after the South Korean president advocated the simultaneous admission of North and South Korea into the United Nations as separate entities. President Kim had denounced the South Korean proposal as an attempt to perpetuate the division of Korea and, instead, advocated the convening of a national conference to establish the "Confederate Republic of Koryo" that should join the UN as an united entity. As the UN Command in the South mobilized 150,000 American and South Korean forces in a military exercise ("Team Spirit of 1979") between 1 and 17 March, the northern side denounced it as "an intolerable challenge and insult to the sincere proposal of our side for peaceful unification,"[17] and no representatives were sent to the meeting called by the South Korean side for 28 March. It was obvious, in any event, that the North Korean leadership did not wish to engage in talks with the South Korean government under President Park Chung Hee. President Kim Il-sŏng had stated in March 1976 that "no relations should be maintained with [the present South Korean government], but it must be thoroughly isolated. Positive support should be given to the people of South Korea in their struggle for democracy so that a democratic government is established in South Korea."[18]

In the wake of the assassination of President Park on 26 October 1979, the DPRK began a campaign that might be characterized as a "peace offensive." Beginning on 9 November *Nodong Sinmun* printed numerous editorials calling for resumption of the North-South Korean dialogue, showing no change, however, on the North Korea formula of talks among representatives of "the people from all walks of life."[19] But in January 1980 the DPRK took a different stance from that in the past. In a letter delivered to the South Korean side on 12 January, North Korean Premier Yi Chong-ok invited his South Korean counterpart, Shin Hyun-hwak, to a meeting for "an unreserved exchange of views." If the dialogue was resumed, the North Korean side stood "ready to have talks between the authorities of the North and South, and furthermore, bring to maturity talks between the high-level authorities, along with the comprehensive political consultative conference already called for by the North Korean side."[20]

As of this writing, North Korean intentions are unclear. Given the fact that the North Korean premier has expressed his willingness to deal with his South Korean counterpart, and the fact that he used the official title of the Republic of Korea for the first time in history, it does represent a departure from the policy of the recent years. On the other hand, the messenger that carried the letter to the South Korean representative also delivered letters signed by Kim Il, the DPRK vice president, and addressed to ten other South Korean political leaders of varied viewpoints. These letters contained clauses that cast doubt on the motives behind the new move. Kim Il's letter to Yang Il-dong, president of the Democratic Unification Party, for example, included the following paragraph:

> As for the dialogue for the reunification of the country . . . it should be a comprehensive, nation-wide dialogue participated in not only by the authorities but also by all the political parties and public organizations and personages of various strata in the North and South and, at the same time, talks between the authorities may be held, if necessary.[21]

Kim Il's letter to Kim Dae-jung, cochairman of the National Union for Democracy and National Reunification, also included a paragraph that said:

> We think we can hold wide-ranging North-South political consultative talks, as well as [among] the authorities, *provided that the authorities are really for the independent and peaceful reunification of the country.*[22]

The mention of the "comprehensive political consultative conference" and various other items cited above caused the

South Korean side to interpret the new "overture" as an attempt to divide public opinion in South Korea, increase political unrest, and isolate South Korea from its major allies, including the United States.[23] In the past the phrase, "independent and peaceful reunification," which appeared in Kim Il's letter to Kim Dae-jung, has signified the North Korean formula of unification, that is, the withdrawal of US forces, rejection of the "two Koreas" formula, and so on. While the South Korean premier agreed to meet his counterpart and several preliminary meetings have been held since then, the outcome of the new move by the DPRK remains to be seen.

At the core of the stalemate in Korea has been the question of whether the de facto division of Korea should be recognized as such and the two societies across the truce line should coexist peacefully until such a time when fears and suspicions on each side are alleviated, or whether the two sides should move immediately toward the formation of a confederation through a "pan-nation consultative conference" of all the political parties and mass organizations. We have alluded to the arguments of the two sides in the beginning of this essay. It should be noted that the issue had come to the fore in North Korea as early as 1954, immediately after Premier Khrushchev advanced the policy of peaceful coexistence with the capitalist camp. President Kim Il-sŏng's various pronouncements indicate that there were elements within the North Korean leadership at that time that wished to extend the principle of peaceful coexistence into Korea. But, while Kim endorsed the principle as "absolutely correct" in the world arena, he was not about to extend the same principle to the Korean peninsula. He said in November 1954 that:

> . . . the idea that Korea could be separated into Northern and Southern parts and that the parts should coexist with each other is very dangerous; it is a view obstructing our efforts for unification. Those holding this view would relegate the responsibility of revolution in South Korea to the South Korean people and relieve of the people in North Korea the responsibility of liberating South Korea.

> This is nothing more than a justification for the division of the Fatherland and the perpetuation of the division.[24]

The DPRK president has not deviated from this stance since then. He has consistently denounced the "two Koreas" formula as well as the proposal for cross-recognition by the respective allies of the DPRK and the ROK.

## CHINESE AND SOVIET INFLUENCE UPON THE FUTURE OF THE KOREAN PENINSULA

In addition to reunification, another key issue has been the disposition of US troops in South Korea. Even since the truce agreement was signed in 1954, the DPRK has insisted on the withdrawal of US troops from Korean territory, and indeed, the expulsion of "foreign forces on a nation-wide scale" was incorporated as one of the political principles in Article 5 of the DPRK constitution adopted in 1972. Until now, DPRK leaders have shown no indication that they would yield on these issues. Only time will tell whether the North Korean leaders will modify their stance.

With regard to these two crucial issues, the ability of either of the North Korean allies to influence the DPRK has been severely limited. In the Chinese context, the PRC leaders have also consistently denounced a "two Chinas" formula and continue to do so. But, in order to achieve the Sino-American accord, they have set aside the Taiwan issue and have made it clear that they would be willing to tolerate the continuance of the ambivalent situation for the indefinite future. There is no talk of bringing about a "democratic revolution" in Taiwan, and PRC authorities have significantly modified their stance toward the government in Taiwan. By doing so, the Chinese leaders have set an example for the DPRK to follow, but it would have been counterproductive for them to suggest a shift in the DPRK policy toward peaceful coexistence between the two parts of Korea. Any attempt to pressure the DPRK leadership would have damaged the friendship between the two countries, and could have served to drive the DPRK toward the Soviet Union, which has been maintaining a cool but correct relationship with the DPRK. Mao's successors in the PRC have been susceptible to the charge of abandoning the cause of revolutionary struggle against imperialism, and they have made extraordinary efforts to seek the understanding of the DPRK leaders with respect to Sino-American rapprochement.

Thus, in May 1978 Chairman Hua Guofeng paid a six-day visit to the DPRK, and Deputy Premier Deng Xiaoping paid another visit in September. Significantly, Chairman Hua's visit was the first trip abroad by a Chinese party chairman since Mao Zedong went to Moscow in 1956, and it was the first stop abroad by Hua in his whirlwind trip. It is to be noted also that during Hua's visit he refrained from using the customary term "hegemonism," a vindictive term against the Soviet Union, and chose the word "domination"—a term more acceptable to North Korea. Interestingly enough, the DPRK president, who was effusive in his praise of the guest, reiterated his "full support" for the Chinese people's "just struggle for liberating Taiwan and achieving the unity of the country,"[25] a matter that was not mentioned in the guest's speech. Between 26 May and 1 June 1979, North Korea also received Deng Yingzhao, the widow of the late premier, Zhou Enlai, to unveil Zhou's statue in Hungnam.[26] In July, after the DPRK rejected the joint proposal of Presidents Carter and Park for a tripartite talk, Chinese Foreign Minister Huang Hua voiced support for the North Korean position.[27]

These visits by high-level Chinese officials are noteworthy, particularly in view of the fact that the North Koreans have not reciprocated them. President Kim Il-sŏng had paid a visit to Peking in 1975, and hence Chairman Hua's visit could be interpreted as a courtesy call in return. Nonetheless, no high-level North Korean officials of Deng's or Madame Zhou's stature have returned their visits. This situation raises the suspicion that it is China rather than the DPRK that has been anxious to win the other's support. Such an interpretation is supported by the fact that the DPRK is the only one among the communist nations in the world that has maintained a close bond of friendship with China for so long—except during the period of the

Great Proletarian Cultural Revolution—and is the only friendly communist country that shares a border with the PRC.

On the issue of US troops, the PRC may have more reasons to disagree with the DPRK, particularly in view of its intensified military connections with the United States, as exemplified during Secretary Brown's visit to the PRC in January 1980. During his May 1978 visit to Pyongyang, Chairman Hua made only a perfunctory reference to the "US policy of aggression and division."[28] During Secretary Brown's visit, the Chinese leaders failed to register their "standard complaint" about US troops in Korea.[29] Nonetheless, for reasons elaborated above, Peking officially continues to support the DPRK position that the US troops should be withdrawn.

Thus, the Chinese ability and desire to affect North Korea's policy toward South Korea is very limited. This is in part because the DPRK possesses the option of siding with the Soviet Union and rejecting China as an ally. Unlike the PRC, the DPRK restored its interparty (as well as its state) relations with the Soviet Union in 1964, after a two-year period of intense hostility.

But the "Russian card" is a difficult one for the DPRK to play. Unlike the Sino-North Korean relations, the DPRK's relationship with the Soviet Union has been formal, perfunctory, and cool. No high-level officials other than foreign ministers and department heads of parties have exchanged visits in recent years, and the majority of the delegations exchanged were concerned with economic matters.[30] Even though President Kim Il-sŏng took an extensive trip abroad in 1975, visiting China and various East European countries, he failed to stop over in Moscow despite the fact that his flight took him over Soviet territory.

The Soviet Union, which had extended a considerable amount of financial credit to the DPRK between 1968 and 1971, has reasons to disapprove of North Korea's economic as well as its foreign policy.[31] The DPRK's pro-China stance was detrimental to Soviet interests, as was its rejection of the peaceful coexistence formula for Korea that caused various economic and political difficulties for the DPRK. The Soviet Union had displayed a fairly clear stand on these various issues.[32] For example, the permission granted by the Soviet Union to the South Korean delegations to attend various international sports events and other gatherings held in the Soviet Union since 1973 was protested by the DPRK, but the Soviet Union did not cease the practice. One of these delegations in 1978 included a South Korean cabinet member who subsequently became the premier in 1979. While Soviet–North Korean trade, which amounted to some 324 million rubles in 1977, subsequently dwindled to barter trade, the Soviet Union engaged in indirect trade with South Korea in 1979 involving some $100 million, according to some sources. Soviet military aid to North Korea has also dwindled substantially since 1975.[33] It should be noted in this connection that whereas the DPRK denounced Vietnam for invading Cambodia, a Chinese ally, it did not find it appropriate to denounce the Chinese invasion of Vietnam. The aggravation of Soviet-American relations in the wake of the Soviet invasion of Afghanistan and the intensified cooperation between the United States and China may cause Soviet leaders to reconsider their attitude toward the DPRK, and the Soviet Union may increase its economic and military aid to North Korea in 1981. These inducements, however, are not likely to be sufficient to alter the outlook of the North Korean leaders toward the Soviet Union and China.

## CONCLUSION

Since the mid-1950s, the DPRK has advanced *chuch'e*, the principle of independence and self-reliance, as its guiding principle in foreign, unification, and economic policies. This principle enabled it to weather the difficult period since then with reasonable success. But its overemphasis on nationalism created numerous problems, particularly in the economic sphere. Autarchy—an extension of nationalism in the economic sphere—was clearly not compatible with an advanced economy, and without an advanced economy the DPRK could not effectively compete with South Korea in the international political, economic, or defense arenas.

It is obvious that similar reasoning persuaded the post-Mao leaders in China to moderate their stand on Taiwan and to enter into a détente relationship with the United States, just as Khrushchev had taken the road toward peaceful coexistence in the 1950s. It is reasonable to assume that the leaders in Pyongyang have been watching these events closely and weighing the alternatives presented to them. For a number of years, since Sino-American negotiations began, the DPRK has attempted to establish direct relations with the United States without modifying its unification and economic policies. The DPRK would have gained considerable advantage over South Korea had it been able to persuade the United States to withdraw its troops from South Korea and establish diplomatic and economic ties with Pyongyang. The defeat of the United States in Vietnam; the enunciation of the Nixon doctrine; and the inauguration of the Carter administration, with its pledge to withdraw US forces from Korea—all these undoubtedly served to encourage the North Korean leaders. The severely strained relationship between the United States and the Park Chung Hee government between 1976 and 1978 probably encouraged the North Korean leaders more. But the mutual interest of the United States and the ROK overcame the temporary strain, and by 1979 cooperation between the two countries had been restored. Even while the relationship was strained, the United States showed no sign of altering its policy of support for South Korea's defense and for its strategy of peaceful unification.

The DPRK also engaged in an extensive propaganda campaign aimed at the South Korean population to alienate them from the Park Chung Hee regime and to persuade them of the rationality and legitimacy of North Korea's formula for unification. Despite this effort, it is doubtful that more than a small minority in the South would support the North Korean formula. A vast majority of the South Koreans see no alternative but peaceful coexistence, and they would like to see negotiations on substantive issues begin on that basis. Inasmuch as this has been Seoul's policy since 1972, there has not been a sharp division within South Korea on the strategy for unification.

As we have already observed, all the major powers surrounding the Korean peninsula also find the peaceful coexistence of the two parts of Korea cogenial to their interest, the contrary verbal statements of official spokesmen notwithstanding. While there is a strong sentiment within Japan for the improvement of relations with North Korea, this does not necessarily result in Japanese support for the North Korean strategy on Korean unification. Japan has been South Korea's major trade partner since 1965, when the relationship between the two countries was normalized, and between 1978 and 1979 Japan and South Korea began to intensify their cooperation on defense matters. In April 1979 the chief of staff of the Japanese Self-Defense Forces visited South Korea, and the Korean-Japanese Parliamentary Conference on Security Affairs was established. In July the director general of the Japanese Defense Agency (in effect, the defense minister) paid his first official visit to Seoul.

It can be concluded, therefore, that neither the four major powers in East Asia nor the ROK are likely to change their policies with respect to relations between the two Korean states within the foreseeable future. Under this situation, North Korea must choose between the two alternatives of continuing the present confrontation or following the pattern established by its Chinese ally. The first choice may be congruent with the ideological viewpoint consistently expounded by Kim Il-sŏng, but the political and economic costs will be heavy indeed. The second course will require a shift in priorities, but, as is illustrated in the Chinese case, much is to be gained from it. It will not be very surprising, therefore, if the DPRK chooses to take the second option in the near future. Such a shift in North Korea's strategy will have an enormous impact on the future of the Korean people in both sides of the truce line.

Should the DPRK significantly modify its strategy on unification, we could then conclude that Sino-American normalization did indeed affect the Korean peninsula in a significant way. This is because such a shift would not have been possible without China having taken the lead by altering its strategy toward Taiwan and entering into a détente relationship with the United States. Preliminary signs indicate that the DPRK has indeed taken a cautious step toward a new strategy in January 1980, but only time will tell the extent and manner of the DPRK's adaptation of the Chinese model.

## NOTES

1. *Nodong Sinmun*, 28 March 1978.
2. *Pyongyang Times*, 14 July 1979.
3. These words appear in the brief congratulatory message sent by Kim Il-sŏng to Hua Guofeng on 24 October 1976. See PR 19:44 (5 November 1976) 14.
4. "New Year Press Conference by President Park Chung Hee," 12 January 1973. Korean Overseas Information Service (Seoul) 9.
5. "Pak Chŏng-hi taet'ongryŏng yŏn-du ki ja hoegyŏn" (New York Press Conference by President Park Chung Hee) 19 January 1979, Seoul, 11.
6. For analyses of these events and their significance see Drew Middleton, "Soviet-Vietnamese Treaty May Alter Sea Strategies," *New York Times* 8 November 1978; David Tharp, "Soviets Stun Japan with Pact with Vietnam," *New York Times*, 6 November 1978; and Douglas Pike, "The USSR and Vietnam: Into the Swamp," *Asian Survey* 19:12 (December 1979) 1159–1170.
7. See Sheldon W. Simon, "China, Vietnam, and ASEAN: The Politics of Polarization," *Asian Survey* 19:12 (December 1979) 1189–1198.
8. I have discussed the events of 1971–73 in "The Impact of the Sino-American Détente on Korea," in Gene T. Hsiao (ed.), *Sino-American Détente and Its Policy Implications* (New York: Praeger, 1974), 189–206; and in "The Détente and Korea," in William E. Griffith (ed.), *The World and the Great Power Triangles* (Cambridge: MIT Press, 1975), 321–396 and 446–453.
9. See the *Pyongyang Times*, 12 May and 26 May 1979, respectively, for President Kim Il-sŏng's speeches.
10. Bradley Martin, "Pyongyang Offers U.S. Guarantees," *Baltimore Sun*, 8 May 1979. *Dong-a Ilbo*, 18 May 1979, quoting John Walluck of the Hearst papers.

11. *Dong-a Ilbo*, 26 April 1979.
12. Ibid., 2 May 1979.
13. *Korea Herald*, 25 May 1979.
14. Ibid., 14 June 1979.
15. *Dong-a Ilbo*, 20 June 1979.
16. *New York Times*, 20 January 1979; *Wall Street Journal*, 22 January 1979.
17. *New York Times*, 1 March 1979.
18. Kim Il-Sŏng, "Talk with the Editor-in-Chief of the Japanese Politico-Theoretical Magazine, *Sekai*," Pyongyang, 1976, 27.
19. *Nodong Sinmun*, 9 November 1979.
20. Foreign Broadcast Information Service, Daily Report—Asia and Pacific (hereafter, FBIS—A&P), 14 January 1980, D1–D2.
21. Ibid., D9 (English translation by the Korean Central News Agency).
22. Ibid., D6 (Emphasis added.)
23. "Seoul Aides Wary of North Korea's Proposal for New Political Talks," *New York Times*, 15 January 1980.
24. "On Our Party's Policies for the Future Development of Agricultural Management," 3 November 1954, *Kim Il-sŏng sŏnjip* (Selected Works of Kim Il-sŏng), (Pyongyang, 1960) IV, 189.
25. For the text of the speeches, see PR 21:19 (12 May 1978) 9–15.
26. For details, see *Pyongyang Times*, 2 June 1979.
27. See "Support Korean People's Just Stand," BR 22:28 (20 July 1979) 27f.
28. PR 21:19 (12 May 1978) 14.
29. *Wall Street Journal*, 14 January 1980, 36.
30. DPRK Premier Pak Sŏng-ch'ŏl visited Moscow in January 1977, but it appears that the primary purpose of his visit was to seek Soviet assistance for North Korea's economy. For details, see Rainer Weichert, "Economic Relations between North Korea and the Soviet Union as Reflected in Soviet Sources," *Koreanische Studien*, May 1977, 22–35, particularly 32.
31. The DPRK refused to participate in the Council for Mutual Economic Assistance (COMECON), the Soviet version of the European Economic Community. The DPRK sought to rely more on imports of plants from the Western countries since 1970, while owing some $700 million to the USSR. For discussion of other points, see ibid.
32. For a more detailed discussion, see Donald S. Zagoria, "The Sino-Soviet Conflict and the Korean Problem," *Journal of Asiatic Studies* (Seoul) (July 1977) 89–104 at 94f.
33. Ibid., 92.

# C. NORMALIZATION AND SOUTHEAST ASIA

**BERNARD K. GORDON**

Professor, Department of Political Science
University of New Hampshire

Our China policy has long provided the best illustration of that special America-centered approach to world affairs: the hubris that believes that when things go right most of the credit should go to US policy and that when things go wrong it must be because Americans have done wrong. In the 1950s it was the fault-finding aspect that was most current: the question then was "Who lost China?" and scapegoats were sought for a development that had most to do with Mao and little, if anything, to do with a State Department conspiracy. Today it is the China normalization decision that illustrates the other side of the point. This is the belief that normalization has been brought about largely by American actions, or that the decision is a particularly bilateral development between China and America.

An example of this is found in the way the president's role has been portrayed to the press. We are told, for example, that when word came from Peking that agreement had been reached on the issue, Dr. Brzezinski strode to the Oval Office and announced: "Mr. President, you have it!" A similar sense of melodrama is also conveyed in the State Department's account of what took place in Peking:

> Vice Premier Teng Hsiao-p'ing [Deng Xiaoping] summoned Ambassador Woodcock to the Great Hall of the People, and in a remarkable and historic meeting, told

> him, in essence, that while the Chinese had in no way abandoned their longstanding position on Taiwan, and the unity of China, they were ready to move forward immediately.[1]

The fact of course is that the event derives as much from China's aims as from ours, and saying that does not detract from the courage and initiative of the Nixon-Kissinger openings to China in 1971–72. But the main point is that normalization was reached because it is deeply in China's interest, and that interest is grounded in other developments—in East Asia and Southeast Asia—that have been given much too little attention by Americans.

It is essential to identify what those other developments were, especially in a discussion of the impact of normalization on Southeast Asia. The reason is that Southeast Asia—as a region of small or vulnerable states—is particularly sensitive to the behavior of Asia's main actors. As Singapore's foreign minister has recently stressed, the security problems of Southeast Asia cannot be separated from what he calls the "broader and globally more crucial problems of security in the Pacific."[2] That interrelatedness is a point most often missing in American analyses, and it is the perspective from which I will begin this discussion.

## THE INDOCHINA SITUATION AND SOUTHEAST ASIA RELATIONS WITH CHINA

The fall of Saigon in 1975 was of course a momentous development for Southeast Asia; from the viewpoint of the ASEAN nations in particular,[3] Hanoi's victory meant that it was imperative to restructure or reassess relations with Asia's communist states. Malaysia and the Philippines had begun to move in that direction even before the US defeat, by normalizing their own relations with China. And within weeks of the Saigon collapse the Thai government played host to a very high-level delegation of the victorious Vietnamese. Singapore and Indonesia, though for not quite the same reasons, maintained somewhat more restraint toward both communist powers in the first few months after the fall of South Vietnam.[4] Nevertheless, it would be accurate to say that ASEAN as a whole began to alter its posture toward both Peking and Hanoi after 1975.

The reflection of this was in a series of meetings in 1976 and 1977 between Hanoi and the ASEAN states, and also between the ASEAN group and China. Among ASEAN's leaders, the main concern was to demonstrate to Hanoi that the group was not anti-Vietnamese and to try to gain some sense of Vietnam's intentions now that its long war with the Americans was over. Although Malaysia especially argued that Hanoi would have no thoughts of foreign adventures—because it now needed to devote its full energies to internal reconstruction—its preponderant military strength was of concern nevertheless. Hanoi's leaders were flushed with victory and had inherited a massive American arsenal—much of it in fine shape as a result of the sudden collapse of the Saigon government. Accordingly, a main ASEAN concern was to avoid any behavior that might seem in any way "provocative" and to hold out a friendly hand to Hanoi. It was hoped that this posture, along with the end of American military involvement in the area, would help reduce the Southeast Asian concerns of the other great powers.

The most specific reflection of this hope was the "neutralization" proposal put forward by Malaysia even before the Saigon defeat; this was a call for the recognition of Southeast Asia as a region of "freedom, independence, and neutrality." It has since become a main plank in ASEAN's overall foreign policy, although Singapore and Indonesia sometimes have been skeptical about its prospects for early realization. The reasons are that Indonesia's army leaders have been generally distrustful of the USSR since the murky coup events of September 1965 (in which the Soviet-aided Indonesian air force was at least somewhat involved), and they have been even more bitterly resentful of the less debatable role that China played. The increasingly bitter Sino-Soviet rivalry since then has not persuaded them that either of the two communist powers would be willing to forgo a major Southeast Asian presence.

Singapore's view has tended to be that the security of small states and weak regions is best assured if there is a competitive, simultaneous "presence" of several great powers. It is for that reason that Singapore Premier Lee Kwan Yew has so consistently urged US leaders not to depart from the region—even after Vietnam.

But even with those two qualifications, and whatever their separate misgivings about the specifics of the "neutralization" proposal, all in ASEAN have hoped that the region would not again become the cockpit of armed conflict, especially among superpowers. Whether under the Singapore notion of a regional "balance" of multiple major power involvement, or the more radical concept of great power forbearance advocated by the Malaysians, their common aim has been to blur the sharp lines of conflict that characterized Southeast Asia in the cold war period.

From the vantage point of 1981, it is clear that that has not happened, and one reflection of the new circumstances is that surface and submarine elements of the Soviet fleet now make regular use of the former US naval facility at Cam Ranh Bay in Vietnam. That development is reminiscent of the first Russian use of those harbor facilities, which occurred during the Russo-Japanese War of 1904–5. More important is the fact that Japan takes increasing exception to this and other signs of the growing Soviet military presence in East and Southeast Asia, and China recognizes it as a direct challenge. Indeed the Chinese have publicly stated that it may be necessary once again to teach the Vietnamese—who make these and other facilities available to the USSR—another "lesson" along the lines of Peking's three-week invasion of Vietnam in early 1979.

Southeast Asian governments, while they hardly can be expected to give open endorsement to those Chinese warnings, do seem to be moving steadily toward the Chinese view of Indochina events—in ways that will quicken polarization in Southeast Asia. Malaysia, for example, not long after the Chinese pullout from Vietnam, sent a very large delegation to Peking, led by its prime minister. Although advertised principally as a trade mission, it is certain that an equal purpose, with the endorsement of others in ASEAN, was to maintain a close dialogue with China in an environment where Soviet and Vietnamese intentions are increasingly suspect.[5] When the Malaysian premier returned home, and despite the fact that his government for so long had championed the "neutralization" concept, that was not his emphasis. He was less concerned to condemn both Vietnam and China for their invasions of others' territory than to report that "China is very concerned, very, very concerned about what is going on in Indochina. . . . China will not be satisfied unless some solution is found with regard to the future of Kampuchea." As a reporter commented, he seemed very "sympathetic" to the Chinese position.[6]

Thailand, another ASEAN member, can be considered the group's "front-line" state in matters Vietnamese, and Thai support for the Indochina cause championed by China has evidently gone beyond expressions of sympathy. Reflecting the fact that China has no overland way to supply the Cambodians ousted by Vietnam in January 1979, Bangkok reportedly has turned a blind eye to China's use of some small ports on the Thai coast. It was Prince Sihanouk, speaking in Peking, who indiscreetly let it be known that while "the Thai pretend neutrality" their practice is anti-Vietnamese.[7]

Even the Philippines leadership, which in recent years has made a career of publicly questioning the continued value to *its* security of the famous US bases there, reversed itself in May 1979. Manila has come to the position long urged by the United States on the matter: that the Philippines bases serve the interests of both nations. (In one of the ironies of contemporary Asia, this is of course the Chinese position as well.) Manuel Collantes, the long-standing Philippines deputy foreign minister, and often among the most vituperative in his denunciations of the American presence in the Philippines, now argues that the bases are "in the interests not only of the Philippines but most certainly of the United States." They are "needed to redress the power disequilibrium" in Asia, and their continued presence "prevents a polarization of Asia."[8]

Each of these recent steps by ASEAN members reflects their concern that far from being a neutral zone or the scene of reduced conflict—as was hoped in the post-Vietnam period—new lines of confrontation have formed in Southeast Asia and are hardening. In that hardening process, the China-US normalization has acted as a catalyst.

## THE PRECONDITIONS FOR SINO-AMERICAN NORMALIZATION

The proposition that I will advance centers on China's assessment of her security relative to the USSR. Specifically, China has been acutely aware and increasingly anxious about the augmented power the Soviet Union has achieved in the 1970s. This increased power is reflected both directly in Russian military strength and indirectly in the widening geographic presence that facilitates projection of that strength. China, as the militarily weaker power by far, and with no realistic prospect in this century to equal Soviet military power, has aimed recently to compensate for that weakness by the only other means available—greatly reducing the potential for conflicts on her other flanks. For China, this meant that it needed to improve significantly its relations with Japan and the United States, and it was precisely this program on which Peking was embarked by 1977.

Into this environment stepped Japan and the United States, each acting from a conviction that its China policy serves not only a sophisticated perception of the individual national interest but the goals of Asian peace and stability as well. I will not attempt here any full-scale analysis of the reasons why in the cases of both Japan and the United States the correctness of these convictions may be doubted; that is not my goal here. What needs to be said is that Japanese foreign policy has never been distinguished for its ability to project beyond the most immediate future and that the present Asian policy of the United States—especially amid the bitterness of the Sino-Russian conflict—has also seemed clumsy to many.[9]

With regard to the United States, what I have in mind of course is the "China card" proposition. This is the view that the United States, itself anxious about the growing power and widening involvements of the USSR, hastened the normalization of US relations with China in order to add to Soviet security concerns. A number of American voices, aware of the deepening relationships already under way between Japan and China in 1977–78, cautioned against a similar US approach in that period. They were sensitive to the likelihood that if the United States appeared to be making a too evident use of the "China card," Soviet fears of "encirclement" would be heightened.

Those Soviet fears in fact have been heightened: by developments that include the massive long-term trade agreements signed in early 1978 by China and Japan; by the China-Japan treaty with its famous "hegemony" clause just eight months later; and finally by the normalization of US-China relations, which came hard on the heels of the two Japan arrangements. The USSR has been at pains throughout and since those developments to demonstrate that it possesses the capacity to respond to such "provocation," for from Moscow's perspective they are certainly destabilizing to the structure of international politics in Asia.

In suggesting these causal connections, I recognize that it has always been the central difficulty in analyzing Soviet-American relations to determine which actions must be considered "initiatives" and which are "responses." A US foreign policy step that Americans believe to be a wholly defensive reaction is just as likely to be regarded by the USSR as an aggressive step, and vice versa. Yet in Southeast Asia, the period immediately following the US defeat in South Vietnam stands out as one in which neither Moscow or Washington was in an active phase. Everything from Carter's announcement of his intention to withdraw troops from Korea to the closure of the US bases in Thailand indicated quite an opposite American posture. And while we certainly know less of Soviet aims in that period, there is little in the Soviets' behavior in late 1975 and 1976 to suggest that Southeast Asia was high on the Soviet agenda.

It would be much closer to the realities of that period to

recognize that for approximately two years after the fall of Saigon something akin to a Soviet-American détente did exist in Southeast Asia. It does not exist today, and while it would be foolish to minimize the difficulty in locating the original sin in the matter, it must be asked what events appear to have set in motion the present heightening of tension in the region.

In my view, the first of the steps involved was the twenty-five-year Treaty of Friendship and Cooperation signed by Laos and Vietnam on 17 July 1977. The treaty called for an intensive degree of direct Vietnamese guidance and oversight in internal affairs and gave legitimacy to the presence of the sizable (40,000) Vietnamese military presence in Laos.[10] Its effect was the annexation of Laos (or at best to make Laos into a Vietnamese protectorate). The arrangement was applauded by the USSR, and though there had been tension before this, involving China's support for Cambodia and the Soviet role in Vietnam (and Laos), this was a development of different magnitude. For China, it meant that for the first time since the US defeat in South Vietnam the distribution of forces in Southeast Asia was materially changed.

It would also be difficult to argue with China's contention that the takeover in Laos was a clear sign that Hanoi does aim to succeed France—to establish in a new form an "Indochina Federation."[11] For both reasons an understanding of the present escalation of tension in Southeast Asia has to start with this little-remarked development in Laos. For China has long believed that its security requires that the Indochina region not be organized into a single political entity, and Vietnam's actions in Laos alone called that into question. To the further extent that it is the USSR that is the dominant external influence in Vietnam, this must represent an anathema to Peking. Accordingly, China's response after 1977 was to become even more steadfast in its support of the distasteful Pol Pot regime in Cambodia (which at least had the advantage of strongly resisting Vietnamese influence) and to take other actions in East Asia—involving both Japan and the United States—that in turn brought other Soviet and Vietnamese counterresponses.

This pattern of action and reaction, which by 1980 has led to an intense and possibly dangerous confrontation, can be seen in a nine-point chronology:

1. *July 1977:* The twenty-five-year Treaty of Friendship of Cooperation between Vietnam and Laos. *A Vietnam initiative*, endorsed by the USSR.
2. *December 1977:* China and Japan announce a five-year, $20 billion "long-term trade agreement," in which China for the first time will accept the equivalent of foreign aid. *A China response.*
3. *July 1978:* Vietnam joins the Soviet bloc economic community, COMECON (Council for Mutual Economic Assistance) as the first new member since Cuba joined in 1962, and the only Asian state to be a full member. *A major Soviet action.*
4. *August 1978:* China and Japan sign their long-delayed peace treaty, including the "antihegemony" clause to which the USSR strongly objects. *A China response*, but Japanese Foreign Minister Sonoda states that "I am now convinced that there will be no Soviet retaliation."
5. *3 November 1978:* The USSR and Vietnam sign a Treaty of Friendship, with a clearly military coloration (Article 6), and several unpublished annexes. *A clear Soviet retaliation response* of major proportions.
6. *15 December 1978:* China and the United States announce that diplomatic ties will be fully restored on 1 January. *A China response.*
7. *27 December 1978:* Vietnam's forces invade Cambodia; on 9 January oust the China-supported Pol Pot regime from Phnom Penh; and with public Soviet endorsement, substitute a new Cambodian government. *A Vietnamese response*, facilitated by its treaty with the USSR.
8. *February 1979:* China, immediately after Deng's return from the United States, invades northern Vietnam and, in a three-week war, causes 50,000 Vietnamese casualties and advertises its own as 20,000. It departs in March after "teaching a lesson." *China's answer.*

9. *10–11 May 1979:* Soviet Deputy Foreign Minister Firyubin and Vietnamese officials announce that indeed regular use of Cam Ranh Bay will be made by the Soviet fleet ("The access of Soviet military ships to Vietnamese harbors is a normal arrangement between countries having friendly relations.") *A major Soviet response.*

There probably will be some response to that latest Soviet escalation, particularly if the use made by the Soviet Pacific Fleet of Cam Ranh becomes so regular, and on such a scale, that it will have been transformed in all but name to a Soviet naval base in the South China Sea. That prospect already has led to considerable Japanese and American concern, and China has stated that it may be necessary to administer another "lesson" to Vietnam. But whatever the specifics of the next or tenth development, the seesaw pattern of mutually heightening escalations is clear. Because it is grounded so firmly in China's concerns over the increasingly close ties of Vietnam to the USSR, the dangers are obvious.

In that connection, I should note that there is a view that Vietnam was not initially inclined, in the period just after its conquest of the South, to adopt this pro-Soviet and anti-Chinese posture. That view stresses Hanoi's interest in "normalizing" relations with the United States after 1975, and its simultaneous invitations to Japanese and Western banking and economic leaders. In this perspective, it was principally the niggardliness of the United States, unresponsive to Vietnam's needs for postwar reconstruction assistance, that cooled Hanoi's enthusiasm and "forced" it to turn to the USSR.

There is some evidence for this viewpoint, but it ought not to be exaggerated. Among other considerations, Vietnam's "openness" to the United States was accompanied—for three years after Saigon's fall—by an insistence on some form of American reparations that was bound to be rejected by Congress. More important, by 1975 Hanoi's stance was already heavily pro-Soviet and its relations with China tense. The USSR paid for most of what was needed to achieve the final drive to take Saigon and was responsible for 60 percent of the military and industrial assistance Hanoi used in the war's final years. The fact that the Chinese connection was in trouble was undeniably evident soon afterward, when Le Duan was scheduled to visit Peking for a week in September 1975. He left instead for the provinces after only two days, and no communiqué was issued. As a German specialist on Soviet-Vietnamese affairs noted, this was "a phenomenon without precedent."[12] Later, when Vietnam took the Laos annexation step, that was the end, so far as Peking was concerned, and it terminated its aid projects in Vietnam.

China's effort significantly to change its Asian posture can be seen most clearly from that point on, and the connections it has forged with Japan since late 1977 (items 2 and 4 in the chronology) are especially important. The trade deal, negotiated in 1977, is by itself of massive proportions. The ink was hardly dry on that text when Deng Xiaoping called for its extension to eight years from five, and it is now certain that the "optimistic" average goal of $5 billion in two-way trade each year will have been exceeded in the first year alone.

Japan's willingness to undertake such a major trade and related investment in China was not a good omen for the USSR, which for years has sought to attract that kind of Japanese interest in Siberian development. More cold water was thrown on Soviet hopes when, despite the sternest of Russian warnings throughout 1978, China then persuaded the Japanese nevertheless to agree to the peace treaty and its hegemony code word.

There are several reasons why Japan was inclined to dismiss or at least discount those Soviet warnings. The most important stems from the fundamental Japanese view that, as between China and the USSR, it is far more important and far more comfortable for Japan to be in a decent working relationship with China. This derives from a host of cultural and historic considerations, often commented on, and that draw Japan to China. Beyond that, and without suggesting the primitive view of Japan as an "economic animal," there is much that is potentially very complementary between the two economies in their present stage. To mention only the most obvious one,

Japan needs to develop alternate sources of oil, which China represents, and Japan has considerable excess steelmaking capacity that China wants. And in overall commercial terms, there was (and is) a Japanese concern to establish a solid economic foothold in China before the United States and the European Economic Community (EEC) countries proceed too far.

These considerations were reinforced by elements of the political environment of importance to Japan—in particular the signs that the United States was itself now ready to greatly improve its relations with Peking. There were plenty of signals in Dr. Brzezinski's visit to China in May 1978, during which he reportedly regaled his Peking hosts with anti-Russian stories and learned some new ones, and even shared with them a US national security briefing based on NSC Document PRM-10. If there was any remaining doubt about the official US position on the issue of the China-Japan treaty, it was then dispelled when Prime Minister Fukuda visited the White House in the same period. From the US viewpoint, there was little to talk about just then, but Fukuda returned home with the seal of approval: President Carter had expressed "no objection" to the treaty and wished the premier "success in the negotiations."

Finally, it was not fashionable in Japan during 1977–78 to believe that Moscow's warnings should weigh too heavily. At one event that I attended while living in Japan, a Japanese audience clearly agreed with a visiting American Kremlinologist that Tokyo should not be deterred from the treaty by Russian bluster. After all, he asked, "What can they [the USSR] do about it?" And as I have mentioned, Foreign Minister Sonoda had assured the nation that "there will be no Soviet retaliation."

Nevertheless, the Soviet response—the 3 November treaty with Vietnam that I have listed as item 5 in the chronology—came soon afterward. Its signing in Moscow was accompanied by much fanfare and was formalized by the signatures of Brezhnev and Kosygin, along with Le Duan and Pham Van Dong. It was a very strong statement to China and also to Japan.

To China it was a statement that Vietnam was not to be

threatened, nor was the new Soviet guarantee to Hanoi to be taken lightly. Article 6 in the treaty is quite important, as is the extension of $3 billion in Soviet and East European aid to Vietnam during the next three years. To Japan it was a statement from Moscow that Tokyo's hopes for a Vietnamese policy of "moderation" in Southeast Asia would not be realized—at least not in the manner envisaged by the *Gaimusho*. The Soviet reaction to the intensifying China-Japan connection was, in other words, an escalation of the political temperature in Southeast Asia. It was a direct projection of the Soviet political presence, and as events have now turned out at Cam Ranh Bay, of its military presence as well.

From that Soviet escalation in Vietnam in November 1978 came China's response in December: the decision to press for normalization with the United States. Just as the USSR, in response to the warned-against China-Japan treaty, had sought to demonstrate that Moscow was not without options, so now it was China's opportunity to show in December that Peking could raise with an even higher card. This was the immediate background for the "remarkable and historic meeting" to which Deng Xiaoping summoned Mr. Woodcock in December 1978. The extension of Moscow's protection to Indochina, by virtue of the truly remarkable Vietnam-Soviet treaty the month before, was to China an intolerable adventure that could not go unanswered. Deng's summons to Woodcock, to convey the message that the time was ripe for normalization with the United States, was China's answer. To believe otherwise, and particularly to suppose that in China's thinking the decision emanated from narrowly Sino-American considerations, is a dangerous delusion.

## SOUTHEAST ASIAN REACTIONS TO NORMALIZATION

To Vietnam, of course, the meaning of the normalization decision was clear:

> Great Nation expansionists and big-power hegemonists [read China], working hand-in-glove with imperialism and other reactionary forces [read the United States and pre-

> sumably Japan] are pursuing a hostile policy against the Socialist Republic of Vietnam.[13]

That has remained Hanoi's rhetorical posture in the months since, and its behavior—backed now more clearly by the USSR—has aimed to consolidate further its leadership in Indochina. Vietnam's invasion of Cambodia came, after all, only two weeks after the announcement of normalization of US-China relations, and there is absolutely no evidence that Hanoi or Moscow was in the least awed by the formal improvement in Sino-American ties. Instead, the opposite seems the case, for despite China's three-week "lesson" in February and March, the government installed in Cambodia by Vietnam remains in place,[14] and Vietnamese-Soviet ties are further intensifying.

That is the main point—the fact that an important product of the normalization decision has been to heighten the Soviet role in Southeast Asia, and with it, the tension level in the area. Southeast Asia's noncommunist leaders have stepped gingerly around this point; after all, a generation has grown up on the idea that American foreign policy was stupid to close itself off from China in the first place. It is, then, difficult to criticize an American administration that decides to put an end to such foolishness, especially when the normalization is advertised as a step that will help facilitate Asian "stability." Nevertheless, there were some leading voices that understood immediately the destabilizing implications of the normalization decision. An editorial in the *Straits Times*, especially notable because it probably reflects leadership thinking in Singapore, sounded this caution just three days after the Carter announcement:

> Recognition of China . . . might have been the American way of warning Vietnam about its activities in Kampuchea and its ties with the USSR. In the short term the Sino-US duet *will probably drive Vietnam closer to the Russians*.[15]

Some other press reactions, especially those focused on the

Taiwan-related implications of the announcement, were more biting. A Bangkok newspaper, after first terming the normalization decision "the most important political development since the end of World War II," then added that it

> raises an important question for other countries which have defense treaties with the United States. The same question came up when North Vietnam overran South Vietnam, and now Israel has sounded the first sour note wondering about the reliability of American commitments. . . . Closer to home, Japan has not asked the question but must be wondering how good is her defense treaty with the United States.[16]

In a grim variation on the same theme, another Thai newspaper remarked that since the United States had been "unable" in the past to meet China's conditions for normalization, it had now reached agreement with Peking simply by "changing conditions":

> One can clearly see that a country's success in world politics depends on its prestige and clever foreign policy. How sincere it is toward another country is the last thing to take into consideration. The severing of the long-established US-Taiwan relations by the United States . . . should teach Thailand a good lesson on foreign policy implementation.[17]

Official comments from the foreign ministries in the ASEAN countries were of course less blunt. Their formal reactions to the normalization of US-China relations were carefully supportive and stressed that it was only logical for Peking and Washington to resume normal diplomatic ties. Indonesia's Foreign Minister Mochtar, however, was in Australia, where he was surprised by the announcement, and his initially spontaneous reaction to reporters was in a different vein. Attempting first to be cautiously "diplomatic," he called it a "very interesting situation [that] alters things somewhat." But then he went to the heart of the matter: the meaning of the normalization will become clear, he said, "only when we learn how the Soviet Union will react to the development."

He had in mind, of course, the issue that has been foremost in the thinking of ASEAN governments since the fall of Saigon: the future posture of Vietnam in the region, and the question of its developing Soviet ties. For as Mochtar concluded, Indochina "had already been affected by the Soviet-Vietnam Treaty of 3 November, and now by the US-China rapprochement."[18] This is the same point made by Singapore's foreign minister and mentioned at the beginning of this essay: that the problems of security in Southeast Asia are inseparable from the "globally more crucial problems of security in the Pacific."

They are crucial because the Pacific is uniquely the domain of all the superpowers. They are uniquely dangerous because the recent pattern of superpower behavior in Asia—in which the Sino-American normalization is a paramount feature—is clearly a pattern of escalation matched by counterescalation. The consequence in Southeast Asia, which hoped for and witnessed a partial softening of its lines of division for two years after Saigon's fall, is that those lines of division have hardened again. As a result, the prospect for new conflicts focusing on this region is greater than it has been for a decade. Moreover, because these now involve the opposing interests of the USSR and China (to say nothing of the awakening concerns of Japan), the likelihood that conflict will be on a wide scale, and at a higher level of intensity than ever before, is considerable.

Southeast Asia's leaders recognize that this hardening process is under way, and while they might hope that each of their nation's security prospects would be enhanced if somehow the tension level could again be reduced, they see no way other than through conventional statecraft to assure security. That is the explanation for the recent warnings by Indonesian leaders that ASEAN members could not "stand idly by" if Thailand was threatened by the large Vietnamese forces now dominating Cambodia, and adjacent to the Thai border. Singaporeans, in another conventional approach, have reminded Vietnam's leaders that even aside from ASEAN, the Chinese "have offered to be Thailand's protector."[19] And Americans, who thought after Vietnam that they would no longer have to hear again of Southeast Asia as a United States-related security issue, must reckon with new facts. The once-spurned Philippine bases are now anxiously sought after, and leading Indonesians are not only asking that the United States guarantee sales of military equipment to the ASEAN states but are calling as well for "close consultation between ASEAN and the US."[20]

These are, in my view, genuinely tragic developments, and run quite contrary to what was hoped would take place in Southeast Asia after 1975. To return to the theme with which I began this discussion, the United States by no means bears the sole or largest responsibility for Asia's growing tensions, but its share has to be recognized. For three years after the fall of Saigon, it seemed hellbent on a posture of withdrawal from Asia; and despite many disclaimers, that is what Asians generally thought and feared was taking place. Then, as part of an effort in 1978 to dispel those fears, the United States both encouraged a Japan-China rapprochement and undertook one of its own, in ways that were bound to heighten the concerns of Moscow and Hanoi precisely to the extent that those in Peking were allayed. It should not have been expected that there would be no Soviet or Vietnamese rejoinder, and the task for statesmanship now is to see whether the resulting tensions can be reduced.

Sadly, that has not been the direction of recent American policy. Among the ASEAN countries there is considerable apprehension that the United States has contributed to the "hardening" process in Southeast Asia to which I have referred, and many believe that it has been intensified since China-US normalization.

I had an opportunity to observe this in early 1980 while on a Southeast Asia visit that brought me to the ASEAN capitals and to Vietnam. My meetings were with foreign ministers, other cabinet members, and a number of other foreign policy specialists in the ASEAN countries. In Hanoi I met with Nguyen Co Thach, the new foreign minister, and with other Vietnamese officials. My visit there may have been the first since the war by an American whose field is contemporary foreign policy in East Asia.

I found that among the ASEAN governments there is a growing concern that since normalization the United States has gone much too far in its relations with China. Many leaders believe that on Southeast Asia affairs—Indochina especially—there is virtually no distinction between American and Chinese policy. The issue involved is the presence of the 200,000 Vietnamese troops in Cambodia, and Hanoi's continuing dominance of Cambodia since it installed the Heng Samrin government there early in 1979.

The ASEAN countries have continued to stress in public that Vietnam must withdraw and that the new government in Phnom Penh cannot be regarded as legitimate. At the same time, however, conversations with ASEAN leaders made it clear that many are interested in negotiating with Hanoi a resolution of the Cambodia problem. Their reason stems from two considerations: first, that so long as the issue remains unresolved, there will be a continuing temptation and opportunity for the USSR *and* China to intensify their involvements in Southeast Asia. Even the possibility of a Sino-Soviet confrontation cannot be minimized. The second consideration is related to the long-standing Southeast Asian view (argued today most openly by Indonesia and Malaysia) that China represents the major and long-term threat to the security of the region. For that reason, no Southeast Asian leader is anxious to do anything that enhances China's role in the region.

This has led to a dilemma on Cambodia, for on the one hand the ASEAN governments have condemned Vietnam's actions there from the outset. Their position has been that Vietnam's behavior constituted aggression and that its fruits cannot be accepted. At the same time, however, China has been the principal and most vocal advocate of the continued legitimacy of the ousted Pol Pot government (though even Peking does not endorse its savagery). The result has been that the ASEAN governments, to the extent that they too condemn Pol Pot's ouster, find that their voice adds to China's legitimacy in Southeast Asia.

Consequently, there have been quiet moves among some in ASEAN to maintain and even widen a dialogue with Vietnam. The hope is that Hanoi will sufficiently loosen its hold on Cambodia so that the government there—probably not one led by Heng Samrin—could be acceptable to all of the countries composing ASEAN. The situation is a stalemate, however, because China insists that no compromise and no negotiation with Hanoi is possible until all Vietnamese troops withdraw from Cambodia. Peking, in fact, proudly announces that its policy is to "bleed Hanoi" until the Vietnamese withdraw. And Vietnam, known, if not for its own stiffness, for nothing else, argues just as firmly that the "situation in Kampuchea is irreversible."

Nevertheless, there are growing signs that the Vietnamese leadership is willing to moderate its role in Cambodia. As I learned, the Vietnamese are prepared to discuss with ASEAN governments certain specific aspects of the composition of the Cambodian government. It is also likely that Hanoi is willing in addition to talk about some form of timetable for the withdrawal of its troops. That, however, is contingent on an end to the Chinese support of anti-Vietnam groups remaining in Cambodia (remnants of the Pol Pot forces, the so-called Khmer Rouge, and other groups that may be no more than bandits). Some of this was no doubt conveyed to the Malaysian leadership (and perhaps to the Thai) in a visit that Foreign Minister Nguyen Co Thach made to Kuala Lumpur and Bangkok in May 1980. No doubt he also made clear Vietnam's main point on the whole affair: that Hanoi will not again allow a government to be emplaced in Phnom Penh that could again forge a close relationship with China, as Pol Pot did from 1976 to 1978.

Into this mixture, the position of the United States has interposed a special difficulty, for the American posture has been to align itself firmly with China's view. Indeed in April 1980 the United States assistant secretary of state (Richard Holbrooke) went so far as to say that "we are not interested in producing a negotiated acceptance of the Vietnamese occupation of Cambodia. . . . Peace will not come to Cambodia until a government exists in Phnom Penh that can be accepted by both China and Vietnam."[21]

It is precisely this sort of statement that has led many in ASEAN to believe that the United States has gone too far in its relations with Peking. ASEAN officials also point to the decision by the Carter administration to authorize sales of "nonlethal" military equipment to China. They see that, along with US policy on Vietnam, as one more indicator that Washington is embarked on an Asia policy that is dangerous to the interests of Southeast Asian states.

Southeast Asian leaders understand, of course, that the reason for this American policy is the hope in Washington that an improved China-US relationship will act to restrain the Soviet Union. They strongly doubt, however, that this can be done by improving China's position in Southeast Asia, or by giving the appearance that the United States endorses China's policy of "bleeding" Hanoi. They add, moreover, that present American policy—which includes a trade embargo on Vietnam—also helps to reinforce Vietnam's dependence on the USSR.

The Hanoi-Moscow relationship, as this chapter has pointed out, is already reinforced by important economic and military agreements, and it appears to have left the Vietnamese with little choice except to accommodate to the evident Soviet insistence on making regular use of the naval facilities at Cam Ranh Bay. By early 1980, for example, it was clear that the USSR had a submarine tender on long-term station there, and it must never be forgotten that this location—only 800 miles due west of the US naval base at Subic Bay in the Philippines—means that the South China Sea can no longer be considered a secure route for Western, and especially Japanese seaborne transit.

Accordingly, it is widely believed in Southeast Asia that US policy since the normalization decision has had two negative results for the security of Southeast Asian states. One is the belief that Washington has helped to enhance China's role in the region (for example, in Thailand, where the Thai appear to allow China to move some supplies to the Pol Pot forces in Cambodia). The second unintended result of American policy has been to make less secure the military facilities of the United States itself in the region. Add to that the view that Vietnam is left with little choice other than to accept Soviet leadership, and it will be understood why, in Southeast Asia, the China-US normalization decision has come to be understood as less than helpful.

While Mr. Phan Hien, who has been Vietnam's deputy foreign minister, will not always be a source of wise or welcome advice to Americans, there are some points worth considering in a recent statement he made:

> Today the US is too fascinated by the meat of the Chinese market. But time will bring people to reality. If the US continues playing the "China card," the situation in Southeast Asia will be influenced. But if America wants a policy of balance and euqilibrium, it's up to them . . . *it's dangerous for countries only to keep their eyes on China.*[22]

## NOTES

1. Quoted in *China and Asia: An Analysis of China's Recent Policy Toward Neighboring States*, Report prepared by the Congressional Research Service for the House Committee on Foreign Affairs, Subcommittee on Asian and Pacific Affairs (March 1979), 3.

2., S. Rajaratnam, "New Cold War in the Pacific," *Asia-Pacific Community* (Winter 1978–79) 3.

3. The Association of Southeast Asian Nations (ASEAN) includes Indonesia, Singapore, Malaysia, Thailand, and the Philippines. The five-nation group was established in 1967.

4. Indonesia, as a charter member of the nonaligned group, maintained relations with North Vietnam throughout the war, but its ardor for Hanoi's cause lessened the more it learned. When the end came in Saigon, Indonesia was a member of the three-nation International Control Commission. The description of North Vietnamese behavior

given to me in Jakarta by a senior member just weeks afterward was not much distinguishable from the US military's.

5. The prime minister said as much, at least with regard to having coordinated with President Suharto of Indonesia his plan to "sound out China's views" (from a report in FBIS—A&P 11 May 1979). Doubts that the week-long visit of seventy-two officials was really to concentrate on trade were prompted by the fact that most of Kuala Lumpur's senior trade people were in Manila that week for the UNCTAD conference.

6. *Far Eastern Economic Review* (FEER), 25 May 1979, 13.

7. *FEER* 27 April 1979, 10f.

8. From a speech to the US-Philippines Mutual Defense Board, 17 May 1979, on the occasion of the twenty-first anniversary of the bases agreement, in FBIS—A&P 18 May 1979.

9. Among the clearest statements of this interpretation of the US approach are the recent writings of Chalmers Johnson. See, for example, his "Carter in Asia: McGovernism without McGovern," *Commentary* (January 1978), and "The New Thrust in China's Foreign Policy," *Foreign Affairs* (Fall 1978). Many have commented on the relative inability of the Japanese to project the consequences of their foreign policy actions. For a discussion that touches on this point, see my "Loose Cannon on a Rolling Deck? Japan's Changing Security Policies," *Orbis* (Winter 1979), especially 998–1005.

10. The importance that Hanoi attached to the treaty was reflected in the delegation sent to Laos to negotiate: Le Duan, Communist Party chief; Premier Pham Van Dong; Vice Premier Phan Hien; and the senior political officer in the Vietnamese army.

11. This is no more exceptionable than the automatic expectation of most of the Indonesian nationalists, in 1945, that they would succeed to the territory of the Dutch East Indies. In fact, the linguistic and other differences in the Dutch domain were no smaller than in "French Indochina."

12. Eberhard Schneider, "Soviet Vietnam Policy, 1975–76," *Aussenpolitik* 28:1 (1977) 15–34.

13. Truong Chinh, in a Hanoi speech on 22 December 1978, reported in FBIS—A&P 22 December 1978.

14. Vietnam and Cambodia signed a number of agreements and a Treaty of Peace, Friendship and Cooperation on 18 February 1979 that is stronger in some respects than the Vietnam-Laos treaty of 1977.

15. Editorial, "Carter's Card," *Straits Times* (Singapore) 18 December 1978; in FBIS—A&P 20 December 1978. (Emphasis added.)

16. *Nation Review*, 18 December 1978; in FBIS—A&P 18 December 1978.

17. Editorial, "Global Politics," in *Siang Puangchon*, 19 December 1978; in FBIS—A&P 22 December 1978.

18. As reported by Antara (Indonesia's news agency) 18 December 1978.

19. Editorial, "Aid for Thailand," *Straits Times* 25 May 1979.

20. Jusuf Wanandi, a prominent member of the Indonesian army-supported Center for Strategic and International Studies in Jakarta, in *FEER* 1 June 1979.

21. From the text of Mr. Holbrooke's speech to the Council on Foreign Relations in New York, 2 April 1980. (Emphasis added.)

22. Quoted by Murray Hiebert, who visited Vietnam in May 1979 as a representative of the Canadian-American Central Committee of the Mennonites, in FEER 15 June 1979, 13. (Emphasis added.)

# D. US-CHINA NORMALIZATION: THE JAPANESE PERSPECTIVE

**DONALD C. HELLMANN**

Professor, Political Science and International Studies
University of Washington

Normalization of relations between the United States and the People's Republic of China is one of a series of events in the last several years that have fundamentally reshaped the role of Japan in the Asian region and in the world. The basic impact on Japan of the normalization of US-China relations is best understood in the broader context of international developments encompassing the oil shocks of 1973 and the consequent economic dislocations, the debacle in Vietnam and the reduced US presence in East Asia, and the deterioration of Japan-Soviet relations. At the same time, the timing and manner in which the normalization occurred also has had significant and lasting influence on bilateral Japanese-American relations. For Japan, formalization of a cooperative relationship between Peking and Washington further signaled the end of the era in which a passive economic diplomacy would meet the basic needs of its foreign policy. Another strand of the web of international politics was extended to Tokyo, drawing the Japanese more fully into the strategic balance in East Asia and the world.

## THE HISTORICAL CONTEXT

Bilateral relations with the United States and with China are the two foreign policy issues that hold the deepest emotional and symbolic importance for all politically articulate groups in Japan. China has been at the center of the Japanese international horizon throughout the twentieth century, and the United States has been the preeminent concern for almost four decades. For the Japanese, China at once stands as a critical key to war or peace in East Asia, as potentially the world's largest market, as a nuclear-armed communist power, and as a nation with which cultural-historical connections are so profound as to cast an aura over things Chinese that transcends immediate political-economic considerations. Prior to the normalization of relations between Tokyo and Peking in the fall of 1972, the Japanese scrupulously followed the policy of diplomatic nonrecognition and economic sanctions dictated by the United States. At the same time, however, Japan cultivated more extensive informal ties with China than any other country and became Peking's largest trading partner. Since 1972 Sino-Japanese relations have broadened and deepened in the areas previously cultivated, and in the euphoria following recognition China replaced the United States as the "most liked nation" in Japanese opinion polls. Accordingly, the manner in which the United States undertook recognition of China was of singular importance to our major Asian ally—a consideration that should have been central to the policymakers in Washington. For the last decade, US policy toward East Asia in general and Japan in particular has been distinguished by twists and turns that have substantially altered our role in the region and raised questions about our long-term commitments there. For Japan, basic doubts about relations with the United States first arose at the time of the so-called Nixon shocks in the summer of 1971, which were brought about by the revelation that the United States had secretly contacted China and begun the process of rapprochement with Peking and that forced Japan to make various economic changes, including a revaluation of the yen. This American initiative was particularly upsetting to the Japanese in view of the high priority given to China in their policies and the years in which they had acquiesced to American demands on this matter. Thus, the end of the post-1945 Japanese-American honeymoon was linked to a sudden shift in US policy toward China, and this linkage in turn magnified the importance of this issue in relations between Washington and Tokyo.

Moreover, the issue of Taiwan retained importance for the Japanese even after they shifted diplomatic recognition from Taipei to Peking in 1972, partly because of extensive economic ties, but also because US policy on this issue was seen as a measure of American strategic credibility in East Asia in the wake of the debacle in Vietnam. The legal and symbolic foundation of the American strategic role in East Asia consisted of a series of bilateral treaties with Japan, South Korea, Taiwan, and the Philippines, plus the Southeast Asian Treaty Organization (SEATO). Following the collapse of Saigon in 1975, the withering away of SEATO in the following years, the prolonged base disputes with the Philippines, and then the announcement in early 1977 of American plans for troop withdrawals from South Korea (since modified), the US-Taiwan Mutual Defense Treaty took on enlarged importance in Tokyo as a measure of American commitment in the face of reduced military presence in the Western Pacific. Because the United States did not move as rapidly as expected to normalize relations with China, the importance of the American tie with Taiwan tended to receive exaggerated importance. Consequently, the Taiwan dimension of American policy was of particular importance to Japan despite the scope of Japanese ties with the mainland.

Finally, to appreciate Japan's posture regarding US-China diplomatic normalization, it is necessary to examine Chinese policy toward Tokyo in recent years. Relations with Japan have long held special importance for Peking, an importance that is rooted in deep cultural-historical ties, in the poignant and bitter experiences of Japanese imperial domination for most of the twentieth century (which directly touched the personal lives of all Chinese leaders) and, most important for our purposes, in the central role of the Japanese in the Asian power balance since 1950. In this last context, the Chinese have viewed Japan as essentially an extension of American power (e.g., the 1950 Sino-Soviet Treaty of Friendship and Alliance was directed against "Japan and any nation allied with Japan") despite the extensive bilateral ties that were cultivated during the two decades in which the United States remained isolated from China. Thus, Sino-Japanese relations developed on two distinct levels, the economic and the strategic. Another unique feature of these bilateral ties is the extent to which they were shaped by Chinese initiatives. Japan has assumed an extremely passive and reactive role in dealings with Peking even after the resumption of diplomatic ties in 1972, despite the leverage offered by Tokyo's economic power. Accordingly, the moves toward normalization of US-China relations fed into a Sino-Japanese relationship that was curiously one-sided.

For China, relations with Japan and the United States held highest priority, beyond the primacy accorded to policy toward the Soviet Union, and by the mid-1970s the Peking-Tokyo-Washington triangle became a central policy concern of the Chinese. This point, along with the demonstrated activism and success of China's diplomacy, needs to be stressed in order to balance the often presented interpretation of US-China relations as a function of American policy initiatives to meet our own geopolitical needs, be they containing the Soviet Union or establishing contact with one fourth of the globe's population. The Nixon-Kissinger opening to China and the Carter-Brzezinski normalization—"playing the China card"—were commonly perceived as exclusively American initiatives. One way of appreciating the extent to which the Chinese shaped the timing and substance of their normalization of relations with the United States is by looking at China's policy toward Japan in the context of East Asian affairs in the period preceding December 1978.

Historically, then, four factors have particular bearing on the Japanese response to US-China normalization: (1) Japanese policy toward China; (2) US policy toward Japan and East Asia; (3) the position of Taiwan in US and Japanese foreign policy; and (4) China's policy toward Japan and the balance of power in East Asia. It is now appropriate to explore how these factors converged in the latter part of 1979 and the implications normalization holds for the future of Japanese foreign policy.

## JAPAN AND THE NORMALIZATION OF US-CHINA RELATIONS

After normalization of Japanese diplomatic ties with the People's Republic of China in 1972, the pattern of Sino-Japanese relations established in the 1960s was continued. It remained essentially a "two Chinas" policy, except Peking replaced Taipei as the location of the official diplomatic mission, and emphasis was limited to the economic sphere despite discussions of international political matters. However, in the summer of 1978 the Japanese finally agreed to a Treaty of Peace and Friendship with the Chinese, a central feature of which was a clause that deplored "hegemonism" of any form in Asia. Japanese acquiescence to this clause, introduced at the insistence of the Chinese and directed at the Soviet Union, was seen by Moscow as a tilt by Japan toward Peking, prior Japanese policy having been built around "equidistance" from both China and Russia, and provoked basic changes in Soviet attitudes and policies toward Asia.

The Japanese appear to have been led to sign the treaty by three considerations: the lure of access to Chinese markets and raw materials, the aforementioned attraction China has traditionally held for Japan, and heavy-handed Soviet diplomacy that reinforced strong anti-Russian attitudes among both the Japanese public and most of the political elite. For the Soviets, this treaty was viewed as a triumph for Chinese diplomacy and as paving the way for a Tokyo-Peking entente that could isolate the Soviet Union in Asia. One immediate result was the Soviet-Vietnam treaty aimed at containing China, which paved the way for Hanoi's invasion of Kampuchea.

Thus, Japan's decision to sign the friendship treaty with China led directly to changes in the East Asian strategic landscape and to a blurring of the economic and strategic levels of Sino-Japanese relations that had been scrupulously separated in the past. This indirect involvement of Japan in regional power politics was a central aim of Peking (there is frequent and continuing mention of a Peking-Tokyo-Washington "alliance"), and it served to magnify the importance of the Japanese-American security tie, especially in the eyes of the Soviets. In this context, the American move to normalize relations with Peking accented this awkward position of Japan and contributed yet further to the success of Chinese diplomacy.

By mid-1978 Japanese-American relations were beset by economic as well as strategic strains and uncertainties. The huge bilateral trade deficit with Japan had stirred the smoldering demands for protectionist measures in Congress and among numerous interest groups. The intensity and depth of this conflict threatened other aspects of the alliance and even extended to Sino-Japanese relations. One of the reasons cited by the Carter administration for the hasty recognition of China was the urgent need to compete with Japan in "the world's largest market." The American security relation with Tokyo was shaken by the reduction of US military capabilities vis-à-vis the Soviet Union, both in Asia and globally.

There were also questions about American credibility that arose in part from the incoherence and inconsistency of US foreign policy in general and in part from repeated breakdowns in bilateral communication. Despite promises to reverse the secretive diplomatic style of Henry Kissinger, the Carter administration did not in any way inform Japan of its intent to remove US troops from South Korea. Moreover, by initially denying the Japanese the right to reprocess spent nuclear power rods, the administration raised doubts in an insulting manner about the intentions of the Japanese to develop nuclear weapons. Consequently, when President Carter informed Prime Minister Ohira of the projected recognition of China less than an hour before he announced it to the American public on television, it was seen in Tokyo as further evidence that the Japanese-American alliance was something less than a real partnership.

The Japanese did not disagree in principle with the American decision to normalize relations with Peking, but the timing and the substance of the agreement provided little assurance that this policy was the result of considered long-range diplomatic planning. It came at a moment when other threads of American foreign policy were becoming unraveled: the Shah was being deposed in Iran; the first deadline of the Camp David accord was not met, to the acute embarrassment of President Carter; and an imminent meeting with the Soviet Union for a "break-through" on SALT (a meeting that was subsequently called off) had brought into the open once again fundamental differences within the administration regarding the usefulness of détente. In this context, the decision to recognize Peking on terms that had essentially been available from the day the president was inaugurated seemed not so much a calculated move to bolster America's position in the world but rather a tactic to arrest the further disintegration of the administration's foreign policy. As previously noted, the secrecy and surprise surrounding the US action further detracted from a policy that, in Tokyo, was seen not only as acceptable but overdue. Consequently, the timing and diplomatic style of the US decision to normalize relations with China had a negative effect on Japan. An issue that, if differently handled, could easily have been used to bolster the Japanese-American alliance at a time of stress and doubt, in fact did little to improve bilateral relations or to provide a framework for broader regional cooperation.

Despite the fact that Japan had also unilaterally broken diplomatic relations with Taiwan in 1972, the American move to terminate its security treaty and to end formal political ties with Taiwan aroused considerable concern in Tokyo. This concern was rooted in Japanese perceptions of the regional security situation. The break with Taiwan was seen in some circles as further evidence of a curtailed US presence in Asia, especially since it was not done in the context of a broad strategy and left undefined the future of the American role. Moreover, the euphoria surrounding normalization provided Peking with singularly salutory conditions to take military action against Vietnam—to defy the Soviet Union and to punish Hanoi for its earlier conquest of Kampuchea. When this occurred, the Japanese were placed in the awkward position of having to condemn the aggression of a country with whom they were assiduously cultivating relations and to repudiate publicly insistent Chinese requests for Sino-Japanese-American collaboration against the Soviet Union. Because the strategic dimension of normalized US-China relations was left extremely vague, Japan's own role in Asia was drawn even more deeply into the shifting tides of events in the region in ways that magnified the passivity and weaknesses of the policy emanating from Tokyo. Again, an inadvertent side effect of America's China policy touched Japan in ways that complicated relations between Washington and Tokyo and raised doubts about whether Japan was truly the cornerstone of American policy toward Asia, as was repeatedly asserted by the Carter administration.

American recognition of Peking stimulated Chinese efforts to strengthen Sino-Japanese ties, especially on the political level. As Lynn Feintech has suggested, the rapid growth in US economic relations with China after January 1979 cannot realistically challenge the already preeminent role of Japanese business, except in special areas such as jet aircraft. Indeed, American competition for the China market remains a secondary consideration for Japan. However, US diplomatic normalization of relations with China did insure that the Japanese "tilt" toward China (and away from the Soviet Union) was pushed still further, and the Chinese have sought to solidify this policy direction through formal arrangements. The Tokyo visit of Vice Premier Deng Xiaoping in January 1979 on his return from his tour of the United States was just the first of many occasions on which the Chinese have attempted to promote an anti-Soviet "united front" in Asia involving Japan, China, and the United States. Peking has also encouraged the expansion of Japanese defense capabilities and, above all, has fed the animosity of the Japanese toward the Soviet Union. Although Japan has avoided outright acceptance of Chinese policies, recognition of Peking without a more comprehensive US Asian policy created an international context in which the Japanese are more susceptible to external pressures—especially those emanating from China.

## RELATIONS BETWEEN THE UNITED STATES, JAPAN, AND CHINA AFTER NORMALIZATION

US recognition of the PRC created as much uncertainty as promise for international stability in East Asia in the future, particularly from the Japanese perspective. Most important, it left political-security relations among the great powers without clear definition. Bilateral ties between Japan and the United States continue to flow in the channels of the Mutual Security Treaty drafted in the early 1950s, the height of the cold war. In view of the recent American emphasis on the Soviet Union as the primary security threat to Asia and the world, at first glance the old bottle of the alliance seems ideally suited for the new strategic wine. However, the significant reduction of American military capacities in the region over the past decade, the previously noted ambiguity of American intent, the pressure on Japan to expand its security role, and the dramatic shift in the status of China from foe to friend leave the Japanese in an indeterminate and awkward situation. In particular, the ambiguities of the security relationship between Peking and Washington is felt in Tokyo. If the United States does share, in the words of Secretary of Defense Brown, "common security interests" with China, and we are willing to sell military equipment to China, then the pressure on Japan to continue to tilt toward Peking (and away from Moscow) is greatly increased. Moreover, the open-ended and undefined nature of our security policy toward China serves both to heighten these pressures internationally and to fuel the internal Japanese security debate.

The costs for Japan to enter into an anti-Soviet alliance with China and the United States would be very substantial indeed. Japan is far more susceptible to direct Soviet political-military pressure than either Peking or Washington, and escalation of Soviet pressure would provide impetus for rapid movement without the promise of alleviation of the problem. Moreover, the efforts of Tokyo to participate in the economic development of Siberia (and at least keep the door ajar for a more balanced policy vis-à-vis Peking and Moscow) would be severely hurt by any move toward an anti-Soviet alliance. In the short run, it is clear that the interests of Japan are better served by remaining aloof from American and Chinese strategic maneuvers, at least until the long-term purpose and commitment of American policy is clarified. Finally, one ironic result of improved American relations with China without a clear overall US Asia policy is to enhance the capacity of Peking to influence Japanese security policy and to reduce the heretofore dominant role of the United States.

There are obvious and substantial benefits for the United States in maintaining friendly relations with both China and Japan. While these were frequently noted by the Carter administration, they should not be exaggerated. There is no assurance that this situation will bring peace to Asia and simplify the strategic calculus of America. Even if the Chinese continue to open their economy to the West and Japan and to stress a "developmental" policy orientation, it is clear that the military capacities of the country will continue to be developed as rapidly as possible and that Peking will deploy such capacity on behalf of her own national interests. If the United States and Japan continue to broaden and deepen their relations with China, it will insure that both nations will be increasingly touched by foreign policy decisions taken in Peking, but there are few assurances that the influence of Washington and Tokyo will be substantially enhanced. Indeed, Japan and the United States have now been drawn more fully into the tangle of international and domestic events that surround the still unfolding story of revolution in China. Whether diplomatic recognition and improved economic relations will dissolve the political conflicts associated with China in this century or merely complicate the already tangled strategic situation for both Japan and the United States is a question that only the passage of time can answer.

# E. STRATEGIC ISSUES IN US POLICIES TOWARD ASIA*

**ROBERT A. SCALAPINO**

Director, Institute of East Asian Studies
University of California, Berkeley

Of the many changes in international politics since World War II, none has been more far-reaching in its consequences than the end of monolithic communism. Rather than use the term "monolithic," we should perhaps refer to the demise of "Russia-centric communism." Even in the period when the Comintern and Cominform dominated the international communist movement, and were in turn controlled by Moscow, communism was never precisely monolithic. Quite apart from splinter groups, of which the Trotskyites were the most prominent, the various official communist parties were encouraged to pursue tactics—specific policies—that supposedly accorded with the unique national circumstances in which they found themselves. Yet international communism remained broadly unified by one iron bond—the commitment to the Great Russian Revolution, and—overwhelmingly—to its contemporary manifestations as well, including that "peerless leader of the global proletariat," Joseph Stalin. One was defined as a communist according to whether one accepted or rejected the USSR as the fatherland of the working class of the world.

In retrospect, it now seems inevitable that as the practice of communism in one state spread to nations other than the USSR, communist policies would diverge and that sooner or

* An earlier version of this essay appeared in the French journal *Politique Internationale*, 4, rue Cambon, 75001 Paris, France. It appears here with the permission of that journal.

later these divergencies would seek ideological sanction. This development in turn would provoke serious trouble in a movement where legitimacy had been conferred from one source and rested upon that source's interpretation of the canons of the Marxist faith. When there was a single source of communist state power, Russian national interests could be defined as the interests of working class everywhere, and hence, the first obligation of any good communist. With the emergence of multiple "national interests" within the communist world, ineradicable fissures were certain to emerge.

In spite of what presently appears wholly logical, however, neither the communists nor the noncommunists were prepared for the explosions that have ripped international communism apart in the past three decades. None of us realized how quickly nationalism would emerge triumphant within a movement so strongly committed initially to international class solidarity. If Marxism is not the only international doctrine to taste defeat in the politics of our times, that defeat must seem the more bitter because of the promise to which several generations of dedicated communists devoted their lives. Communist nationalism, moreover, has proved to be particularly formidable, partly because the long-pent-up patriotic emotions of the educated ex-colonial elite liberated from foreign control can combine with the historic xenophobia of the masses in those same societies. And it can be given immediate effect via the proficient organizational tactics upon which communists have rightfully prided themselves. No nineteenth- or early-twentieth-century leaders of the West except Hitler were ever able to mobilize their citizenry so fully and effectively under nationalist banners as have the communist leaders of the recent decades.

It would be difficult to overestimate the impact these developments have had upon the course of international politics, including the foreign policies of the United States. Especially in a region like Asia where the Sino-Soviet cleavage now influences almost every other aspect of the international scene, the advent of communist nationalism has provided both opportunities and dilemmas. On the one hand, it has ended the threat that an intimate and enduring Sino-Soviet alliance would dominate the Eurasian continent. Yet, on the other hand, it has raised the most profound issues of strategy, and also the question of whether US foreign policy can or should retain the type of ethical or ideological underpinning that previously provided the basis for broad support from the American people.

It is thus not surprising that in recent times two basic and interrelated issues have emerged with respect to US policies in Asia, impinging upon every specific proposal. While these issues have not always been articulated or even fully comprehended by our practitioners of foreign policy, not to mention other elements of American society, they are increasingly becoming the crucial questions that will determine our course—and quite possibly, that of much of Asia.

## THE CASE FOR A "UNITED FRONT" POLICY

Put in its most elemental terms, the first issue is whether we should follow a "united front" or an "equilibrium" policy. We can define a united front policy as one dedicated to the emergence of a Sino-Japanese-American entente, the underlying purpose of which would be to prevent further Soviet expansion in Asia. The support for such a strategy relies upon the following theses:

First, as "the other superpower" the Soviet Union is the only nation that can wreak great physical damage upon the United States. Given the fact that it is rapidly augmenting its military power on a global scale, conventional as well as nuclear, and that profound differences continue to separate us, the USSR must be regarded as our principal threat.

Second, the Soviet Union intends to be major Asian as well as European power. Not only is it seeking to develop Siberia and Central Asia, both militarily and economically; it is also extending its involvement throughout East and South Asia, in a variety of ways. Unchecked, the USSR will continue its multifaceted expansion, to the detriment of Chinese and Japanese as well as American interests.

Third, no nation of the Pacific-Asian region is prepared to

challenge this expansion effectively alone. China will be militarily and economically weak beyond the end of this century, whatever gains it may make under its new policies, and thus no match for Moscow. Japan, while beginning to stir under a combination of Soviet threat and American confusion, faces a complex economic and political future and is unlikely to assume responsibilities of a strategic nature other than those relating to self-defense. And the United States, still traumatized by its defeat in Indochina, is in no mood to accept a unilateral obligation to uphold the security of Asia, even Northeast Asia. Thus, only a collective effort can succeed. It must be an effort short of alliance, since such an alliance is unacceptable to any of the states involved. It cannot be a duplicate of NATO or even the European Economic Community. Yet, as a sustained interaction aimed at promoting and aggregating the strength and stability of each party, it will serve in some measure as the counterpart of these Western organizations.

If these arguments have a classical ring (aligning with the enemy of one's enemy in the quest for a balance of power), their proponents believe that they fit the contemporary scene well. And they have gained strength recently as American-Soviet relations have deteriorated. The current trend may stabilize or be reversed, but one need not be an unmitigated pessimist to note that the political horizon is dominated at present by issues that divide Washington and Moscow, some of them exceedingly dangerous.

Above all, a gnawing anxiety grips many Americans—even those committed to détente—as the Soviet Union approaches that status that we vaguely call military parity. The United States has lived with global power for decades at this point. It has been party to successes and failures; gauged events correctly and made serious mistakes; endured the glory and the frustrations of the mighty. Gradually, the combination of experience and institutional safeguards has made power acceptable if not entirely comfortable. As the USSR now approaches military parity—and hence coequal global power—Americans wonder what further experiences Russia will have to undergo and what internal institutional constraints it will need to fashion in order to moderate its newly gained power. In sum, can Soviet leaders and the Soviet system handle great military power without grave danger to the rest of the world? Against the psychological uneasiness flowing from this uncertainty and fed by recent events in Africa, Indochina, and Afghanistan, a policy on Sino-Japanese-American "collaboration" acquires added attractiveness.

## THE CASE FOR AN "EQUILIBRIUM" POLICY

What is the alternative? The equilibrium strategy is based upon a conscious effort to keep relations with Russia and China in rough balance, cognizant of the fact that the two relationships must be significantly different, the USSR being a global power while the PRC is a regional power at most. This strategy requires that the United States avoid a sustained tilt toward either Moscow or Peking, eschewing the concept of alignment with one against the other. Rather, it is based upon the premise that maximum flexibility is preferable for the United States in both cases. The aim would be a broadening of each relationship, but with a clear understanding that major differences between us will continue to prevail. Hence, the American preparation must be for involvement in intensive, protracted negotiations with an insistence upon two principles: reciprocity and accountability. The arguments favoring this strategy can be set forth as follows:

First, irrespective of any differences, an American working relationship with the Soviet Union is critical to the future of all states and people. Issues such as strategic arms control cannot await some later golden age. Ultimately, moreover, a comprehensive peace for the Middle East may well hinge upon Soviet cooperation, and that is likely to be true for Africa and Asia as well. None of this indicates that Washington should lower its guard or proffer a series of unilateral concessions to Moscow. However, to confront the Russians with an anti-Soviet entente in Asia, coupled with NATO in the West, inevitably raises the specter of a two-front challenge reminiscent to the Russians of the 1930s, when Moscow faced Germany on its western flank and Japan in the East. Could this not lead to a return of the cold war or, at a minimum, to intensified Soviet retaliation expressed in a variety of unpleasant ways? Thus, the risks of stalemate or retrogression on many fronts would increase, as would the threat of conflict, at least via surrogates.

Second, although it is true that the Soviet Union is en route to strengthening its military power in Asia as elsewhere, and undoubtedly will further develop its military installations in its own Asian territories, notably Siberia, it remains very questionable as to whether the USSR can parlay military power into political influence in Asia.

Observe the status of the Soviet Union in this region today. As Donald Hellmann has observed, its relations with Japan have not been worse since World War II. China, from the viewpoint of Moscow, is a debacle. Even with North Korea, as Chong-sik Lee has indicated, relations have been distinctly cool. In South and Southeast Asia, the situation is only moderately better, with much hinging upon internal developments over which Moscow generally has marginal influence, as Bernard Gordon pointed out. Thus, recent gains with respect to Afghanistan are offset by the heightened efforts of India to seek an equidistant position. Vietnam, of course, represents a Soviet "success," as do Laos and Kampuchea by extension. But this is clearly a marriage of convenience for Hanoi, not of love—the quest of a small but expansionist-minded nation living cheek-by-jowl with a huge nation en route to power for a meaningful source of external assistance.

When one examines the scene as a whole, Soviet successes in the East have been few, including those within the various communist movements of the region. The Soviet Union is not the wave of the future in Asia. Russian diplomacy has been too rigid, Russian culture too foreign, the Soviet developmental model too inapplicable, and the ethnic differences too striking to provide the USSR with extensive political access to this vital region. There is always the possibility, to be sure, that an effort will be made to substitute sheer military power for the economic and political approaches to influence, as Russian intervention in Afghanistan so graphically illustrates, but is that temptation not heightened by confronting Moscow with what appears to it as a de facto alliance brought together solely by anti-Soviet concerns?

Third, is it not likely to be China rather than Russia that presents the greater problem for other Asian states in the long run? At present, China is weak—the prototype of a massively backward society. It is plagued by the serious mistakes of the past decade that not only exacerbated its economic deficiencies but bequeathed deep political fissures that have not yet been healed. Yet even in its weakness, China manifests its future potentials in its quarrel with Vietnam, its involvement with the communist guerrilla movements of the region, and its "special relations" with North Korea. Like any major state striving to improve its security, China intends to develop a buffer state system to the extent that conditions permit. It is bound to consider such a region as Southeast Asia as its appropriate sphere of influence. Hostility will not be tolerated. Even neutralism will not be accepted without a strenuous effort to cultivate another "friend of China."

To these ends, Peking is not without means. The nation of China contains a billion people at this point, dwarfing every neighbor including the Russians. While a huge population constitutes a weakness as well as a strength, the psychological impact of China's dimensions, especially upon small, nearby states, should not be minimized. Chinese diplomacy, moreover, frequently demonstrates a subtleness and sophistication distilled from a long history of interaction with peripheral Asian peoples. The use of "carrot-and-stick diplomacy" is an art Chinese rulers perfected centuries ago. Now, new instrumentalities are available. The capacity to raise or lower assistance to communist guerrilla movements, for example, constitutes leverage upon such hard-pressed states as Burma and Thailand. On the other hand, the techniques used to induce support can also be loving if paternal, as in the current cultivation of North Korea.[7]

In truth, classical Chinese culture shaped the major traditions of many of the countries of East Asia, Japan included.

This heritage is not without its impact upon the political propensities of the present and, one may presume, the future. Even in its revolutionary form, China has a relevance denied Moscow. The issue of modernizing a massive peasantry, of coping with the urban-rural gap, remains for much of Asia the central challenge. Only Japan is well beyond this issue, with (ironically) Taiwan close behind, and societies like South Korea moving rapidly up, albeit with some strains ensuing. While there is good reason to debate whether the PRC's approach provides satisfactory solutions, there can be little doubt that the peasant antecedents of many of its leaders and the concern expressed for agricultural modernization carry with them an image distinctly different from that conveyed by the USSR in recent times.

All of the signs thus indicate that China will play an ever larger role in the politics of Asia as conditions permit. Two questions follow. Will that role accord with the interests of the other Asian states, and with those of the United States? And what will be the impact of extensive assistance ot China at this point, associated or unassociated with the concept of containing the USSR? Can it not be argued that a powerful, strongly nationalist China will inevitably gravitate toward hegemonism in East Asia, its pledges notwithstanding? Are the warnings not present in the current struggle for influence in Indochina, the adamant Chinese stand on disputed territorial issues stretching from the north (involving the USSR, Japan, and even the two Koreas) to the south (involving Vietnam, the Philippines, and of course Taiwan)? Are they not equally present in the complexities engendered by China's relationship with current guerrilla movements and the overseas Chinese as well as to the existing governments of South Asia?

It can be asserted, of course, that to involve China in extensive economic and military relations with Japan and the West will provide a leavening influence, not only making any restoration of a Sino-Soviet alliance less likely but inhibiting future Chinese leaders from threatening these sources of support by actions considered aggressive. It may also be asserted that by thrusting China upon the path of modernization with all due speed the energies of this people will be wholly consumed in indigenous tasks, reducing the interest in, and potential for, external adventurism.

These arguments, while persuasive, are not conclusive. As we shall shortly note, many factors make a restoration of a Sino-Soviet alliance unlikely; and while economic aid and even military sales to the PRC may be warranted, these acts do not guarantee fidelity to the purposes of the donors, as the recent history of international relations should have demonstrated conclusively. Moreover, many nations heavily engaged in modernization have found sufficient energy for external expansion—indeed, that is the history of Western imperialism.

In sum, China's interests in Asia are not the same as those of the United States, Japan, or most if not all other Asian states. The common denominator of the present is a negative one—concern over Soviet policies. While legitimate, that is not sufficient to warrant an alignment of the type advocated by the united front theorists, assert the doubters.

The issues just introduced raise a final argument by the equilibrium proponents, one relating to the issue of future Sino-Soviet relations. At one point, it was argued that only if the United States quickly normalized its relations with the PRC, prior to the death of Mao, could we prevent a shift in Chinese foreign policy, a drive to restore the Sino-Soviet alliance. The united front proponents also used this argument initially. As events turned out differently and antagonism between the PRC and the USSR rose to new heights after Mao's death, the argument was reversed. Now, a united front was necessary to prevent China from being attacked by the USSR.

In point of fact, neither of these two arguments is viable according to equilibrium advocates. While efforts may well be made from time to time to reduce the current level of tension between Russia and China, possibly with some success, the restoration of a 1950-type alliance is most improbable. (One might note, incidentally, that the Chinese have recently abrogated their security treaty with the USSR.) The forces now operating within each of these societies and, more important, the diverse nature of the two societies themselves, preclude a return to an earlier era. Two empires are moving toward each other with accelerating speed as each seeks to populate and develop its border regions, and with no buffer state system to separate them, as was available in Central Europe. These are also empires having different cultural traditions, differing timings of revolution, different stages of development, and different levels of power. Hence, each has a very different definition of national interest, a separation that a common ideology cannot bridge. On the contrary, as we have noted, the national interest of each, defined by leadership, is now clothed in nationalist array, with patriotic sentiments marshaled on both sides.

What could possibly bring Russia and China together again in intimate alliance? The alliance of 1950 was not only consummated when the concept of international communism still had considerable vitality (and Chinese experience with Soviet collaborators was very limited); it was also born at a point when both parties perceived a common threat—the United States. It is in the nature of international relations, indeed, that two major neighboring states are likely to unite only when they feel themselves seriously challenged by the same opponent. Today, the United States has no desire to play that role.

To be sure, there is a lesson to be learned from the Sino-Soviet alliance and its collapse. When Peking decided that Moscow was no longer credible vis-à-vis the United States, the alliance lost its raison-d'être. This decision was reached in the course of the second Taiwan Strait crisis of 1958 and was confirmed in the Chinese mind by the Cuban missile episode and other events that followed. At present, Peking evidences concerns over American credibility vis-à-vis the Soviet Union, as do many noncommunist nations. If we were to cease being credible in global terms, if the patterns of withdrawal and isolation were to prevail, then the PRC along with many other states might be forced to reexamine the basic tenets of its foreign policies. Unquestionably, the pressure for an accommodation with the Soviet Union would mount, at least for a tactical accommodation.

While this constitutes a warning against isolationism or

weakness, however, it does not require a policy aimed at confrontation with the USSR. It is not in the American interest to lend support to that old Chinese adage featuring the monkey who is able to sit on the mountaintop and watch two tigers fight. Nor is it necessary to pursue such a course in order to prevent a Sino-Soviet alliance.

What of the other supposed risk—that of a Sino-Soviet war? The strong improbability of such a war issues from one elemental consideration: neither side could possibly win. Taking the Russian perspective first, the time for a surgical nuclear strike is past. Such a gambit would leave a boiling cauldron of rage in its wake; nothing could be calculated to mobilize Chinese nationalism against Russia more fully. But beyond this, it would fall short of full success, the Chinese having dispersed facilities and weaponry.

The costliness of an all-out war would be extraordinarily high. However ill equipped the People's Liberation Army is today, it would unquestionably exact a heavy toll, and while a people's war is at root a primitive concept, the capacity to mobilize a goodly portion of 1 billion people in defense of their villages and land is probably the best defense available for a nation in the PRC's stage of development, particularly when coupled with a nuclear retaliatory capacity of growing importance.

Suppose, however, that the mechanized forces of the Soviet Red Army—in combination with massive Russian air power—were able to seize great portions of China. How would the Russians govern and for how long would a mighty occupying force be necessary? Undoubtedly, the aim would be to create a faithful Chinese government operating under Soviet aegis, but the memory of the Japanese experience in these respects cannot be cast aside lightly. And if border regions alone were seized, would not the Russians face endless guerrilla warfare, with the drain upon manpower and resources extremely serious over time?

As for China, can anyone truly imagine that Peking's leaders would risk a full-fledged conflict against a neighboring state so vastly superior in military power? Surely this would be an act of madness, and while irrationality plays a role in politics, it has rarely if ever reached these proportions.

Border violence—recurrent incidents—these are certainly possible. But total war is on the outer perimeters of possibility. The Chinese interest in acquiring modern military arms is understandable and will no doubt result in an increased offensive as well as defensive capacity over time. These arms will presumably be acquired from Western Europe. While some Americans have advocated US sales—yet another potential facet of a united front strategy—such a course of action has thus far been avoided, although some military-related technology—for example, sophisticated computers and a domestic satellite—has been made available, and now nonlethal military equipment is to be sold. The Japanese government has also been skittish about military sales, but visits among ranking military men have been exchanged, arousing Moscow's concern.

In point of fact, however, Western military assistance to the PRC, whatever its dimensions, will not fundamentally alter the Soviet-Chinese strategic balance. No nation is about to furnish the Chinese with its most advanced conventional weaponry or with nuclear weapons. By some estimates, moreover, it would cost upward of $50 billion to upgrade China's conventional arsenal to "modern," but not superpower, status. There is some merit, therefore, in the Soviet claim that Western military aid to China, rather than threatening the Soviet Union, will constitute additional pressure on nations in Asia.

Given these circumstances, it is the view of the equilibrium proponents that a united front strategy would have to rest primarily upon the military capacities of the United States. The additive power of the PRC and Japan would relate almost wholly to strictly defensive operations—now and for the foreseeable future. Consequently, the increased strategic strength derived from the united front policies could not offset the increased costs and risks of that strategy, especially since gains would be essentially limited to Chinese inputs, the US-Japan Mutual Security Treaty being already in effect.

We have set forth these two strategic alternatives in their "pure" form, fully cognizant of the fact there is little chance that either will be adopted in that condition. The ultimate product, expressed in American policies, will be some mix as ongoing developments make clear.

No combination of actions toward Peking and Moscow, however, will resolve the strategic debate outlined above, a controversy that has progressively expanded in recent years. Behind the support or reservations advanced toward each specific policy affecting Russia and China, one is able to discern the shadow of the broader strategic cleavage. Rarely are such considerations discussed openly, but they have not been absent from the policy debates of the past five years and they will not be absent in the future. Thus, even though the policy outcome at every stage is likely to represent some degree of compromise, it is essential here to explore the polar alternatives and the arguments advanced to sustain them with as much precision and clarity as possible. Only thus can trends be understood and critiqued.

With this understanding in mind, let us proceed to explore a second interrelated strategic issue, one broader in scope than the first, and once again, having particular relevance to Asia. This second issue can be capsulized as follows: Shall the United States place primary reliance upon communist nationalism in fashioning its strategic position or shall it adhere to the centrality of its existing alignments and alliances? Once again, we shall set forth these alternate strategies in "pure" form, acknowledging that in the real political world compromises will ensue.

## THE CASE FOR RELIANCE ON COMMUNIST NATIONALISM

Those who would place ever greater reliance upon communist nationalism see a world in which the old ideological lines have disintegrated, making the alliances of the 1950s largely meaningless. Their analysis of global trends runs as follows. Despite the various experiments in internationalism under way, nationalism remains the primary motive force in world politics today, and those states labeled communist have carried nationalism to its furthest point. Consequently, the ability of such nations to operate collectively on behalf of any cause has been greatly diminished, if it has not entirely vanished.

The only significant trend offsetting the global nationalist wave is the growth of regionalism. A broad tendency toward regional aggregations—economic, political, and strategic—is to be seen, and that may well be an accelerating development. Such a trend, however, begets both stability and strife. On the one hand, it produces incentives for cooperation in the economic, political, and military fields. On the other hand, it can—and sometimes does—result in a struggle for dominance. Once again, moreover, the divisions are not necessarily between communist and noncommunist states. Witness the current struggle for influence in Indochina between Vietnam and China and the rival efforts of both to woo the Association of Southeast Asian Nations (ASEAN) community.

In this setting, it is asserted, the United States can and should help to build or participate in coalitions that cut across ideological lines, aggregations grounded in a commonality of perceived national interests. It can also profitably create a series of bilateral relations with communist states resting upon the same premises as those earlier governing relations with various noncommunist states. These new ties should involve economic, political, and military assistance of diverse types—so proponents of collaboration with communist nationalism urge. Such relations, whether multilateral or bilateral, would not be alliances of the formal type established shortly after World War II. But that type of alliance is fading away in any case, because circumstances have rendered it impossible and unnecessary to sustain. Thus, American relations with former allies should gradually rest on the same basis as those with certain communist states. What are the principal arguments sustaining this view?

First, by working closely with communist nationalism, a more permanent and favorable balance of power will supposedly have been created. Never again will the American people face the threat of united opposition from a coalition of the most tightly organized, highly mobilized states in the world. As various communist societies are increasingly interrelated economically and strategically to the United States and other advanced "capitalist states," a reestablishment of monolithic, or even cohesive communism on a broad international scale will become ever more remote. Meanwhile, existing bonds like those symbolized by COMECON (Council for Mutual Economic Assistance) and the Warsaw Pact will gradually loosen. In this fashion, the heavy responsibilities currently borne by the United States for its own security and that of its allies can be set aside. The threat to all liberal societies will have been significantly reduced.

Moreover, the argument goes, as the advanced world helps the developing nations, including various communist states, strengthen their economies and raise the living standards of their people, the authoritarian character of the prevailing political system will gradually soften. A rising quotient of political openness will mark the evolution of such societies, concomitant with their own heightened security and material well-being.

The latter theme introduces an ethical note, suggesting that the United States can advance the timetable of human rights and freedom by a program of both protecting and assisting select communist societies. Nor does the ethical defense of combining American power with communist nationalism stop there. At present, violence or the threat of violence marks the relations of various communist societies with each other. In these situations, it is submitted, the task is to identify the aggressive force and then, according to the circumstances, contribute to the assistance of the real or potential victim. Only if a network of deterrence can be built up, one that includes active cooperation of states drawn from a broad ideological-institutional spectrum, can the threat of cumulative violence be met.

As will be noted, the arguments presented above can be used not merely with respect to the China issue but to cover relations with other communist states as well—precisely which states depending upon events and evaluations. These themes can also be used in the effort either to dismantle or radically change the current alliances to which the United States is a party. In its pure form, the strategy of placing extensive reliance upon communist nationalism in fashioning American strategic policy and the historic policies fashioned by men like George Marshall, Dean Acheson, and John Foster Dulles stand at the antipodes. The policies of the latter men led not only to our alliance structure in West Europe but to that in Asia, establishing close ties between the United States and Japan, South Korea, Taiwan, the Philippines, and other noncommunist states of the region.

## THE CASE FOR THE MAINTENANCE OF EXISTING ALIGNMENTS

Let us turn now to the position of those who would have the United States concentrate upon maintaining and strengthening those ties, with minor modifications dictated by new circumstances. What are the major arguments supporting such a policy? The adherents of this strategy would agree with a substantial portion of the general political analysis advanced earlier. They would acknowledge that nationalism is rising almost everywhere, affecting all relationships and particularly those within the once unified international communist movement. They would accept the fact that all alliances, including those to which the United States is a party, have suffered some degree of erosion and must be viewed in different terms than during the cold war era. Nor would they deny that most of the hot and cold wars taking place today are among communist states, some of them having far-reaching implications for the international order.

Their differences with the strategists banking on communist nationalism, however, commence at this point. A sharp line, they argue, must be drawn between utilizing communist nationalism and being dependent upon it. If the United States appears to be relatively indifferent to the deterioration of its older network of ties and alliances, or reshapes its alignments so as to encompass noncommunist and communist forces more or less equally and indiscriminately, various adverse results will follow, some of them extremely serious in their implications.

First, older relationships will be damaged, even poisoned, by a rising feeling that the United States at a minimum is neglecting, at a maximum betraying those who have placed their trust in it. From this perspective, many of those doubtful of the strategy of reliance upon communist nationalism would trenchantly criticize the initial Asian policies of the Carter administration, offering the following evaluation. The abandonment of Vietnam (which preceded Carter), coupled with the rush to Paris to negotiate with representatives of the government of Hanoi immediately after Carter came to office, created a profound sense of mistrust throughout noncommunist Southeast Asia, particularly in countries like Singapore and Indonesia. Did the United States intend to withdraw from the region strategically, meanwhile giving aid to those whom it had once opposed as aggressors and adversaries of freedom? Was it now more interested in cultivating former opponents than in preserving its ties with old friends?

Policies in this region, moreover, were paralleled by those in Northeast Asia. There were suggestions that Taiwan might also be abandoned at Peking's insistence as the price for normalization, and the decision to withdraw American ground forces from South Korea was announced, with no quid pro quo from the communist states requested. The impact of these developments upon Taiwan and South Korea was understandably sharp. Meanwhile, relations with Japan—ties once defined as the cornerstone of the US East Asian policy—progressively deteriorated, largely but not wholly because of economic issues. Yet on this front, a curious malaise ensued.

In fairness, it should be noted that the Carter administration finally awoke to the fact that at least some of these policies required rectification, but critics would argue that serious, possibly irreparable harm had already been done. In any case, relations in Asia hinge not merely upon matters of power but upon intensely personal considerations involving trust, faithfulness, and respect for one's dignity. When these tenets are violated, or are perceived to have been violated, a relationship changes quickly.

"If the old ties are neglected or consciously undermined, what will succeed them?" ask the proponents of strengthening the present alliance structure. The thesis that we have reached a stage in international politics where states—especially major states—can act in a purely random fashion, either individually or bilaterally, or via ad hoc coalitions created on an issue-by-issue basis, they dismiss as both dangerous and romantic. Global politics will continue to be coalition politics like its domestic counterpart, they insist, and the firmer, the more cohesive the coalition, the more likely its goals to be achieved.

The new polyglot coalitions built out of a mix of noncommunist and communist states can be only weak, they assert. Lacking a commitment to common political institutions or economic systems, devoid of any unifying ideology, such clusters are certain to be highly unstable. At most, the new grouping will share nationalism—but nationalism alone is a precarious basis upon which to build long-range cooperative endeavors. Expressed negatively, it is the fear of an external foe; expressed positively, the quest for economic development. But development for what? A rapid enhancement of state power to what ends? Can it be assumed that governing elites believing in radically different political creeds, operating under significantly different institutional systems will move toward each other, accepting a common set of policies, procedures, goals, and values? And even if this trend unfolds over the long run, is not a foreign policy based upon this premise today woefully premature, thus likely to break down the element of consensus within the noncommunist community, and particularly within the community of advanced industrial societies, without being able to underwrite a comparable consensus to take its place?

These represent the beliefs—and the fears—of those who find the strategy of reliance upon nationalism to be deeply flawed. But there is an additional concern. If the United States appears to discount ideological and institutional differences in favor of a strict balance-of-power formula on the international stage, how is an American consensus supportive of US policies to be achieved? This issue has already been a troublesome one. With the end of monolithic communism, it became increasingly difficult to build a simple yet meaningful set of values into American foreign policy, to give it the ethical foundations sufficient for mass support. And the American people have always demanded such a foundation in exchange for the risks and costs of activist foreign policy. Whether in war or peace, irrespective of the nature of the assistance, our people have been united in support only when they believed that they were combating an evil of the dimensions of a Hitler or a Stalin, and contributing to the general cause of democracy and freedom.

It was partly for this reason that the Carter administration cultivated the human rights issue. In the aftermath of the Vietnam debacle, when the moral questions surrounding the Vietnam War became entangled in fierce domestic debate, the American people moved quickly into division and disenchantment. By advancing the commitment to human rights, might it be possible to rebuild an American consensus supportive of continued international leadership?

This experiment has not been without its difficulties, and indeed, after an initial exaggerated debut, for which the media must bear its usual share of responsibility, human rights has been adjusted so that it is not made to appear the sole or even necessarily the foremost priority in the shaping of American foreign policy. Yet it remains a concern, both in the administration and among the American people.

How could it possibly be reconciled with a policy of primary reliance upon communist nationalism? One does not need to dwell upon the atrocities that have taken place and are taking place in Cambodia; or the Stalinist-type silence that emanates from North Korea where critics were long ago liquidated. Let us refer only to those more outgoing communist governments like Vietnam and China. How many hundreds of thousands of individuals remain in the concentration camps called reeducation centers in Vietnam, and how many thousands have died of illness or malnutrition? And what of the noncommunist leaders of the past—not merely the supporters of Diem and Thieu but the other nationalists, Buddhists, Cao Dai, and Hoa Hao leaders? Tran Van Tuyen—liberal assembly leader of the opposition—"died in prison." Thich Tri Quang—once a favorite of the American media—was cast into oblivion.

It is ironic, moreover, that American visitors to China are currently told more horror stories about events taking place in that nation between 1966 and 1976 than the staunchest anticommunist could have imagined—stories now officially sanctioned, many of them told by the people who suffered the abuse. But is repression over, or are the political trials and lengthy imprisonments for political offenders merely directed toward a new clientele?

In sum, given our political culture and the antecedents of American foreign policy, it is not possible to eliminate considerations of ideological commitment and political values from international alignments and expect to retain strong grass-roots support from the American people. It is quite true that purism on this score is equally impossible, and the charge of American support for "corrupt dictatorships" has been a recurrent one, often with reason. Yet in general, proponents of strengthening the present alliance structure argue, Americans believe that most quasi-authoritarian governments of the Third World type receiving American assistance have a far better record with respect to human rights and an acceptance of pluralism—political, economic, and social—than their communist counterparts. Of at least equal importance, they also believe that such societies have a better potential for political evolution in the direction of more openness. If as a result of a conscious policy emphasizing alignment with communist nationalism, this issue became hopelessly confused, one can foresee the new strategy lending massive, albeit unwitting support to American withdrawal from international leadership, since there would be no understandable ethical reasons for commitment—so it is argued.

A final thesis is advanced, possibly the most critical to the proponents of strengthening current alliances. If reliance upon communist nationalism to effect an international equilibrium were to progress, at some point the noncommunist components within the coalition, including the United States, would cease to control either the policy initiatives or the general direction of events. Increasingly, a dependence upon the mercurial course of the political tides flowing in Peking, Hanoi, Pyongyang, and elsewhere would have been forged, and since each of these societies is controlled by a tiny elite, changes of their policies and alignments can be both abrupt and extreme, permitting little time for adjustment. Thus, the strategy of reliance upon communist nationalism represents a course endangering control of one's own policies and conducive to permanent instability.

Once again, it must be reiterated that the strategic alternatives connected with communist nationalism and existing alliances have been presented here so as to delineate the cardinal issues in the sharpest possible manner. In reality, most if not all advocates of increased reliance upon communist nationalism are opposed to an abandonment of certain current alignments if the issue is posed to them in this manner. And the proponents of maintaining and strengthening existing ties would not deny the importance of taking advantage of communist nationalism in a variety of ways, even to the extent of advancing aid or fashioning alignment under certain conditions.

Nevertheless, the arguments advanced above are not artificially constructed ones divorced from the real debate in Washington and elsewhere. Often unarticulated, they lie beneath the surface of a wide range of specific policy decisions. And because the differences frequently appear to be those of degree rather than of kind, one should not assume that they are lightly held or easily reconciled. Since any course of action entails risks and costs, moreover, and since ours is an extremely complex, volatile world—frequently involving the unexpected—a strategy pertaining to alignments and alliances will not be *finally* settled in the foreseeable future, irrespective of certain near-term decisions. As in the case of the united front versus the equilibrium strategies, one may expect trends and countertrends to ensue.

## THE FUTURE OF US ASIAN POLICY

Given these caveats, can we venture some broad predictions about US Asian policy in the immediate future? With reference to the first strategic debate, one development is clear. During the past few years, as American-Soviet relations have deteriorated, support for the united front strategy has grown. Since normalization of relations, the United States is actively assisting the People's Republic of China in many ways. Economically, it is making a wider range of advanced technology products available, and it stands ready to provide both credit and technicians as these are desired, together with an ample supply of grain. A new era of cultural relations is opening, with Chinese students coming to the United States to acquire training in science and technology, and American students going to China for education in other fields. Meanwhile, Washington maintains a public silence on political issues where differences exist, refraining from any public criticism of the PRC (a posture not yet fully reciprocated by Peking). The United States has also interposed no objections to Chinese explorations of military equipment on the West European market, nor to the military mission exchanged between China and Japan. Indeed, Washington actively encouraged the Fukuda government to sign the Sino-Japanese Treaty of Peace and Friendship (1978), seemingly forwarding the united front strategy in a very direct manner.

As previously indicated, however, Carter hoped to be able to couple advances on the China front with progress in American-Soviet relations, at least as these related to SALT II and trade pacts. Beyond this, the United States and the USSR are aware of the fact that we have not yet really entered into the type of negotiations that will determine the nature of the future world. Arms limitations are not arms reductions, or even arms stabilization. The last step in a Middle Eastern peace will not have taken place until the Soviet Union is involved, much as this may be regretted by many Americans. This is also likely to be true in Africa. Thus, any American administration—while finding the "China card" useful at this point—will avoid entering fully into the united front strategy if it is wise. The long-term American interest—and that of the world—lies with the equilibrium strategy, and we may expect that to be the determining factor in the final analysis.

It is also likely that American ties will remain centrally with those nations sharing the greatest commonality of interests, economic, political, and strategic. In the first instance, this means West Europe and Japan. There will be no absence of problems in these relations, as recent events have demonstrated, but there are also no substitutes—as every party to them knows well. In volume of economic intercourse, in basic political compatibility, in level of development—hence, in capacity to communicate—these relations have an innate validity that cannot be duplicated.

Increasingly, however, a number of other countries—many of them in Asia—will become equally important to the United States. Taken as a whole, the Pacific-Asian region is rapidly becoming the most significant area in the world for American foreign policy. Our economic relations with Asia now exceed those with Europe. Our political concerns here are also vital, given the fact that many of the world's major societies—Russia, China, Japan, and ourselves—come into the closest contact in this region. Moreover, it is not just the major powers that are of importance here. With many smaller nations of the Pacific-Asian region—from South Korea to Australia and New Zealand—our economic, cultural, political, and strategic ties have steadily grown, despite periodic crises in bilateral relations.

The nations most likely to be drawn into the circle of more intimate, sustained relations with the United States are those modernizing rapidly with a reliance upon mixed economies and pluralist sociopolitical systems. It is with these societies—and these societies alone—that the United States is equipped to interact in a comprehensive fashion. We shall always be interested in communist nationalism tactically—and our relations with some communist states may be relatively intense on certain fronts, for certain periods—but until the evolution of these societies makes possible the type of economic, political, and cultural interaction that underwrites a total relationship, such ties will continue to be tactical in nature for both parties, held tentatively and subject to alteration when the objectives of one side or the other appear to have been attained. Perhaps the early twenty-first century will witness a more profound change—a sufficient progress in socioeconomic development to enable more and fuller communication and interaction with ideological-systemic barriers greatly reduced, but that era will not be reached in the next several decades. A complex, transitional stage in such relations must first be successfully traversed.

Thus, in my view, American strategy in Asia will not gravitate toward a primary reliance upon communist nationalism, important though this factor is in the contemporary scene. International relationships will continue to grow in complexity, both to take account of the new circumstances within communist Asia and the altered circumstances in noncommunist Asia as well. The primary reliance, however, will continue to be upon traditional relationships—reshaped, broadened, and made more flexible to fit the requirements of the late twentieth century.

# ISSUES IN US-EAST ASIAN POLICY

## A Comment on the Symposium, US-China Relations as Viewed by the Major International Actors in the East Asian Region

**ADMIRAL NOEL GAYLER, USN (RET.)**

The five authors hold views that are rich in their interest and diversity, yet they have a great deal of coherence. There are no flat contradictions, but rather the differences in perception and emphasis of the fabled blind men describing the elephant.

From the many broad issues and illuminating details presented here there are ten, I think, of enduring importance and interest. Each deserves deep scrutiny. Because my comments here are brief, they are inevitably incomplete.

First, the issue raised so clearly by Professor Scalapino: Can and should foreign policy retain an ethical content? My answer is an unqualified yes. US policy cannot command support, in the long term, if it is not seen to be right and just. America must not be perceived to be a twin superpower to the USSR. We and the Soviet Union hold in common great power and very little else. However difficult it may be in detail and in practical politics (the question, "Why must we support all those dictators?" is continually raised), the American commitment to freedom is our main strength in world politics.

A second great question is the proper role of military strength—force, coercion, or violence—in world affairs. It is easy to suggest that force is legitimate when used for protection and illegitimate when used for aggression. But who is to define these circumstances? One man's "necessary defensive measures" are another's "blatant preparations for aggression."

Security lies in the eyes of the beholder. Yet there is an objective definition: freedom from coercion, or the threat of coercion, by violence. To that end we Americans have no choice but to make our own decisions toward our own security; that of our allies; and, so far as we are able, that of nations generally.

For us, this means the ability to protect and hold open the sea lanes and the air, to hold ground in Europe and Korea, and to project power at very great distances. We are not now in very good military shape, partly from neglect and distaste stemming from the Vietnam War, partly from overreliance on nuclear weapons, and partly from confused and inconsistent policies and resource support.

A third major issue is the apparent primacy of nationalism in world politics. In my view, nothing could be more absurd than the fiction of 150-odd "sovereign" states, ranging in size from China to Nauru, occupying this small planet.

Unbridled nationalism and unexamined crusading ideology are the major twin causes of war and all the misery it brings. Formal international organizations in their present forms tend to be politically defective, but they can still pave the way toward a more rationally organized world. Regional associations—ASEAN is a good example—give promise of an integrative evolution. Developments in recognized international law, such as the Law of the Sea drafts, are promising. International business has a major role to play, and it can be constructive rather than predatory.

The necessary missing ingredient is to put real power and muscle behind the consensus of international law.

In Asia, the striking policy alternatives for the United States are either alliance with the weaker power, China, to redress the balance with the Soviet Union, or else an equidistant policy toward those two countries. We seem to be implicitly committed to the former policy, but I think it a grave mistake to go too far. There is little we can do to alter the Chinese capability to resist the USSR. The mass of China is in place irrespective of what we do. The best place for America is to be on better terms with each of these powers than they are with each other.

In our relationship with the USSR, its relationship with China, and between both and Vietnam, much is made by Professor Gordon of an initiative-response chronology. The argument is interesting, but I think considerably overdrawn. In my own view, Sino-Japanese economic cooperation, Vietnamese ambitions for hegemony in Southeast Asia, Russian desires for a Vietnam naval base, and the American rapprochement with China are all major strategic objectives of the various powers concerned, quite unrelated, except perhaps in timing, to tit-for-tat tactics.

A sixth issue is the notion implicitly held in many places—and there is some flavor of it in these essays—that relationships with the USSR are always a zero-sum game. That is, that which hurts the USSR helps the United States (or China) and vice versa. Of course, that is not always or even generally true. There may be a negative-sum game: the Olympic and grain boycotts hurt the United States as well as the Soviet Union. And there may be positive-sum games. SALT II, discouragement of nuclear proliferation, suppression of international terrorism, an accepted Law of the Sea are examples of "games" in which both the USSR and the United States stand to gain. We should look for more of them, and there are plenty of opportunities, in Asia as elsewhere.

A seventh issue for policy is: Do we see the Pacific-Asian–Indian Ocean–Middle East theater as an integrated whole, where every action in one area has a consequence throughout the theater, or do we treat the incredible complexities in each country in exhaustive detail? My answer is that somehow we must manage to do both, for both are necessary. The trick will be to bring our country and area specialists into a close and symbiotic relationship with the grand strategists (if there are, in fact, any grand strategists!).

An eighth issue—possibly the most important of all—is the absolutely essential search for "ground truth." If the United States is to have an ethical foreign policy—and again I think it must have—then the need for fact is basic. This should, of course, be the professional preoccupation of journalists and historians. But it is far more important than that. It is the bedrock upon which policy must rest. It is most disturbing to see the lying effrontery of North Korea in claiming that they "had not initiated the war in 1950" accepted in a serious foreign policy paper without either rebuttal or comment. Perception depends on the observer, but fact is not relative. In a very real and profound sense in foreign policy, "the truth will make you free"—at least sufficiently free to make judgments corresponding to the real world.

This is not to say that the United States is always right or fully informed. It is to say that we must always strive to be, and be tireless in our reliance on truth. We have no other weapon against the big lie techniques of the Hitlers, Stalins, Kims, Khrushchevs, Khomeinis, and Khadafis of this world.

The ninth issue is closely related to the above. It is the extraordinary and dangerous misperceptions that the countries have about each other. To read the press in countries like India, Algeria, and the Soviet Union is to see the United States portrayed as a dangerous and power-hungry behemoth. The Third World extremists of the Libyan and Iranian stripe see us as a surreal monster allied with Satan himself. In spite of perhaps the best press in the world, and one that attempts to be objective, we too are not immune. There is certainly no evidence that the Russian seizure of Afghanistan is a precursor to their seizure of the Persian Gulf, yet this is accepted as an article of faith in many American circles.

What is most disturbing of all is that even Russian specialists on the United States, such as Georgi Arbatov, entertain weird ideas on what makes the United States run: "ruling imperialist circles." Soviet policy can hardly be grounded in reality when their "experts" are so far off the mark.

How to cure all of this? It is difficult, and the traditional conferences, exchanges, and reporting do not seem to help much. One basic problem is that many a regime "needs" an external threat to justify its illegitimate hold on power.

And the last issue of my list: Can our relationship with foreign states in Asia as elsewhere be regarded as a constantly shifting kaleidoscope seeking a balance of power, along the lines of Metternich and his disciple Kissinger? History on this is mixed but predominantly bad. Sooner or later the scales unbalance, and too often war results.

Or can we strive for some system, some stability, that will be insensitive to ephemeral changes? My own answer is that we can and we must. Certainly, Asia will not accept Russian hegemony or Chinese hegemony. Most might prefer America as the least of three evils, but we have no such ambitions to rule. Yet there does seem to be opportunity, for the four greatest powers are involved in the Pacific, and if each and all can become convinced that stability or peaceful evolution are positive-sum games, then collectively we should be able to make it happen.

And a footnote, not related to all of the issues raised above: two of the essays refer, in a common but slipshod way, to the "American defeat in Vietnam." If one wishes to refer to a "political defeat" or a "policy defeat," I have no objection. But militarily defeated we were not. Through the military ignorance and mismanagement of Lyndon Johnson and Robert McNamara we expended blood and treasure with little to show for it. The military contributed much pedestrian leadership and a distressing propensity to "lead with the infantry"—a danger Omar Bradley had warned against more than a decade earlier. But let the record show that American forces were never defeated in battle. In fact, in December 1972, in a nine-day air and naval blockade of Hanoi and Haiphong, the North Vietnam was brought to its knees, with remarkably little loss of life on either side. The political battle had already been lost, so the military victory was nugatory.

The importance is not to refight the Vietnam War, or to justify our role in it. It is rather, again, in a plea for precision and accuracy, to specify the sort of defeat America suffered, for the fiction that military power cannot be effectively applied in Asia is just that: a fiction.

# III. SCIENTIFIC, TECHNOLOGICAL, AND CULTURAL RELATIONS WITH CHINA

## Chapter 3

# DEVELOPMENT, ISSUES AND PROSPECTS OF SINO-AMERICAN CULTURAL, SCIENTIFIC, AND TECHNOLOGICAL EXCHANGES*

**JOYCE K. KALLGREN**

Professor, Department of Political Science
University of California at Davis

### INTRODUCTION

In mid-1980 Chinese authorities were forced to suspend applications for study abroad by Chinese scholars who had managed to arrange their own financing, though government programs were not affected. The reason for their decision was relatively simple. The enthusiasm of Chinese scholars, together with the helpfulness of foreign institutions, and the assistance of the overseas Chinese community threatened to drain away too many Chinese scholars at one time and therefore to negatively influence the teaching and research programs of the nation. At the same time, Chinese scientific institutions

* I wish to thank the Ford Foundation for providing a grant to assist in research travel for this issue: Nancy Hearst, Librarian at the Fairbank East Asian Research Center, and C. P. Chen and Anne Huang of the Center for Chinese Studies were generous in their time with respect to various research problems.

and research units were inundated with applications from foreign scholars (many of whom were prepared to pay their own expenses) to visit, lecture, and study with their Chinese counterparts. Scientific and technological as well as cultural exchanges were undergoing dramatic expansion. What were the implications of this development for Sino-American exchanges?

As we have seen in the preceding sections, despite impressive progress, there are still difficulties to be resolved in Sino-American bilateral relations. In the commercial domain, while textiles quotas may be agreed upon, patent difficulties or payment of pre-1949 bondholders pose problems in reconciling differing economic systems. While statements of friendship in international meetings are frequent, working out the relationship between and among the United States, the Soviet Union, and China, as well as other East Asian countries, will take time. Differences of emphasis remain.

In matters of scientific, cultural, and technological exchanges, however, disagreements and disputes have been less serious and rancorous, and controversies seem capable of resolution. There are several reasons for this. Many Americans consider exchanges to be of low priority in bilateral relations and, therefore, of less interest. While the Olympic controversy shows the willingness of authorities to use sports boycotts to register political opposition, in general, exchanges draw relatively little attention except from the interested participants. On the other hand, there is a long tradition of American interest and faith in exchanges, or a version of people-to-people contact. In the Chinese case, there remain many senior Chinese academicians whose degrees were from, and whose academic experience was in, the United States. There are many Americans who have lived and worked in China. They and their children support exchanges. American missionaries, though redefining their tasks in less religious terms, still want to work in China. And most important, there is the overseas Chinese community well represented in American academic and scientific circles that has provided assistance and has facilitated the exchange programs. All of these groups, constrained during the period of the Chinese Cultural Revolution, found their own interests happily matching the priorities of the Four Modernizations campaigns and the contemporary China political leadership.

Prior to the normalization of diplomatic relations, exchanges often served as a litmus test of the state of Sino-American relations as well as the state of internal political struggles in China or the United States. In the post-1949 years there were periods of time when Chinese authorities rebuffed American attempts to initiate exchanges, and there were times when American authorities were not receptive to Chinese efforts to explore exchanges. Following normalization, the exchange programs and the negotiations associated with them seem to have functioned separately from other aspects of the renewed bilateral relations—in a sense, to have assumed an independent life and priority of their own. For American scholars, the development of long-term research opportunities in China through a national program, together with individual research unit-to-research unit relations seem to be progressing with real cooperative spirit. The number of Chinese scholars in the United States, although not matching the enthusiastic estimates of 1978, is still substantial and, perhaps more important, growing. The constraints on a more rapid expansion of government-supported scholars from China seem to be monetary—a shortage of dollars—rather than based on policy considerations. Certainly the number of invitations for short-term American visits to China has increased simultaneously with the cutback in plans to send Chinese to the United States.

This chapter looks at several aspects of the matter of exchanges with China. First of all, how is the term "exchanges" to be construed in cultural as well as in scientific and academic terms? Second, what is the nature of the organizations that have administered the exchanges—both the formal programs and the informal ones—and what are the practical difficulties and issues these organizations have encountered in developing exchange programs? Finally, how should we evaluate the total effort to date? Are there unresolved problems inherent in current Chinese exchanges or that posed themselves to the participant in such exchanges?

## THE NATURE OF EXCHANGES WITH THE PEOPLE'S REPUBLIC OF CHINA

> "Can you develop and give me a copy in sixty seconds?" asked the impatient Kazakh herdsman standing by his circular yurt in the remotest part of northwest China. "No, I'm sorry, this is not that kind of camera," I had to explain apologetically, while a small boy played with a plastic film cartridge left behind by a group of tourists three days earlier.[1]

The growing sophistication of Chinese who come in contact with visiting foreigners is apparent to those who visit China. In 1977 a Chinese International Travel Service (CITS) official visiting the United States spoke of plans for some 15,000 Americans to visit China the following year. Some of those visitors were tourists, interested travelers on escorted trips often arranged through American airline, steamship, and travel companies. Other "visitors," though touring historical monuments and scenic spots, also met with their professional counterparts in China, lectured, gave seminars, and discussed technological developments in industrial processes, surgical techniques, or computer programming. When they returned home, they sent materials to Chinese colleagues met during the course of their trips and frequently received information in exchange. They saw themselves as participants in an exchange program.

Virtually all visitors to China travel in groups. Though a significant number arrange their travel through the agencies mentioned above, many others visited China as members of "study tours" arranged by the US-China People's Friendship Association (USCPFA).* They travel as "self-paying guests,"

* This chapter does not discuss the role of the USCPFA in the prenormalization period, since there were no mutual exchanges. In recent months the USCPFA, while retaining an interest and effectiveness in sending groups, has also diversified activities to include more educational programs in the United States.

and are often required to have participated in USCPFA activities prior to their trip, or to commit themselves to lecturing for the association upon their return. Many such self-paying guests expect to reciprocate hospitality by receiving Chinese guests in return and actively try to arrange such return visits while traveling in China. The same effort to organize reciprocal visits by Chinese to this country is often true for business visitors, athletic delegations, as well as professional groups.

Those travelers who could thus be designated as participants in "exchanges" with China are quite numerous, but the number of Americans traveling under formal sponsorship is much smaller. Since 1972 nongovernmental organizations and, since 1977, governmental units have established yearly goals for exchanges with China, often specifying topics or participants. These exchanges are more concerned with such issues as equivalency in number of trips, participation, and cost. Three American organizations have controlled and directed these exchanges. They are the National Committee for US-China Relations (NCUSCR), the National Council for US-China Trade (NCUSCT), and the Committee on Scholarly Communications with the People's Republic of China (CSCPRC). The latter organization, although a subcommittee of the National Academy of Science, also represents the Social Science Research Council (SSRC) and the American Council of Learned Societies (ACLS).

The trips arranged by these organizations have emphasized topics and problems appropriate to their respective constituencies. The NCUSCT has sent and received delegations primarily concerned with commerce, foreign trade, and specific industrial interests. The NCUSCR has exchanged public affairs delegations, athletic teams, and performing artists. The CSCPRC has selected and received academic delegations in the basic, natural, and social sciences, as well as in the humanities. All three organizations routinely exchange leadership delegations with their Chinese counterparts to negotiate annual goals, to establish and reaffirm ties, and to update their knowledge of China and the United States through travel following the completion of formal negotiating sessions. Comparable to these officially facilitated visits, but at an even more formal level, are the trips of American congressional delegations who visit as guests of the Chinese. The participants typically discuss domestic Chinese developments and Sino-American foreign policy questions or international problems with Chinese Communist Party and government leaders in Peking and follow these discussions with travel to other points in China.

In a somewhat separate category, and of increasing importance in recent years, are the numerous faculty and university delegations that visit China. The trips of these groups, especially important since 1977, have often been facilitated initially through the good offices of Chinese-American faculty members, who have worked to reestablish contact between American academic institutions and the Chinese community.

Prior to 1977 the work of all of these groups was frequently hampered by the generally anti-intellectual and antiforeign policies of the then dominant political leadership. When Chinese domestic policy changed in 1976–77 and new emphasis was placed on the revitalization and modernization of Chinese universities and research centers, the opportunities for exchange with universities, with institutes of the Chinese academies of science, agricultural, medical and social science, and with other educational and research units multiplied. During the last three years, genuine exchanges of information, materials, and views by university delegations have become more and more common, making this category likely to increase in importance.

At virtually every level of exchange, experiences during the past seven years have varied enormously. Consequently, assessments of the exchange process have also varied. Initially, the diverse groups mentioned above had highly stylized trips, virtually always limited to the well-known successful model units in China that were routinely visited by all foreign travelers. Only gradually did the specialist delegations find their schedules sharpened to focus on briefings and meetings with appropriate counterpart units. After 1977, not only the participants in officially facilitated exchanges, but also professionals traveling under other auspices increasingly had the opportunity for real exchanges of views and ideas with their Chinese counterparts. By the late 1970s American scientists, humanists, and social scientists were engaged in efforts to facilitate specific research projects.

During the last three years progress in academic exchanges has been considerable. Chinese research institutes receive visitors, foreign physicians are invited to medical conferences, linguists tape-record different pronunciations in the various regions of China, and historians visit archives and discuss interpretations with their counterparts. Even social scientists manage to arrange research opportunities: an anthropologist team has spent a number of months observing village life, and two groups of political scientists have carried out collaborative research with the assistance of Chinese authorities in villages and county seats. In the summer of 1980 the Chinese Academy of Social Sciences received a delegation of American, Canadian, and British experts on the life and political thought of Mao Zedong. Though many participants were frustrated in implementing some aspects of their plans, the overall impression is one of considerable progress.

As regards the reciprocal of this flow, there has been an increase in the number of Chinese visiting the United States, but nothing comparable to the number of American tourists visiting China. While a few Chinese citizens have come to the United States on private matters, the vast majority of Chinese visitors are sponsored by their government, and they are virtually always organized in groups. The sponsoring agencies in China have become diversified, now including universities and academic departments, enterprises, and local governments, such as those of provinces or municipalities.

During 1979 and 1980 American faculty members saw an increase in the number of Chinese scientific groups visiting their facilities. The American sponsors were diverse. Some Chinese trips were facilitated by American scientific organizations, some through formally negotiated programs of Chinese and American counterpart organizations, some by return invitation of members of American delegations, and some as guests of US corporations or laboratories. The visits of these groups were usually fully programmed according to the specialization of their members. While these Chinese visitors occasionally gave lectures and made contact with former colleagues or teachers, their principal task was to continue a survey of the American scientific establishment, understand its operation and current priorities, and reestablish relationships that had lapsed during the thirty-year break in relations between the two countries. Groups making the short three- to four-week trips were usually composed of senior scholars accompanied by department heads or their deputies.

In addition to three- and four-week survey trips and visits by participants in international meetings, a growing number of Chinese scholars and research personnel have come to the United States for periods of a year or two to observe and participate in the ongoing research programs at American universities and institutes for the purpose of updating their training. In so doing, they were normally classified as "visiting scholars." At the outset of their stay many of these men and women found themselves working to overcome language handicaps that limited their direct participation in ongoing research projects. The arrangements to normalize this process of extended research were largely carried out under bilateral agreements between American universities and Chinese academic institutions. Other Chinese scholars have formed informal relationships with a bureau, center, or some similar unit in a university.

With respect to technology, visits of Chinese to the United States, together with demonstration projects in China, are numerous. The commitment to modernization in China has made this a high-priority area for exchanges. Visits by corporate representatives are reciprocated by Chinese specialists in areas of mutual interest. Participation in these trips to the United States are not confined to technicians and engineers; a number of high-ranking Chinese political leaders, as well as middle-level bureaucrats, also take part.

Cultural exchanges have been negotiated by specific organizations and by the appropriate American governmental institution. The 1979 Sino-American cultural agreement envisaged a broad number of exchange possibilities between the two countries, with emphasis upon broadly defined reciprocity. Prior to the signing of this agreement, the Chinese Performing Arts Troupe toured the United States in 1978, and the Boston Symphony Orchestra visited China in 1979. The expectation for cultural exchanges embodied in the 1979 agreement went far beyond these rather conventional exchanges, and involves single performers, delegations to study dance performance, staging techniques, filmmaking, and scriptwriting and translation. All of these projects are to be conducted jointly where possible. Finally, by 1979 one after another US cabinet member, from what was then called Health, Education, and Welfare to Agriculture, as well as leaders of other governmental agencies, proposed and negotiated separate programs to exchange information and facilitate participation in a wide range of ongoing activities in the two countries. While it remains to be seen how successfully these paper agreements will be implemented, the opportunities for the exchange of visitors have increased almost daily.

## MAJOR EXCHANGE ORGANIZATIONS

By 1980 the methods for arranging American travel to China or Chinese travel to the United States have become quite diverse. Host organizations have multiplied. The length of trips, the places to visit, and the conditions for travel were also widely disparate. While the "facilitated exchanges" by national organizations with special courtesies and programs remained the most honorific of the various alternatives, flexibility exists, and optional programs seemed to proliferate.

The diversification of organizations on the American side might not seem surprising. After all, the backlog of interest in travel, work, or study in China was substantial in 1972, and developments since then guaranteed that it would increase. American travel agents in collaboration with interested and enterprising American companies, universities, alumni associations, and other special-interest groups rapidly learned what the Chinese expected and devised means and organizations that would be responsive to apparent Chinese guidelines. Although China is a socialist country, American organizations have had some prior experience with the travel programs of socialist countries. This experience was helpful in adjusting to Chinese expectations and practices.

As regards the reverse flow of visitors, up to 1980, in neither number nor interest has there been evidence of Chinese applications matching the American deluge. On the other hand, within the framework of Chinese goals, there has been very substantial innovation and expansion of travel. The proliferation of connections through academic or professional organizations, together with the overseas Chinese relatives and friends, has assisted the enterprising Chinese scholar-professional in his or her quest to reestablish ties abroad. The large and diverse Chinese community in the United States has made it easier for assistance to be extended.

Before considering the exchanges themselves, it is essential to examine the core organizations, because in arranging travel, scheduling, and similar matters the key issue is the "unit," or sponsor, of the individual. Just as American political scientists and sociologists have noted that within China itself status and political standing is determined by the answer to the question "What is your unit?" so, too, in international circles the core organizations established the procedures, means, and criteria out of which further exchange programs have grown. With respect to bilateral exchanges, the Chinese had organizations (established in the immediate post-1949 period) in place when the Sino-American thaw occurred. These "mass" semiofficial organizations issued invitations, acted as hosts in China, sent delegations to international meetings, received "friendly personages," and organized the travel of sports teams—all as part of China's contact with the outside world. They ran cultural and political exchanges during the first few years of renewed American ties. A slight complication in the pre-1978 period was the fact that government-to-government relations were not possible, and therefore the efforts always had to be described in terms of "people-to-people" diplomacy. On the American side, in 1972 there were no immediately obvious units to serve as the counterparts to these Chinese organizations.

By 1972 the Chinese had five major organizations conducting exchanges. In addition, of course, the Chinese Communist Party, the All-China Women's Federation, the trade unions, and the Youth Federation had all sponsored delegations from China and received visitors. But for the United States exchanges, these organizations did not enter into the picture until late 1979.

The Chinese People's Institute for Foreign Affairs (CPIFA) receives important foreigners and groups that cannot appropriately be received by the Ministry of Foreign Affairs. The institute has assumed responsibility for receiving all congressional delegations, certain delegations of public affairs leaders, and some academics determined by the Chinese to be of particular importance. The CPIFA did not send a delegation to the United States until 1977, and that delegation was the highest-ranking group received until the visit of Vice Premier Deng Xiaoping following normalization.

A second organization that receives foreign guests is the Chinese People's Association for Friendship with Foreign Countries (CPAFFC). This organization sends and receives official delegations at the nongovernmental level. As is the case in many socialist societies, these delegations include personages considered "friendly" to the country, or favorably disposed toward its socialist goals. In China the task of the CPAFFC is broader than that of comparable organizations in other socialist countries. This organization has sponsored and hosted most cultural groups. It is also the Chinese counterpart of the USCPFA. It received those American delegations whose American sponsors were considered to be friends of China.

Sports have played an important role in Chinese cultural diplomacy. The Chinese table tennis team initiated the first invitation to an American group, and other sports groups have subsequently traveled to the United States. The importance of the All-China Sports Federation (ACSF) is thus obvious. Each individual sports group in China is a part of this federation, which acts to facilitate all exchanges of sports groups with other countries.

Under the Four Modernizations program, relations with the international business and commercial communities assumed an increased importance in China. Exchanges in this area are the responsibility of the China Council for the Promotion of International Trade (CCPIT). The CCPIT facilitates travel, organizes exhibits, provides opportunities for companies to make presentations, and organizes special programs to enhance the understanding of industrial and commercial procedures. Many industrial nations now have a counterpart organization to the CCPIT to handle reciprocal arrangements.

Operating under the Chinese State Scientific and Technical Commission, the Science and Technology Association of the PRC (STAPRC) coordinated exchanges for the Chinese Academies of Science, Agricultural Science, Medical Science, and Social Science. The specifics of technical and academic exchange are formalized through meetings between STAPRC and its American counterpart, the National Academy of Science Committee on Scholarly Communication with the PRC (CSCPRC). By 1979 a number of Chinese research institutes and the various academies of science were developing their own plans, but the STAPRC still remains the vehicle for negotiating formal exchange programs in the sciences at the government-to-government level.

Closely related to each of these special organizations, and yet separate, is the China International Travel Service (CITS). It is this organization that plans programs and arranges housing and guides for foreign tourists. This agency has primary responsibility for travel of all tourists to China. Since many of the self-paying guests are also sponsored by other organizations, CITS works closely with these organizations to coordinate their programs.

All of these Chinese organizations were in place and operating when a new era in relations with the United States was initiated with the invitation to the American table tennis team for noncompetitive play in China. The need to reciprocate the invitation necessitated American groups to direct and coordinate Chinese travel in the United States.

As the head of the American Table Tennis Association was pondering the problem of how to reciprocate the Chinese invitation, he received word from the NCUSCR that it was willing to assist the Table Tennis Association. This brought the NCUSCR into the forefront of exchange negotiations for the first few years of Sino-American contacts.

The NCUSCR was established in 1966 to encourage a public debate in the United States on China policy. The committee was initially composed of American academics in the China field, businessmen, and labor leaders, all of whom wished to encourage a national discussion of new alternatives in American foreign policy. The committee was carefully balanced to include individuals with differing views regarding America's relations with China. It included those advocating immediate positive steps toward establishing contacts with the PRC as well as those who believed that no changes should be made in the basically pro-Taiwan stance of the American government.

Unfortunately, the decision to form the committee coincided with the onset of the Cultural Revolution in China, and the committee's opportunities to initiate policy reviews were severely limited by the increasing chaos that seemed to characterize Chinese politics. In assisting the Table Tennis Association, the NCUSCR, at the initiative of its staff, assumed a new responsibility in addition to the educational function that had been envisaged in the early days of the organization. Taking this initiative brought about an ongoing reconsideration of goals by the committee's staff, pressured as it was to respond to demands for development of public information programs (particularly in the area of the prospects for increased US trade with China) and to demands imposed by the developing possibilities for an active exchange program with China. Until 1975 the annual mission review reiterated the committee's continued "commitment to the public understanding of China and US-China relations through an active program of conferences, advisory services and cultural exchanges." But the pressure on staff and the limited financial resources finally resulted in a shift. In 1975 the National Committee altered its orientation:

> The Board formally endorsed the proposal that the Committee henceforth concentrate on the conduct of education exchanges with the PRC and on related activities. . . . In the coming months the Committee will also work with the Asia Society, a New York based educational and cultural organization, on its new public education program on China and US-China relations. The [Asia] Society's China Council is being expanded to include China scholars and civic leaders across the country, who will guide the development of a comprehensive program to study and stimulate discussion of contemporary China and its relations with the US.[2]

Since that policy decision, the NCUSCR has hosted or cohosted with other sponsoring organizations various cultural groups, sports teams, and other groups. Each year the NCUSCR, initially in close cooperation with the Department of State and more recently with the International Communication Agency (ICA), negotiated a package of exchanges and developed its own programs. It has sent delegations to China composed of representatives drawn from the NCUSCR board of directors. The financing of the committee has varied over the years, as to both amount and source. It has included special donations for special projects, foundation grants, corporate assistance, and governmental support from ICA and its predecessor organization, the US Information Agency.

As we have seen, between 1972 and 1975 the NCUSCR included among its activities special programs for members of the American business community, some of whom were excited at the prospect of renewed opportunity at a China market and yet uninformed about the possibilities for commerce or the means for instituting inquiries. Early on, however, American government encouragement, together with business community interest, resulted in the formation of an organization specifically devoted to the problems of trade with China. On

22 March 1973 a meeting of senior businessmen hosted by Secretary of Commerce Frederick B. Dent and chaired by Donald Burnham, chairman and president of Westinghouse Corporation, planned the establishment of the National Council for US-China Trade (NCUSCT). This organization, intended to be funded through membership dues, is said to have been modeled after the Sino-British Trade Council. Initially, the NCUSCT and the NCUSCR cooperated in certain educational programs. Over time, however, the NCUSCT developed a clientele and full program of its own and the NCUSCR withdrew from activities in this field.

The NCUSCT is a private, nonprofit membership organization of small and large firms. The council program is directed from its headquarters office in Washington, D.C., with branch offices in New York, Hong Kong, and Peking. The first delegation from the council went to China in November 1973, at the invitation of the CCPIT. Discussions in China resulted in a joint agreement that recognized the NCUSCT in the United States as the counterpart organization of the CCPIT, that the two organizations would exchange trade exhibitions on a reciprocal basis, and that they would carry out joint exchanges of trade and business missions.

The effect of the joint agreement and the legitimization it conferred became especially important when the Four Modernizations program was translated into Chinese interest in foreign investment and foreign trade. Since then the council has been intimately and actively involved in assisting the Chinese in their search for high-technology firms capable of presenting their products and services to potential Chinese users. It has arranged for and assisted a number of groups traveling to China from the American business community and staffed reciprocal visits from China. The close contact between the NCUSCT and the American government was well illustrated by the active involvement of the Council in financing and hosting parts of the visit to the United States of Vice Premier Deng in January 1979.

As a private organization with a close working relationship but no formal financial ties to the US government, the council has taken on an active role in the promotion of trade with, and the transfer of, technology to China. With the development of bilateral arrangements between agencies of the US government and their Chinese counterparts, this role may be somewhat diminished in the future. Over the near term, however, both business and government will continue to depend on the close ties that have been developed between the council and its Chinese counterpart.

In addition to the NCUSCR and the NCUSCT, the third key organization involved in facilitating Sino-American exchanges has been the Committee on Scholarly Communication with the People's Republic of China (CSCPRC). Many of the initial exchanges were in the field of science—an emphasis that has been strongly reinforced following the adoption of the Four Modernizations program. Consequently, the role of the CSCPRC has been of key importance in the development of exchange programs with China. In 1966, at the same time that the NCUSCR was being formed, the National Academy of Science recruited Alan T. Waterman, former president of the National Science Foundation, to become chairman of a newly formed Committee on Scholarly Communication with Mainland China. Convened at the urging of a group of American scientists and China scholars who sought to develop means for interacting with the scientific community in China, the committee was composed of representatives of American foundations, major universities, and scientific institutes. There was some overlap in membership with the NCUSCR. The committee's staff was located in the offices of the National Academy of Sciences, but the committee itself represented the interests of the SSRC and the ACLS as well as the academy. Thus, all the major components of the American scholarly community were represented on, and then interests forwarded by, a single committee.

Like the NCUSCR, the CSCPRC was established just as the Cultural Revolution broke out. Between 1966 and 1969 only three meetings of the committee were held, and in 1969 a cutback in the committee's staff was made. Following the initial Sino-American contacts in 1971 the committee was renamed the Committee on Scholarly Communication with the

PRC and a series of letters was sent by the committee to Chinese science officials inviting them to send delegations to conferences to be held in the United States. When provision for exchanges was included in the Shanghai Communiqué, another letter was sent to China, this time conveyed by a Chinese-American scientist. Shortly thereafter an American medical delegation visited China and a Chinese scientific delegation visited the United States. The latter group was jointly hosted by the American Federation of Scientists and the CSCPRC. Thus began the current work of the CSCPRC in the development of academic exchanges. Partly on its own, and partly through formal government-to-government negotiations at the highest levels, the CSCPRC developed a program of exchanges with the STAPRC. Exchanges were initially limited to month-long surveys.

Between 1971 and 1979 other organizations sponsored delegations to China. Some individuals organized themselves, adopted a title, and negotiated directly with the Chinese. Some travelers met with their opposite numbers and gave lectures and presentations. By 1976 organizations such as chambers of commerce, the American Bar Association, and various political organizations were visiting and often extending invitations for a Chinese visit. Some American physicians and scientists who had traveled to China were able to arrange a Chinese return trip to the United States. In the main, however, the NCUSCR, the CSCPRC, and the NCUSCT were responsible for the programs of Chinese visiting the United States. Only when the serious efforts to place visiting scholars in US academic institutions began did the sponsorship of Chinese delegations visiting the United States begin to diversify.

The effort to insure equity over the long run, to match interests between organizations, to expand the opportunities for exchanges beyond those of survey trips, and to increase the number and range of sites visited by Chinese and American travelers was made by the three main American organizations. Although two of them—the NCUSCR and the CSCPRC—were established for purposes other than the administration of exchange programs, as we have seen, circumstances subsequently involved them centrally in the exchange process. In order to meet their responsibility, each has had to develop expertise, procedures, and policies for exchanges and to do so under often difficult circumstances. After normalization, some of the roles of these organizations have altered, and aspects of their programs have needed reevaluation. New institutions, primarily academic ones, have entered into the exchange field, often in the process adopting procedures developed by the NCUSCR and the CSCPRC.

Regardless of the sponsorship of the delegations, certain aspects of travel in China or in the United States were similar: how and who determined the composition of a delegation to be sent and received; how long a group would stay; what an appropriate itinerary was; and who would pay the costs involved. Planning by American hosts for the initial Chinese delegations was at least partially influenced by the way in which American visitors were received in China. Up to 1980 certain issues were fundamental to the arrangements for these formal exchanges: appropriate recognition of status and prestige, equity with respect to treatment, sensitivity to political issues implicit or explicit in the travel arrangements, and provision for bearing the costs of travel.

In both the formal negotiations and informal arrangements, funding has been a matter of particular importance. In the case of the facilitated exchanges, the custom has been that the visitors have been responsible for international travel costs, while the hosts assume in-country costs. Because of the proliferation of groups traveling in both directions, some change in this practice has occurred. Although formally negotiated survey trips still provide for this division of costs, in the past three years some American delegations have visited China as self-paying guests. They have been hosted by an academic unit, a mass organization, or one of the five Chinese organizations described above, but the delegation covered its own expenses in China. In some cases, the travel was possible only on these grounds; in other cases, members of the group traveling wished to travel as self-paying guests. Similarly, with the proliferation of groups and the increase in costs in the United States, some

Chinese travelers, though hosted by an American institution or organization, have been expected to cover the cost of their domestic travel in the United States. American hosts have then assumed local expenses. In the newly developed programs of scholarly exchange between US and Chinese academic units there are a variety of financial arrangements. Chinese "visiting scholars" are supported by their government, though American funding is gratefully received.

Little is known about the budgetary process within the Chinese exchange organizations. Some of the component units within the STAPRC have their own funds and may invite guests in accordance with the resources available to them. Some self-paying guests in China have found that a part or all of their costs are assumed by their Chinese hosts during the course of their trip.

On the American side, there has been an ongoing problem for organizations in funding their delegations' travel to China and the costs of receiving Chinese guests in return. In the initial years of exchanges, when each traveler or delegation could emphasize the special nature of the opportunity and the contribution that the trip would make to improved Sino-American relations, funds from foundations and corporations were relatively easy to obtain. As travel has become more common, however, the availability of such funds has been sharply curtailed. As a result, two American organizations (the NCUSCR and the CSCPRC) have found themselves more and more dependent upon federal funds. The degree of this dependence varies. When opportunities for research to China developed in 1978 and afterward, the role of government funding agencies, as well as that of private scholarly organizations such as the SSRC and the ACLS, have been essential for the start-up and maintenance of the national program. In bilateral university exchange programs, request for federal funding to supplement university support have as yet been rare. As the importance of federal funding increases, new problems are raised with regard to the autonomy of private exchange organizations. Just as private research organizations in the United States, such as the Brookings Institution, have tried to diversify the sources of their support to limit their dependence on government funding because of the possible compromise of their autonomy, so too efforts by exchange organizations to diversify their funding sources have been evident since 1972.

Since 1979 some American foundations such as Ford and Rockefeller, or organizations formerly active in China such as the Yale-China Association, have been exploring a variety of organizational arrangements with various Chinese institutions. These arrangements do not generally emphasize the support of American research scholars in China, though in fact the side effects of the efforts may be to assist researchers. The Chinese program to recruit teachers of English as a second language will produce some new scholars in the Chinese field. Some American China scholars have negotiated their own arrangements to teach in China together with an ongoing research program. In general, however, the major research support for American students and faculty who wish to carry out research or language training has been managed through the national program.

This virtual monopoly of financial resources for in-China research has scaled down possibilities for American research in the diversity of programs that had been originally supported by the NEH and the SSRC or the ACLS. When the national program was established in the aftermath of Chinese overtures, the emphasis was upon redirecting funds from whatever source, in order to maximize the resources available for the departing faculty and students. Not unexpectedly, the consequences have been to limit funds for library research or non-China programs. Furthermore, the CSCPRC naturally wished to have some part in the determination of awards which it would administer. This has meant that the CSCPRC became a focus for all applications no matter where they might initially have been submitted.

In addition to funding considerations, a common problem of formal and informal exchange organizations has been the composition of the groups to travel to China and those to be received from China. In the case of the American organizations, lists of proposed delegations have been prepared and transmitted to the Chinese counterpart organizations during the course of annual visits to arrange exchange programs. Chinese proposals for reciprocal visits were also received during these negotiating sessions. The problems inherent in the development of these lists and negotiating their acceptance were numerous, and only gradually did organizations develop the experience required to do so effectively. First of all, each side had to take into account the current realities of Sino-American relations, as well as the strength and standing of the groups that were being proposed. American hosts became sensitized to the issue of Taiwan—the potential for clashes with Taiwanese groups in the United States, for gifts produced in Taiwan mistakenly being offered to Chinese hosts, or for the wrong flag being raised to salute a PRC delegation. On their part, the Chinese altered the lyrics of songs they performed that would otherwise have offended their American hosts, and, in the course of their conversations downplayed differences in policy between the two governments, and they emphasized common themes and common enemies, the importance of "people-to-people" relationships, and the enduring advantages of international understanding.

Each side retained the right to select the members of its delegations. The Chinese were unable to alter the composition of one CSCPRC delegation, for example, despite their objections to the inclusion on it of certain China scholars they regarded as unfriendly. In the case of one NCUSCR delegation, a trip was canceled at virtually the last moment when a satisfactory resolution of a problem with the composition of the delegation could not be found. With these exceptions, delegates formally proposed by one side were generally accepted by the other.

The establishment of itineraries and sites to be visited posed significant problems for both Chinese and Americans. Chinese knowledge of the American business and professional communities was initially very limited. Their requests were thus confined to the best-known institutions. Efforts by American hosts to encourage their Chinese guests to visit other, less well known centers have been only partially successful. American travelers to China initially faced much the same problem of limited knowledge of the Chinese organizational structure. One of the initial purposes of the early surveys was thus to map the Chinese academic and governmental systems. Improvement in matching requested itineraries with actual travel experience was gradual, frequently influenced by political considerations, and finally fostered as American and Chinese counterpart organizations developed confidence and knowledge of each other. Where initial proposals had been quite vague, occasionally out of date, and sometimes based on incorrect information, subsequent proposals on both sides became more precise and accurate as mutual knowledge increased through experience. In the academic sphere, American scholars in the natural and physical sciences as well as in medical science have developed quite detailed knowledge of the Chinese academic establishment in their fields. In addition, since some CSCPRC delegations focused on topics in the humanities, some expertise was developed in these areas. Because of the paucity of social science delegations, American social scientists lagged far behind their colleagues in developing a knowledge of Chinese personnel, research activities, and archives in the social science fields.

At the same time that the American exchange organizations were developing the experience and background necessary successfully to prepare American delegations for travel in China, they were also forced to develop, virtually from the ground up, the necessary knowledge to propose appropriate sites for visiting Chinese. In connection with this task it was always necessary to be sensitive to the problems of security and of "proprietary knowledge"—that is, research peculiar to a particular industrial concern—when scheduling Chinese travelers.

These problems of itinerary, delegation composition, and funding were slowly resolved as both sides in the formal negotiations worked out accommodations and procedures to maximize the satisfaction of travel participants on each side. While members of the initial trips, whether by the NCUSCR, the NCUSCT, or the CSCPRC, were often obliged to devote considerable time to protocol and ceremonial duties, this aspect of travel began to decline in importance as domestic priorities in China changed and as American counterpart organizations gained confidence in their assessments of Chinese interests. Though certain Chinese delegations did and do merit special treatment because of their composition—for example, the CPIFA delegation headed by a distinguished former Chinese ambassador—most recent programs have been considerably less concerned about protocol and ceremony. On the Chinese side, the need for special treatment of US congressional delegations is accepted without question. Other delegations with special interests, however, while being treated courteously, are nonetheless increasingly scheduled with more attention to substantive interests than to protocol.

## CHARACTERISTICS OF SINO-AMERICAN EXCHANGES

American experience with exchanges with the PRC falls into two distinct periods: 1972–77, when Maoist goals and leadership dominated Chinese politics and exchanges, and the post-1977 period, when the campaign for the Four Modernizations meant a reoriented and expanded program. During the first five years, decisions regarding the size, direction, and scope of exchanges were taken almost exclusively by the Chinese authorities. Though the first initiative was made by the Chinese in their invitation to the American table tennis team, much of the subsequent pressure for exchanges was largely American in origin. Why was this so? Many policies forcefully stated in the Cultural Revolution were antithetical to, or at least suspicious of, exchanges, of visitors, and of the dangers of cultural and technological transfers. The exchange proposals of the American side, especially in the humanities and social sciences, were constantly circumscribed or limited, the scope of travel only gradually expanded, and political conflict over some symbolic aspects of travel quite common. On the basis of slowly accumulated experience, American negotiators developed a working set of assumptions about programs likely to be accepted by the Chinese prior to formal diplomatic recognition. Exchange students were not acceptable; the Taiwan issue was a constant worry; and cultural exchanges, especially of printed material and films, were almost beyond imagination. Joint participation in scientific programs and cooperative conferences and seminars was rare. Virtually every one of these possibilities was raised, mentioned, formally proposed or explored by the American side, and either delayed or denied by the Chinese in the course of negotiations during the first five years. American organizations exercised ingenuity and enthusiasm in maintaining a program, not so much in the face of explicit opposition in China, but rather the face of great caution, hesitation, and a broad set of regulations and restrictions.

With the decision for rapid modernization in China and the repudiation of many of the Cultural Revolution values, the initiative for exchange programs shifted somewhat. The transformation of the Chinese education system and the upgrading of the scientific organizations of the country had immediate consequences for programs in the exchange package. Chinese participation in the international scientific community increased markedly, and interest in foreign technology and its possible application to China was apparent, not only on the part of Chinese scientists, but also on the part of representatives of Chinese industrial circles. Chinese interest in Western culture, ranging from music and the arts to pop culture, has been more surprising. It was announced that a significant number of Chinese students would be sent to study in foreign universities and colleges. Scientists would be encouraged to establish close ties and working relationships with foreign colleagues, as well as to develop access to advanced technical instrumentation. All of these decisions implied increased contact with the United States.

In place of earlier official caution about exchanges, the new emphasis in China has been on expansion. Americans on the exchange organizations, as well as citizens who had long been supporters of informal exchange programs or return courtesy trips found a different attitude and outlook on the part of their Chinese colleagues. Where pressure had come from the Americans, it now became more evenly balanced. In 1980 the expansion of scientific exchanges continued, and there was a surprising receptivity on the part of the Chinese to exchanges in the humanities and social sciences. As social science and humanities organizations were reestablished in China, they became constituents for continued Chinese government support.

On the American side, the initial five-year experience was managed and directed principally by the NCUSCR, the CSCPRC, and the NCUSCT. There is no question that close relationships existed between the leaders of these exchange organizations and officials of the US government. Official participation in high-level receptions and meetings would have been unthinkable in the absence of a commitment to improved China relations on the part of successive administrations in Washington. On the other hand, few American government officials were directly drawn into the programs. To be sure, some members of the NCUSCR were recruited from the ranks of former State Department personnel, but there was no equivalent to the ties that had developed between the US government and the Taiwan Research Institute. Instead, there was the assumption by essentially education-oriented committees of the tasks of administering exchanges. The procedures for recruitment of staff and appointment and selection committees, the standards for financing travel, and a number of aspects of the day-to-day bureaucratic life of these organizations was significantly different from those characteristic of the government. The personnel of these organizations were and still are largely drawn from the ranks of advanced students and young faculty in Chinese studies. In the pre-1977 period, because the organizations had not intended exchanges to constitute so important and crucial a part of their work, committee members and leaders served on a part-time basis, sometimes without prior experience in the China field, though sympathetic to exchanges in general. As a result, direction and guidance of the exchange program often rested in the hands of a limited number of individuals. Little attention was paid to regularized rules with respect to recruitment and committee turnover. When Chinese priorities changed, the pressure of events, the need for care in pursuing the exchange opening, and the requirement to make rapid decisions accounted in large measure for the ensuing centralization of authority. Whatever the disadvantages, the result has been a strong and effective set of organizations presenting and administering the American side of the exchange program.

A key factor in the successful arrangement of informal exchanges was the assistance and intervention of Chinese-American scientists, who acted out of an interest in facilitating ties between the United States and China. That story has yet to be fully recounted, but with almost every organization and on virtually every campus Chinese-American scientists played essential roles in establishing ties and forwarding programs. In addition, there were other Americans who, for a range of reasons, had maintained good relations with the Chinese. These individuals formed the nucleus of a gradually widening circle of persons who worked to foster informal exchanges.

This ad hoc quality on the American side contrasted sharply with the highly organized Chinese staffs that interchanged personnel among the Foreign Affairs Ministry, the CPIFA, the CAFFC, and other units.

Throughout the post-1972 period, the issue of rough equity or reciprocity in the exchange process remained paramount in the minds of American negotiators. They were sensitive to the special aspects of a relationship with a socialist society. They were well aware of the very tough negotiating that had been involved in the establishment of American-Soviet exchanges. Outside observers constantly warned about the importance of maintaining equity in a developing relationship. Some aspects of the problem were rather easy to arrange. As indicated earlier, the establishment of balance with respect to funding was based largely on equivalent services. Indeed, the routinization of trips arranged by the NCUSCR and the CSCPRC came rather easily. In the CSCPRC experience, equity could be maintained by a rough equivalence in the total number of trips in each direction during a given period of time.

The problem was viewed in a different light in the case of the NCUSCR and the NCUSCT. In the latter case, there were no means for insuring equity in technology transfer, since there was so substantial a technical gap between the two societies. Furthermore, the NCUSCT was involved in effecting some of the transfer through commercial means. Companies did not see equity in transportation as important, since their interests often lay in sales and in long-term relations. In the case of the NCUSCR, the early years of exchanges found the Chinese unwilling to return American trips to China on the grounds that the continuing US relationship with Taiwan precluded such travel. Though the political changes of 1978 made these arguments seem less persuasive than they were in the sterner period of 1974–75, they posed significant problems in establishing reciprocity at the time.

While important, reciprocity in cultural exchanges has never been a primary goal. When cultural relaxation occurred in China, however, it was also reflected in the Chinese interest in foreign cultural visits. The NCUSCR, which had been somewhat unsure of its relationship with the Chinese authorities, now found itself receiving many requests for assistance. Chinese groups traveling as self-paying guests in the United States sought the advice and assistance of the NCUSCR. Committee members found many of their relationships with the Chinese Liaison Office in Washington increasingly cordial and productive and even more rewarding after normalization.

One final aspect of their development needs comment before turning to the prospects for the future of US-Chinese exchanges. As this section has suggested, much of the exchange program resulted in the first instance in response to Chinese preferences and constraints, especially during the 1972–77 period. American strategy and tactics were also influenced by the US-Soviet experience. Chinese reluctance to approve social science research and their very cautious attitude toward the humanities had seemed to indicate that the very centralized and tough American negotiating posture that characterized the development of Soviet exchanges would be necessary in the Chinese case as well. The CSCPRC, where evidence of this problem was most common, tried to insure at least limited access to China for social scientists and humanists by assigning a social scientist or humanist to each of its delegations. So did the NCUSCR. The CSCPRC took very seriously its obligation to forward the interests of the humanities and social sciences, as well as those of the National Academy of Science.

The centralization of programs diminished when Chinese science and technology began to reach outward in 1977. The diversification of program content suggested by the Chinese in 1977–78 harked back to earlier proposals of the CSCPRC. Discussions now revolved around bilateral seminars, lecturing programs, and a variety of enrichment proposals. While these interesting options did not require a change in organizational structure on the American side, some changes nonetheless became apparent in the fall of 1978. Long-range exchanges were suggested to various American universities, colleges, and research units by Chinese universities and research units. While the CSCPRC remained an effective and important part of Chinese exchanges, a new feature of potential importance was the wide-scale effort to establish direct unit-to-unit exchanges.

In the fall of 1978 the Chinese government sent a high-ranking education delegation to the United States to discuss additional exchange programs. The delegation visited a number of American universities. Expectations were that this delegation would expand the CSCPRC exchange program to include long-term arrangements for visiting scholars and students. The final statement of that delegation (initially viewed merely as a statement of intent rather than as a formal agreement) spoke of Chinese interests and intentions. It did not provide a specific role for the CSCPRC or the American government in the long-term program. The American side, however, did propose a set of specific figures to suggest the scope of an American national program to send scholars and graduate students to China.

Why did the Chinese authorities not request, let alone insist upon, formal assumption of responsibility by the US government for the implementation of the exchange effort? One part of the answer to this question was funding. Placement of scholars and students would require expertise, experience, and testing. Since the sending side has typically assumed responsibility for funding, the Chinese were concerned about the potential costs. Second, some Chinese-American scientists and some American scholars counseled the Chinese that US governmental implementation would be not only costly but also inefficient. The Chinese thus began to discuss exchanges with American universities on an individual basis and have continued to do so.

On the other hand, the Americans retained, indeed reinforced centralization on their side by expanding the work of the CSCPRC to include establishment of a centralized clearinghouse for testing and selecting candidates for research travel to the PRC. The CSCPRC was required to act as both a facilitator of exchanges and as an awards administrator. The program was to include all disciplines, just as the CSCPRC had represented the humanities, social sciences, and the National Academy in establishing its exchange program.

The possible conflicts that were foreseen in the administration of the exchange programs have proved to be quite modest in practice. While technology transfer may yet provide difficulties in terms of the possible military application of some hardware, the cultural programs have generally been well received. At present, there are a variety of proposals for exchange programs with China, representing a variety of interests that would have been difficult to imagine some five years ago.

## THE FUTURE OF US-CHINA EXCHANGES

Should the US government continue to encourage, finance, and administer exchange programs with the PRC? Should the government foster certain activities and eschew others? What guidelines are applicable for the coming decade? Which programs are best arranged through governmental organizations and which through private groups? What problems are the exchange program likely to encounter, and how will they be resolved?

Under present conditions, there is reason to be optimistic

about the likelihood of continued exchanges, formal and informal, with China. China's efforts to borrow technology, its interest in selected aspects of American culture, its encouragement of English-language instruction, and its expanded program of tourism all suggest a basically positive outlook with respect to foreign contacts. In addition, the Chinese are confident of their ability to shape what they borrow to the needs of China. On the American side, even discounting those whose interest in China is exclusively faddish, there is substantial scholarly interest in China that, together with the enthusiasm of the sizable Chinese community in the United States and the long history of cultural interaction with China, suggests a fertile setting for exchanges.

The performing arts, film, and sports demonstrations and competitions are an ongoing part of American cultural diplomacy as well as that of the Chinese. The ease with which athletic exchanges have been developed, together with contemporary Chinese interest in international athletic competition, suggests that this area of shared and reciprocal competition will be easy to maintain and will be beneficial to both sides. Chinese sports organizations and their American counterparts may be successfully matched. The NCUSCR has had extensive experience in facilitating such arrangements.

In other cultural areas, it is somewhat premature to assess the likelihood of significant expansion. The cost and logistics problems involved in the exchange visits of groups such as the Performing Arts Troupe and the Boston Symphony Orchestra (BSO) make this type of program especially complicated to arrange. Because of these considerations, nonprofit organizations such as the NCUSCR may not be able to continue to negotiate effectively and to direct such programs. Chinese interest in the past was said to center on maximizing the number of Americans able to see Chinese performances. It remains to be seen whether or not that outlook will be retained when the Chinese dollar earnings from performances might be enhanced by higher ticket prices. From the American side, it is also a question whether the costs of a trip such as that of the BSO—estimated at $750,000, not including the services rendered by the Chinese—represents the best use of limited funds. In the case of the BSO, federal funds were not involved; the NCUSCR assisted in facilitating the trip and funds were raised privately. Nonetheless, the questions remains: should it have been encouraged, even with a Chinese invitation?

Assuming that American theatrical entrepreneurs will eventually seek to participate in the larger and more lucrative aspects of cultural performances, a governmental role might be to provide support and encouragement to diverse smaller participations in the arts, not only in performances in China, but also in education programs and exhibitions. In many of these cases a smaller investment might result in a broader segment of the Chinese population having the opportunity to observe aspects of American culture. These questions are being considered by the US International Communications Agency, which is responsible for coordination and leadership in this field. In fact, by 1980 the ICA was beginning to seek to facilitate the participation of smaller troupes and groups in exchange.

Past experience in this and other areas of exchange suggests that disagreement or disputes will inevitably arise. Consequently, it is necessary to have in place a mechanism for dispute resolution that would obviate the need to refer an issue to the very top levels of political leadership. One possible avenue for such a procedure will be the use of a Sino-American bilateral commission, such as the one that reviews agreements already signed by the United States and China in the field of scientific exchange. The American commission has a part of its membership drawn from the public sector. Continued appointment of "public" members will develop responsible community ties that can serve to raise support for the exchange programs when financial priorities and emphases shift to other areas. But bilateral commissions often become merely ceremonial in function and honorific in the selection of their members, and thus of little use unless well prepared and staffed for meetings.

With respect to science and technology, there are some perplexing problems in the development of these programs, even though many difficulties initially expected have failed to materialize. There are two general areas of exchange in the science field. There is the broadened CSCPRC program of survey trips, cooperative seminars, and senior lectureships originally proposed and ultimately accepted by the Chinese. In addition, there is the American national program to send students and scholars to conduct study and research in China.

It is important to keep in mind that the announced national program that the Chinese have accepted is not matched by an equivalent national program for which the US government has responsibility to facilitate. Although the proposals of American scholars and students for extended research programs in China are subject to negotiation and approval by the Chinese Ministry of Education, the plans of Chinese scholars for extended training and research in the United States are not subject to similar scrutiny by the US government. The CSCPRC does not place Chinese students in American institutions; it does not facilitate their admission; and it does not provide formal referral services. In that sense, reciprocity is lacking in one part of the science and technology effort. Only with regard to short-term trips, seminars, and lectureships is there a rough equality in the administration of the program. Here stylized measurements of reciprocity including such terms as "man-months" to measure equality have been developed.

There are other considerations that must be looked at in an analysis of the likely future of the national program. To begin with, however, it must be recognized that there is little experience yet with the program of sending scholars and students to China. Only three sets of US awardees have been selected and sent to China at this writing. Furthermore, there is no longer doubt that problems of logistics, the shortage of housing, and related matters will necessarily affect the program in these early years. Setting aside these considerations, however, there remains the question of the nature of the research supported. Many American scholars believe that certain proposals are not appropriate because they will be unacceptable to Chinese authorities or infeasible in contemporary Chinese society. Sociologists and political scientists believe aspects of their work are of such a nature that they cannot be carried out in the framework of a socialist society. Normally such scholars do not apply for support. Therefore, self-selection in applications occurs in the initial stages of the program. As presently administered, a second level of appraisal of acceptability is then made by the US committee charged with ranking applicants. Preliminary ranking is made by an SSRC or an ACLS committee, which then sends on its judgments to the CSCPRC Committee on Advanced Study in China. These organizations are area committees. Formal peer review in the discipline was agreed upon in 1980. How it will be integrated into the area committees of the SCRC and the ACLS remains to be seen.

In the early exchange programs, where the trips were normally of only one month in duration, the advantages of selection were primarily honorific. Each group member had an opportunity to see his specialty in a new society, to contact new personnel, and to contribute to a general trip report on the present state of the discipline in China. The 1981 national program is quite a different matter; and selection for, and participation in, it carries much more substantial research rewards. Moreover, the national program currently pays the costs of the scholar for the period of study or research in China. At present the academic marketplace is a difficult one, and the advantages of a successful application for a graduate student entering the job market or for a scholar seeking a research opportunity to improve his or her chances of being granted tenure are substantial. In this setting the issue of equity and reciprocity is a two-directional one: toward the Chinese side with whom the exchanges are undertaken, and toward the American scholarly community from whom the applications are drawn.

Until 1979 the opportunities for research support in the China field were largely confined to small programs of the ACLS and the SSRC, together with government programs of the National Science Foundation and the National Endowment for the Humanities. The latter two were more discipline oriented than area programs, though China scholars in a specific discipline did receive support from them. In addition, there were Fulbright awards to Taiwan and occasional government-supported research generally directed at specific policy questions or analyses of specific developments. These latter projects were generally based on State Department, occasionally CIA, and other government funding sources.

The review procedures for each of these grants were quite disparate, their orientation and problems diverse, and their expectation of research proposals quite varied. When the national program was initiated, with a commitment for fifty scholars and students to be sent to China in the fall of 1979, a key matter became the problem of financing such a program. Should the funds of all agencies be directed toward the national program as administered by the CSCPRC, or should diversity with respect to approach and award be maintained? What would be fair with respect to American applicants? Should the CSCPRC simply approve the awards made in other agencies (then often involving peer review)? Should another set of review procedures be superimposed on those already in place in the specific agency? Would maintenance of the diversity of sources for applicants' funding compromise the effectiveness of the Americans in the China program? Initial decisions were influenced by the need to place individuals in the field quickly and hence had an ad hoc quality to them. Emphasis was upon seizing the long-desired opportunity to initiate research and study in China. For that reason many funds were channeled to the national program to support those selected, and the CSCPRC, using a somewhat expanded committee apparatus, was charged with the administration of these funds.

Decisions to have the program operate in this manner were understandable and probably wise in the short run. What now remains is to continue to adapt the decision-making mechanism to insure that selection and appointment committees and procedures are capable of meeting the responsibility to American applicants as well as the responsibility to the Chinese receiving the scholars. A decision to require that all China research be funded and reviewed through one central committee was originally urged by those who feared that, lacking a unified stance, American scholars would be unsuccessful in their efforts to work in China. This argument was based largely upon experience with the Soviet Union. There is some reason to believe that it applies to China as well. Evidence, still very limited, now seems to support the view that an American academic advisor in the American Embassy is invaluable.

The argument for centralization of selection procedures, though, seems to rest upon effective use of limited resources. This argument is a strong one, but successful implementation will require, at a minimum, the assurance of a diverse and broadly representative selection committee. For reasons suggested earlier in this chapter, the establishment of that type of committee and procedure has not yet received much attention.

Apart from government and foundation funding, the other option available to American students and scholars is the bilateral exchange between American universities and Chinese universities and research organizations. It is much too early to appraise such programs. Still, some cautious comments are possible. The university-to-university experience reflects ingenuity, innovation, and considerable goodwill. One problem does seem certain, however. If these programs result in increased costs for the Chinese in the United States or the Americans in China, then early enthusiasm will be subject to university budgetary constraints. American universities generally have been responsive to the possibility of involving themselves in exchanges with Chinese educational institutions. By 1980 American universities were trying to institutionalize the procedures for sending and receiving participants. Such efforts are important in a time of limited resources. There is, however, one unavoidable limitation of such programs. Many of the current generation of American faculty in Chinese studies are placed in smaller colleges and schools that are not currently participating in bilateral exchanges with China. Lacking an institutional exchange program, they will inevitably be disadvantaged in their effort to undertake research.

A question of fairness, equity, and moral obligation rises in considering the reverse side of the problems of American participants in research programs. What obligation, if any, do American programs and their participants have toward the Chinese scholars who collaborate in research work or toward the participants who are subjects of research? This problem is an exceedingly difficult and complicated one. In past years the American scholarly community has been subjected to repeated criticism for its attitudes with respect to field work. In India, for example, local scholars criticized American visitors for their eager acceptance of assistance with no recognition of the contribution of their Indian colleagues or the individuals who assisted in the work. Sensitive to this problem, many American foundations and the Fulbright Committee have attempted to encourage joint projects or have at least insisted upon recognition of the assistance of native residents. By 1980, however, there is evidence that some scholars are using means to facilitate their work that can only compromise national-local relations in China, and possibly relations between scholars. These cases are not common—but they do exist.

There is another aspect to the problem, especially pertinent to research in many socialist societies. What moral responsibility, if any, should a scholar accept for the consequences of social and political research? There is considerable evidence in the political histories of countries that today's friends may be tomorrow's enemies. Research into attitudes, personal backgrounds, and anecdotal evidence all leave the respondent or interviewee open to criticism in his or her own milieu after the visiting scholar has departed. The Cultural Revolution gives ample evidence of this. The 1980 fluctuation of attitudes on questions of "security" suggests the issue is by no means resolved in China. It would seem essential that some degree of responsibility for this eventuality be accepted by the American funding agencies, the selection committees, and the individual scholar.

Social scientists in American society have been wrestling with this problem for some years. There is ongoing conflict over the need for social research unfettered by the government, similar to the freedom accorded the press, as against the counterposition that emphasizes the responsibility of the scientist to the subject. Committees on university campuses confront this problem in many aspects of clinical research. That is not the problem here. In this case, the issue is centered in the society. Developing a balance between scholarship, responsibility, and moral obligation will be an ongoing task.

It does seem that certain steps can be taken to reduce potential criticism. Selection committees might well be limited to faculty members, or at least specialists separated from the agencies that rely upon classified research. Discussion of potential social problems should probably be a standard part of the briefing program for those going to China. Some policy limiting contact with intelligence agencies immediately prior to assumption of an award might well be adopted. Though reliance needs to be placed upon the moral responsibility of each individual, there are some policies that may assist in the matter and signify the awareness of the responsible American agencies to the difficulty.

A new period in Sino-American exchanges and relations is now under way. Exchanges are seen as potentially valuable to both sides, and hence there may be increasing opportunities to expand exchanges in the next decade. On both the American and the Chinese sides, the decision to maintain, or to allocate anew, scarce resources to the operation of such exchanges will ultimately rest upon the degree to which each side finds itself benefiting in scientific, technological, and cultural terms.

Problems of social responsibility, selection, and like matters indicate how much progress has been made. But in these formative growth years, attention and responsiveness to possible cultural and political differences will likely pay good dividends. Considering how far the programs have come, it would be a mistake not to insure continued growth.

## NOTES

1. *Christian Science Monitor*, 17 July 1979, 2.

2. *Notes from the National Committee on U.S.-China Relations*, July 1975.

# SINO-AMERICAN EXCHANGES
## A Comment on the Chapter by Joyce K. Kallgren

**GLENN T. SEABORG**

Associate Director, Lawrence Berkeley Laboratory
University of California, Berkeley

The rapid development in the scope and number of exchanges between the PRC and the United States during the last eighteen months is a heartening sign for those looking to the development of people-to-people ties between the two countries. Whether viewed from the perspective of cultural exchanges; the proliferation of scientific contacts, both formal and informal; or sports competition and individual trips, the growth of programs and interchange is part of the reawakening of American and Chinese interests in one another that go back to the virtual beginnings of contact in the late eighteenth century.

As a scientist with a nearly lifelong commitment to the encouragement and facilitation of scientific exchange, it has been particularly gratifying for me to participate in these developments. Since the early 1970s, when exchanges once again became possible, there has been interest in contact with China by the scientific community. In the early years, the Chinese leadership was, for a variety of reasons, rather more cautious about the topics and areas for exchanges than their American counterparts. That hesitation has moderated considerably as I have observed in the course of my two trips to China[1] and in hosting various Chinese delegations in the United States. By 1979 international cooperation in science was a high priority in Chinese scientific circles, not only in the research institutes themselves, but also in Chinese educational institutions. It has been reinforced in governmental statements and policies that call for the development of ties with international organizations, research centers, and graduate training facilities.

In this time of activity, enthusiasm, and optimism, it is important to stress the need for sound program development so that the maintenance and continued growth of these programs will persist when political differences or shifting economic or cultural priorities may be more prominent than is currently the case. This long-range concern was one of the considerations underlying the thinking of the UNA-USA National Policy Panel to Study US-China Relations Subpanel on Scientific, Technological and Cultural Relations. The recommendations of the subpanel, which I chaired, were framed with these considerations in mind.[2] Professor Kallgren, consultant to our subpanel, addresses a number of issues implicit in the work in her analysis here. Her emphasis upon the programs and difficulties in establishing exchanges and the selection of participants, together with such considerations as equity in goals and personnel, was of particular relevance to our subpanel's interest in institutionalizing and routinizing the emerging programs.

The current development of Sino-American exchanges takes place after a hiatus of nearly thirty years. Yet there was a long pre-1949 experience when both Chinese and American exchange participants traveled back and forth between the two countries, studied in each other's institutions, and made contributions to the advancement of science and scholarship in the humanities and social sciences. That experience needs to be kept in mind when looking at contemporary activities. During the period 1949–72, though American relations with the Chinese scientific community were few, and contacts with cultural circles and educational institutions minimal or nonexistent, there were vigorous international exchanges by the Chinese with other nations. Chinese experiences with these other nations play a role in the contemporary Sino-American programs. From the American perspective, there has been some inclination to draw upon the history of US-Soviet programs as a possible guide for the burgeoning Chinese exchanges. It now seems that some past experiences may be of limited use. From the American side, the Soviet model appears to be somewhat restrictive in application. From the Chinese side, current program developments appear to be going beyond what might have been predicted on the basis of prior bilateral exchanges. In this sense, both participants are moving into new and challenging areas where past history may be less help than expected, and primary reliance should thus be placed on practical common sense to facilitate the goals of both parties.

In contemporary programs, it is wise to keep in mind that a substantial portion of the top leadership in Chinese scientific circles was trained abroad between the 1920s and 1950s in the United States as well as in Western Europe. At the same time, some American-financed and partially staffed institutions in China played roles in the scientific, cultural, and economic developments of the pre-1949 years. These institutions and many of the individuals affiliated with them were then criticized in the immediate post-1949 period. The institutions were characterized as examples of neocolonialism, and some of their graduates have suffered seriously at various points in the past thirty years. Whether or not one agrees with the institutional criticisms that have been made in China, it is important to keep in mind that exchanges, especially in the scientific and technological fields, will inevitably be related to the priorities of contemporary China, in political terms as well as in the basic scientific sense. When westerners assist in the development of high technology or in the training of physicists or biochemists, they become inevitably linked to the products that will eventually emerge and the criticisms as well as accolades that may result. In the United States, American scientists differ among themselves about various scientific policies, the wisdom of financial supports, and the role of science in the life of the nation and its citizens. It is not likely that these same American scientists will be able to avoid such criticisms in Chinese society. Furthermore, participants in exchange programs, including science but also cultural and educational as well, will always find themselves related in one form or another to very difficult and sensitive decisions in the host country. Accordingly, it is important to emphasize the need for Chinese determination of priorities and science alternatives. Westerners and certainly Americans should be drawn into the programs only when the Chinese themselves determine priorities, just as we expect the Chinese to allow us to make similar determinations for ourselves in terms of our exchange goals.

There is considerable publicity in American media sources about the Chinese students, particularly those in the United States. Americans are, and quite understandably in my view, concerned with the two-way nature of exchanges. Professor Kallgren points out the important current differences in the exchange programs between the two countries. Chinese students come to the United States from a highly bureaucratized and centralized society, but they are not formal participants in a government-to-government program. The American government, through the National Academy of Sciences unit, negotiates with the Chinese governmental ministers for placement and training of Americans. The American government finances and selects the American participants. The Chinese students go to American universities, on the basis of either individual applications or of bilateral arrangements between their home institution and the American counterpart organization. In the not-too-distant future, the Chinese visitors may be drawn from the undergraduate and graduate student population in China rather than the more advanced "visiting scholar" group presently attached to research units in American educational institutions. Because of the different means by which the educational affiliation is made, the nature of the training undertaken and the research begun, there may well be some differences of view about the symmetry of the programs. As long as scholars on both sides are hardworking and students are evenhandedly treated whether formally enrolled or facilitated in their work by informal means, it seems wise to downplay the exact reciprocal features of the program. With many other countries of the world, the United States has served as a center for advanced scientific and technological training without insistence upon a one-to-one arrangement. It seems only just, therefore, to continue that procedure in the current situation.

In the light of the brevity of current experience, it is not prudent to predict the course of exchange development. Reversals of policies have occurred in the past thirty-year period in both the United States and China. However, it may be enough to say that developments to date make Sino-American exchanges seem similar to those presently sustained with most of the major nations of the world. This very normalcy about their development is a positive sign.

## NOTES

1. Details of these trips, including an interview with Premier Zhou Enlai, are found in Glenn T. Seaborg, "China Journal, May 22–June 10, 1973," and "China Revisited: May 14–June 11, 1978."

2. The subpanel was composed of Dr. Matina S. Horner, President, Radcliffe College; Phillips Talbot, former Ambassador to Greece and President, Asia Society; Mrs. Margaret B. Young, Chairman, Whitney M. Young, Jr. Memorial Foundation; and was chaired by myself.

# IV. LEGAL CONSIDERATIONS IN THE EVOLUTION OF US-CHINA RELATIONS

## Chapter 4

# THE LEGAL STATUS AND POLITICAL FUTURE OF TAIWAN AFTER NORMALIZATION

**VICTOR H. LI**

President, East-West Center
University of Hawaii

I am delighted that normalization of relations with the People's Republic of China (PRC) has finally taken place, after eight years and so many fits and starts. But normalization still leaves many political and legal problems to be resolved, including the status of Taiwan.

After 1 January 1979, we know what the United States does *not* regard Taiwan to be: it is not the de jure government of the state of China. Much less clear, however, is the question of what Taiwan *is*.[1]

We also know that US–Republic of China (ROC) treaties do not automatically lapse upon withdrawal of recognition. In a 30 December 1978 memorandum for all departments and agencies, President Carter declared:

> Existing international agreements and arrangements in force between the United States and Taiwan shall continue in force and shall be performed and enforced by depart-

> ments and their agencies beginning January 1, 1979, in accordance with their terms.[2]

Similarly, Section 4(c) of the Taiwan Relations Act states:

> For all purposes, including actions in any court in the United States, the Congress approves the continuation in force of all treaties and other international agreements, including multilateral conventions, entered into by the United States and the Republic of China prior to January 1, 1979, and in force between them on December 31, 1978, unless and until terminated in accordance with law.[3]

But the United States has not explained the legal rationale for preserving treaties and maintaining commercial, cultural, and other relations with an unrecognized entity.

## TWO POSSIBLE CHOICES

*Successor Government.* One possible basis for future US-Taiwan dealings is that the United States has treaty and other relations with the state of China. Prior to 1 January, that state was represented by the ROC government. After the switch of recognition, the United States regards the PRC as the successor government to the ROC. As such, the PRC assumes the rights and obligations of its predecessor.

The successor government theory is well known. For example, in 1971 the PRC was recognized by the United Nations as the only legitimate representative of China and succeeded to the seat belonging to that state.[4]

Some scholars argued that the successor government theory should be applied to the China situation.[5] But such an approach would produce some highly unsatisfactory results. First, the PRC would succeed to the Mutual Defense Treaty and other agreements with the United States. These treaties would remain in force because the PRC would agree, in an implied manner, that they should continue to serve as the bases of American relations with the Chinese territory of Taiwan. This means that at some later time China could withdraw its implied agreement and terminate American treaty relations with Taiwan. In addition, the United States would be in the absurd situation of having a mutual defense treaty with the PRC for the purpose of defending Taiwan from being attacked by the PRC.

In addition, since the PRC would be the sole legitimate government of all of China including Taiwan, the United States could have no direct relations with the authorities on Taiwan, unless the PRC consented, even if only in an implied manner. Taiwan would have no capacity to conduct foreign affairs, except again insofar as the PRC consented. Alternatively, the United States might be able to continue direct dealings with Taiwan by explicitly asserting that Taiwan is not part of China. This policy position would be extremely difficult to maintain.

*De Facto Entity with International Personality.* A second possible description of the legal status of Taiwan after withdrawal of recognition is that it is a "de facto entity with international personality." That is, while no longer regarded by the United States as the de jure government or state, nevertheless Taiwan continues to control a population and territory and to carry out the usual functions of government. Section 4 of the *Restatement, Second, Foreign Relations Law of the United States* (hereafter, *Restatement*) provides:

> Except as otherwise indicated, "state" as used in the Restatement of this Subject means an entity that has a defined territory and population under the control of a government and that engages in foreign relations.[6]

In other words, whether Taiwan is regarded as a "state" or as a juridical person in international law depends on whether it carries out the usual functions of a state, not on whether it is recognized de jure by other states.

If Taiwan is a de facto entity with international personality, it may carry out the full range of foreign relations, including entering into international agreements and sending and receiving official missions. With respect to preexisting treaties and agreements, international law does not require that treaties entered into with a once recognized government, the terms of which are limited to the territory actually controlled by that government, must lapse after that government loses de jure recognition while still exerting de facto control.[7] In such an unprecedented situation, the United States could make a political decision to maintain these treaties on the ground that it may continue to deal with the authorities in actual control of Taiwan.

## THE AMERICAN POSITION

The PRC obviously views the switch of recognition as a successor government situation. In its unilateral statement of 15 December 1978 the Chinese government said:

> As is known to all, the Government of the People's Republic of China is the sole legal government of China and Taiwan is part of China. . . . As for the way of bringing Taiwan back to the embrace of the motherland and reunifying the country, it is entirely China's internal affair.[8]

The American position is less definitive. In the Joint Communiqué of 15 December 1978, the United States "acknowledges the Chinese position that there is but one China and Taiwan is part of China" and "recognizes the People's Republic of China as the sole legal Government of China. Within this context, the people of the United States will maintain cultural, commercial, and other unofficial relations with the people of Taiwan."

One possible interpretation of these statements is that the PRC is the successor government to the ROC: there is a state of China that includes Taiwan, and the PRC is the sole legal government of this state. Moreover, since the United States can deal with Taiwan only "within this context," the United States acknowledges the PRC's ultimate legal authority over Taiwan, including the right to approve future US-Taiwan relations.

An alternative interpretation is that "acknowledgment" of the Chinese position is not tantamount to accepting it. With regard to this term, there is, however, a potentially serious linguistic discrepancy between the English and Chinese texts. The Chinese text uses *chengren* for "acknowledges." In this context, the Chinese term carries a clear connotation of acceptance or agreement. Moreover, the Shanghai Communiqué states: "The United States acknowledges that Chinese on both sides of the Strait agree that there is but one China and Taiwan is part of China. We do not challenge this position." In this instance the Chinese text uses a correct equivalent, *renshi*, for "acknowledges." Reading the Chinese texts of the two communiqués together, the United States has increased the degree of its acquiescence in the Chinese position from *renshi* (acknowledges or takes note) to *chengren*. Administration officials have stated that in interpreting this phrase, the United States will adhere only to the English version.[9] Of course China will adhere only to the Chinese version. If, based on the American interpretation of the terms, the United States does not accept the PRC position on Taiwan, then the status of Taiwan would remain "undetermined."[10]

In selecting between the successor government theory and the de facto entity theory, I believe that the former is not workable and does not serve American interests. The need to obtain the PRC's consent, even if only implied, for continued dealings with Taiwan constantly places the United States on the defensive. Serious difficulties would arise if, at a later time, the PRC should object to some aspect of US-Taiwan relations. In addition, one of the reasons for moving ahead with normalization is to bring American policy into accord with reality, a laudable goal. Structuring our dealings with Taiwan as though it were a politically subordinate unit of the PRC would be a departure from reality.

I believe the United States should follow the theory that Taiwan is a de facto entity with international personality. Such a stand accurately reflects reality: derecognition has not affected the manner in which the authorities and 17 million inhabitants of Taiwan conduct their affairs. The United States simply is acknowledging the fact that Taiwan continues to manage its affairs in an autonomous manner.

I should note that the above proposal does not violate the principle of one China. The de facto entity concept deals with present political realities and does not either require or preclude eventual reunification or any other outcome. Indeed, Vice Premier Deng's indications that Taiwan may retain its own political and economic systems as well as maintain separate armed forces acknowledges the same realities.[11]

The United States may derive some short-term benefits from refusing to clarify the legal rationale for continued dealings with Taiwan. After all, explicitly calling it a de facto entity might annoy the PRC, while adopting the successor government theory would damage Taiwan. This policy of international ambiguity will be difficult to maintain for an indeterminate time.

Indeed, a great deal has already occurred that requires the United States to be increasingly specific about its view of the status of Taiwan. For example, Taiwan has deposited in American banks several billion dollars of its foreign exchange reserves. If the PRC is the successor government, it could assert that this money belongs to the "state of China" and should be handed over to the proper representative of that state, namely the government of the PRC. The transfer of such a vast sum would undercut any policy to insure that the people of Taiwan "face a peaceful and prosperous future."

The Taiwan Relations Act has dealt with this problem by providing in Section 4(b)(3)(B) that the PRC does not succeed to the property of the ROC:

> [R]ecognition of the People's Republic of China shall not affect in any way the ownership of or other rights or interests in properties, tangible and intangible, and other things of value, owned or held on or prior to December 31, 1978, or thereafter acquired or earned by the governing authorities on Taiwan.[12]

A related problem that is not completely resolved concerns the ownership of the former ROC Embassy at Twin Oaks, and perhaps other diplomatic and consular properties. The Senate version of the act excluded diplomatic real property from the application of the section quoted above, and hence would have resulted in the PRC taking over Twin Oaks.[13] The act, however, follows the House version, the legislative history of which indicates that this section applies to all property, including diplomatic real property.[14]

The PRC considers the obtaining of the state of China's diplomatic property an important symbolic act. The executive branch may want for political reasons to allow this property to pass to the PRC. Ultimately, the courts may have to decide whether the PRC is the successor government to the ROC, and if so, whether Section 4(b)(3)(B) should be narrowly construed so that it is consistent with international law rules regarding the rights of successor governments.[15]

The issue of whether the PRC is the successor government to the ROC has come up and will do so repeatedly in the future. For example, under what structure will athletes from the PRC and Taiwan participate in the Olympic Games? What are Taiwan's rights and obligations under bilateral and multilateral international agreements on civil aviation?[16] When Chinese assets were unfrozen in 1979, which party was entitled to the assets belonging to the "state of China"?[17] If the PRC objects, can American commercial, cultural, and educational bodies legally have direct dealings with the Taiwan government? Each instance would require a specific response from the United States and also would set a precedent for future dealings.

Although with considerable reluctance and awkwardness, the United States has begun to give some formal indications that it regards Taiwan as a de facto entity with international personality. In his 30 December 1979 memorandum,[18] President Carter directed that:

> [W]henever any law, regulation, or order of the United States refers to a foreign country, nation, state, government, or similar entity, departments and agencies shall construe those terms and apply those laws, regulations, or orders to include Taiwan.

Similarly, Section 4 of the Taiwan Relations Act provides:

> The absence of diplomatic relations or recognition shall not affect the application of the laws of the United States with respect to Taiwan. . . . Whenever the laws of the United States refer or relate to foreign countries, states, governments, or similar entities, such terms shall include and such laws shall apply to Taiwan.

Even more explicitly, the report of the Senate Committee on Foreign Relations states:

> Considerable discussion has occurred concerning the status of Taiwan under international law. The Committee concluded that it was unnecessary, in drafting this legislation, to address this issue since, for purposes of United States domestic law, the Executive Branch can be empowered, statutorily, to treat Taiwan as if it were a state. This is, in fact, precisely what the bill does.[19]

The formulation "de facto entity with international personality" is awkward, both semantically and substantively. But since both the PRC and Taiwan agree on the principle of one China, it is hardly appropriate for the United States, as an outsider, to propose any other position. Having to operate within this principle, the United States must use the de facto entity concept if it is to maintain economic, cultural, and other ties with Taiwan for the indefinite future. My guess is that in the coming months and years the United States will be increasingly explicit in asserting that Taiwan is such a de facto entity.

## ATTRIBUTES OF A DE FACTO ENTITY WITH INTERNATIONAL PERSONALITY

In order more fully to understand the status of Taiwan after derecognition, this section discusses the capabilities and disabilities of a de facto entity, comparing them with the attributes of a de jure recognized state. It should be pointed out at the outset that the de facto entity concept is not new or unfamiliar. Prior to 1 January 1979, the United States dealt with the PRC on exactly such a basis. Although we did not extend de jure recognition, official missions were exchanged, agreements were reached, American presidents visited the PRC, and a considerable amount of trade and travel was carried out. No one seriously questioned the capacity of the United States or the PRC to engage in such relations.

*International Law Perspective.* A de facto entity has the capacity to have treaty and other foreign relations, even with countries not extending it de jure recognition. Section 107 of the *Restatement* provides:

> An entity not recognized as a state but meeting the requirements for recognition [of controlling a territory and population and engaging in foreign affairs], or an entity recognized as a state whose regime is not recognized as its government, has the rights of a state under international law in relations to a non-recognizing state, although it can be precluded from exercising such a right if
> (a) the right is of such a nature that it can only be exercised by the government of a state, and
> (b) the non-recognizing state refuses to treat the purported exercise of the right as action taken by the government of the other state.[20]

In recent years, the United States has entered into agreements regarding a wide variety of subjects with de facto entities such as the Socialist Republic of Vietnam, the German Democratic Republic, and the PRC.

As discussed earlier, international law does not require that preexisting treaties with Taiwan lapse upon derecognition.

The American decision to conduct future relations with Taiwan through quasi-governmental corporations rather than through formal official channels does not affect the status of Taiwan in international law. This decision reflects political factors in US-PRC-Taiwan relations and is not the result of some inherent disability of de facto entities.

*Existing Legislation.*[21] There are very few provisions in American legislation that specify that de jure governments and de facto authorities should be treated differently. For example, officials of the former are exempted from having to register as foreign propaganda agents.[22] Transfers of property by the Federal Reserve Bank from the account of a de jure recognized country to a duly qualified representative of that country is conclusively presumed to be legal.[23] Official representatives of de facto recognized entities coming to the United States receive a different class of visas, and special provisions have to be made regarding diplomatic immunity.[24]

In most other instances, terms such as "foreign country" or "foreign government" usually apply to both de jure and de facto recognized entities. An examination of congressional enactments leads to three conclusions. First, Congress regards governments firmly in control but not recognized de jure as having a definite existence and a certain degree of legitimate authority. Second, Congress contemplates and permits dealings with such entities. Third, for most purposes, the legislative approach has been to treat de jure and de facto recognized entities similarly unless there is a specific provision to the contrary.

A de facto entity—in this case, Taiwan—does encounter difficulties, however, in specific areas. A number of important statutory schemes involving economic and military aid apply only to "friendly countries." These programs include military sales and assistance,[25] the Overseas Private Investment Corporation (OPIC),[26] sale of American agricultural surplus on credit terms or for foreign currency by the Commodity Credit Corporation,[27] loans to small farmers of predominantly rural countries,[28] and expenditures of funds received pursuant to the Agricultural Trade Development and Assistance Act of 1954.[29] Interestingly, nowhere in these statutes are the terms "friendly" or "country" defined. However, a de facto entity might not be a "country," and withdrawal of recognition might be interpreted as resulting in a loss of "friendliness."

A related problem is that several statutes impose sanctions upon countries with which the United States has severed diplomatic relations. The Foreign Assistance Act, which affects both economic and military aid, includes the blanket provisions in Section 2370(t):[30]

> No assistance shall be furnished under this chapter *or any other Act*, and no sales shall be made under the Agricultural Trade Development Act of 1954, in or to any country which has severed or hereafter severs diplomatic relations with the United States or with which the United States has severed or hereafter severs diplomatic relations.

Finally, some statutes place restrictions on dealings with "communist countries." If Taiwan is considered part of a "communist country" after withdrawal of recognition, then the Export-Import Bank,[31] the generalized system of preferences,[32] and tariff rates,[33] among other things, might be affected.

*Judicially Developed Rules*. Judicially developed rules impose few serious disabilities on de facto entities. They are entitled to claim sovereign immunity to the same extent as de jure recognized states. In *Wulfson* v. *Russian Socialist Federated Soviet Republic*, 23 N.Y. 372, 138 N.E. 24 (1923) the RSFSR was "an existing government sovereign within its own territory," but unrecognized by the United States. Immunity was granted on the ground that a foreign sovereign, even if unrecognized, cannot be sued in an American court without his consent. The Foreign Sovereign Immunities Act of 1976, 90 Stat. 2981, makes no explicit mention of unrecognized entities, but instead refers generally to "foreign states." The absence of a specific provision implies that preexisting cases law remains valid.

The act of state doctrine provides:

> Every sovereign state is bound to respect the independence of every other sovereign state, and the courts of one country will not sit in judgment on the acts of the government of another, done within its own territory. *Underhill* v. *Hernandez*, 168 U.S. 250, 18 S.Ct. 83 (1897).

In *Salminoff & Co.* v. *Standard Oil Co. of New York*, 262 N.Y. 220, 186 N.E. 679 (1933) (refusal to examine the validity of a law confiscating property located in the Soviet Union), the court applied this doctrine to acts of the Soviet government, which was unrecognized but in actual control.

The "constitutional underpinning" for the act of state doctrine is the separation of powers. The judiciary is reluctant to interfere with the conduct of foreign affairs by the executive. (*Banco Nacional de Cuba* v. *Sabbatino*, 376 U.S. 398, 84 S.Ct. 923 [1964].) Courts should be especially wary of making politically delicate pronouncements about the possible invalidity of actions taken by de facto entities. The act of state doctrine should be applied, leaving such determinations to the executive. (*First National City Bank* v. *Banco Nacional de Cuba*, 406 U.S. 759 [1971], *Bernstein* v. *Van Heyghen Frères Société Anonyme*, 163 F. 2d 246 2nd Cir., [1947].)

The only disability imposed by the courts on de facto entities is that they may not have standing to bring suit in an American court. In *Russian Socialist Federated Soviet Republic* v. *Cibrario*, 25 N.Y. 255, 139 N.E. 259 (1923), the court held that allowing an unrecognized government to sue would undermine the executive decision not to extend de jure recognition.

Yet even this rule, has eroded substantially over time. A Soviet-owned corporation organized under the laws of New York was allowed to bring suit. (*Amtorg Trading Corp.* v. *United States*, 71 F.2d 324, 2nd Cir., [1934].) In *Upright* v. *Mercury Business Machines*, 13 A.D.2d 36, 213 N.Y.S.2d 417 (1961), an American assignee of a corporation controlled by the unrecognized German Democratic Republic also was permitted to sue.

More recently, in *Federal Republic of Germany* v. *Elicofon*,

358 F.Supp 747 (E.D.N.Y., 1972), *aff'd*, 478 F.2d 231, 415 U.S. 1931 (1974) *reh. denied*, 416 U.S. 954 (1974), the court did not allow the Weimer Art Collection, an East German museum that was an arm of the East German government, to bring suit. However, the court added in a footnote:

> It is unclear whether this reasoning supports a rule invariably denying standing to unrecognized governments. There may be special circumstances in which action by the President can be interpreted as creating an exception to the rule. For example, it may be argued that the act of the Executive in permitting American nationals to engage in commercial relations with unrecognized governments or their instrumentalities carries with it a grant to those governments or instrumentalities of standing to litigate claims arising out of those transactions in United States courts.

The *Upright* case dealt with both the act of state doctrine and the question of standing to sue. The starting point for the court was that a "foreign government, although not recognized by the political arm of the United States government, may nevertheless have de facto existence which is juridically cognizable." The court looked to "the realities of life" and noted that an unrecognized government carries on many routine activities and that trade between the two countries is not forbidden. The legal consequences of nonrecognition should be narrowly construed unless they "can be properly related as inimical to the aims and purposes of our public and national policy."

Thus, although there is no definitive case on the subject, judicial doctrine seems to be evolving to a position where unrecognized entities have standing to sue, at least in cases involving economic and cultural relations.

## THE TAIWAN RELATIONS ACT

A basic American policy in which the executive and the Congress are in full agreement is that all preexisting commercial and cultural ties with Taiwan should be preserved after normalization of relations with the PRC. I believe that the Taiwan Relations Act has achieved this goal.

As discussed earlier, the act states that the absence of recognition or diplomatic relations will not affect the application of US laws with respect to Taiwan. The act also provides that rights and obligations concerning contracts or property interests, ownership of property, choice-of-law rules, Taiwan's standing to sue or be sued, and eligibility for export licenses for nuclear materials also remain unchanged.

The president is authorized to grant, on a reciprocal basis, such privileges and immunities to personnel of the instrumentality to be established by Taiwan (the Coordinating Council for North American Affairs) as may be necessary for the performance of their duties.[34] In addition, the legislative history specifically refers to the Arms Export Act, the Export Administration Act, the Export-Import Bank Act, the Foreign Assistance Act of 1961, the Trade Act of 1974, the Foreign Sovereign Immunities Act of 1976, the Agricultural Trade Development and Assistance Act of 1954, and the Federal Reserve Act, and explains that these laws and programs should apply to Taiwan in the same manner as before derecognition.[35]

The effect of the Taiwan Relations Act is the removal of the statutory and judicially developed disabilities imposed on de facto entities discussed in the previous section. For purposes of domestic American law, Taiwan will be treated as a de jure recognized state or government in the commercial and cultural areas. Relations in these areas should continue without change. Indeed, Taiwan even gained one unexpected commercial advantage from derecognition. In the normal course of events, it would have become ineligible for OPIC insurance in 1979 because the island's per capita annual income exceeded the $1,000 limit. In order not to have this additional economic blow fall at a time of political uncertainty and tension, the act extended Taiwan's eligibility for OPIC insurance for three years.[36]

As discussed earlier, President Carter's 30 December 1978 memorandum and the Taiwan Relations Act declares that treaties between the United States and Taiwan remain in force until terminated in accordance with law. Fifty-nine of the sixty treaties and executive agreements in force as of 31 December 1978 remain unchanged (although many have long had no operational effect).[37]

The sixtieth agreement is the Mutual Defense Treaty,[38] which terminated at the end of 1979.[39] In my view, the termination of this treaty does not substantially alter the security relations between the United States and Taiwan. The name Mutual Defense Treaty suggests a commitment to come to the defense of Taiwan. But that is not what the terms of the treaty required. Article 5 states that in the event of an armed attack on Taiwan, the United States "would act to meet the common danger in accordance with its constitutional processes"—a vague commitment indeed. In light of the limitations imposed on the president by the War Powers Resolution, the post-Vietnam public and congressional attitudes toward American involvement in an Asian war, the American response under Article 5 most likely would have been limited to making protests plus supplying arms and other logistical support.

Very similar actions will be taken by the United States if an armed attack were to occur now that the Mutual Defense Treaty has terminated. The unilateral US statement of 15 December 1978 declared:

> The United States is confident that the people of Taiwan face a peaceful and prosperous future. The United States continues to have an interest in the peaceful resolution of the Taiwan issue and expects that the Taiwan issue will be settled peacefully by the Chinese themselves.

At a White House background briefing for the press the same day, an "Administration Official" was asked:

> *Q*: Can we continue to sell arms directly to Taiwan during this next year or for any period of time?
>
> *Administration Official*: I think it is quite clear from the statement that is being made that the United States will continue the full range of commercial relations with Taiwan. As the treaty is being abrogated, we will continue

> to deliver to Taiwan all the items that have been committed or have been contracted for. And beyond 1979, we will, of course, make our judgments in the light of the prevailing situation, which we hope will be peaceful. But we will, as I said earlier, retain the full range of commercial relations with Taiwan.
>
> *Q*: Which includes military weapons?
>
> *Administration Official*: Which includes, if necessary and the situation warrants it, selected defense weaponry. . . .
>
> *Q*: Do we reserve the right to supply military equipment to Taiwan?
>
> *Q*: We just asked that. He answered.
>
> *Administration Official*: Let me answer it again so that there is no doubt about that. The treaty will be terminated at the end of 1979. We are giving a one-year notice in accordance with Article 10 of the treaty of its termination. After the treaty is terminated at the end of 1979, the United States will give Taiwan access to arms of a defensive character and do so on a restrained basis so as to promote peace and not interfere with peace in that area.

Similarly, Cyrus Vance, then secretary of state, speaking at a briefing for members of the National Council for US-China Trade and the USA-ROC Economic Council on 15 January 1979, said:

> [A]fter the termination of the Mutual Defense Treaty on December 31, 1979, we will continue our previous policy of selling carefully selected defensive weapons to Taiwan. While the PRC said they disapprove of this, they nevertheless moved forward with normalization with full knowledge of our intentions.[40]

The Taiwan Relations Act is even more explicit about future US-Taiwan security issues:

> Sec. 2(b): It is the policy of the United States: . . .
>
> (2) to declare that peace and stability in the area are in

the political, security, and economic interests of the United States, and are matters of international concern:

(3) to make clear that the United States decision to establish diplomatic relations with the People's Republic of China rests upon the expectation that the future of Taiwan will be determined by peaceful means;

(4) to consider any effort to determine the future of Taiwan by other than peaceful means, including by boycotts or embargoes, a threat to the peace and security of the Western Pacific area and of grave concern to the United States;

(5) to provide Taiwan with arms of a defensive character; and

(6) to maintain the capacity of the United States to resist any resort to force or other forms of coercion that would jeopardize the security, or the social or economic system, of the people on Taiwan. . . .

Sec. 3(a): In furtherance of the policy set forth in section 2 of this Act, the United States will make available to Taiwan such defense articles and defense services in such quantity as may be necessary to enable Taiwan to maintain a sufficient self-defense capability.

(b): The President and the Congress shall determine the nature and quantity of such defense articles and services based solely upon their judgment on the needs of Taiwan, in accordance with procedures established by law. Such determination of Taiwan's defense needs shall include review by United States military authorities in connection with recommendations to the President and the Congress.

(c): The President is directed to inform the Congress promptly of any threat to the security or the social or economic system of the people on Taiwan and any danger to the interests of the United States arising therefrom. The President and the Congress shall determine, in accordance with constitutional processes, appropriate action by the United States in response to any such danger.

The net result of the above statements is that the United

States will continue the sale of defensive arms to Taiwan[41] and will also strongly object to the use of force in the Taiwan area—essentially the same result that could have been expected under the Mutual Defense Treaty.

Looking at US-Taiwan relations as a whole, therefore, economic and cultural ties are not affected; our treaty relations remain unchanged except for the Mutual Defense Treaty; and the substantive security relations remain the same. Some adjustments must be made in the manner in which we deal with Taiwan, since there no longer are "official" relations. The United States has no embassy in Taipei, but instead operates through the American Institute on Taiwan; similarly, Taiwan is represented in this country by the Coordinating Council for North American Affairs.[42] These are ostensibly private corporations. However, they are staffed by foreign service officers temporarily on leave, are funded by the respective government, are entitled to certain privileges and immunities accorded foreign representatives and organs, and carry out an assortment of familiar "governmental" activities such as processing visas and taking depositions.

In sum, we may be unable or unwilling to call Taiwan a government or a state. In terms of our actions, and for purposes of our domestic law, however, we are treating Taiwan like a de facto government or state with virtually all the attributes normally possessed by such entities.

It also should be noted that the act of extending de jure recognition to the PRC, in and of itself, grants the PRC few rights and privileges. At this point, we should at least ask why we continue to use the concept of recognition if the extending or withdrawing of recognition produces few or no legal consequences of importance. Could it be that this concept, which so shaped the US-China relations debate for so long, has only symbolic content? If so, perhaps we should consider whether it would be simpler and better for countries merely to "deal" with each other without being tied to the ritual of recognition.

## A PERSPECTIVE ON TAIWAN[43]

In this last section, let me turn to a political, rather than legal, problem concerning the status of Taiwan. I am not an expert on this subject, but I see some very disquieting developments to which people in this country should pay greater attention. My concern is that changes may take place in Taiwan that will lead to an entirely new political situation in US-PRC-Taiwan relations. Neither the United States nor the PRC has much control over these changes, nor is either country well prepared to respond should changes occur.

One aspect of this problem is that during the past thirty years the United States has viewed Taiwan as a passive party that did essentially what we told it to do. Sometimes we had to tighten the reins, and at other times we had to offer incentives, but control and initiative were in our hands. Up until now, this perception of Taiwan has been correct. In the past several years, however, a new internal political dynamic has been developing in Taiwan that may lead to Taiwan initiating, rather than merely reacting to, change.

The leadership of the central government on Taiwan is getting very old. For example, the average age of the members of the National Legislature (which is the equivalent of our Congress) and the National Assembly (which meets periodically to elect the president and vice president) is around seventy-five. Obviously, they will soon be replaced by a new generation of leaders.

These two national bodies possess a second special characteristic besides elderly membership. More than 90 percent of the members of the Legislature and more than 95 percent of the National Assembly were elected in 1947, thirty-four years ago. These persons have not stood for reelection since that time. After all, it was hardly possible for the person representing Shanghai to return to his district and constituents after 1949.

Incidentally, this peculiarity concerning the status of elected officials of the central government explains in part why it is so difficult for the Taiwan government to abandon its claim to be the government of all China. Such an adjustment, while fully in accord with realities, would undercut the basis of legitimacy for many officeholders in the central government.

The net result is that the people on Taiwan, including both the "Taiwanese" (the term used to describe persons whose ancestors came from China to Taiwan over the past several hundred years) and the "mainlanders" (persons coming from China to Taiwan after 1945), vote for only a tiny fraction of these national-level bodies. In addition, some Taiwanese are dissatisfied because although they constitute 85 percent of the population, they nonetheless hold only a small number of important government and party positions.

Perhaps the passing of the older generation of leaders opens the way for new ideas about the future of Taiwan. Or perhaps the island's great economic achievements have freed people to think about broader social issues rather than just issues of survival, and equally great educational achievements have given people the intellectual tools for dealing with the process of change. It also may be that so much change has occurred since 1971—expulsion from the United Nations, the Nixon visit to the PRC, the normalization of Sino-Japanese relations, and the death of Chiang Kai-shek—that further change does not appear especially unusual or uncomfortable. In any event, there has been a growing call for a redistribution of political power that would more accurately reflect the realities of the island.

The electoral process illustrates how the internal political dynamic is developing. Taiwan is basically a single-party state, consisting of the Guomindang (Nationalist Party) and two small and tame parties. In the past, running for public office was not an effective means by which persons outside the Guomindang might attain political power. Several opposition candidates did win on occasion, but the election process was basically dominated by the Guomindang.

An important change occurred, however, in the 1977 local elections for provincial, county, and municipal offices. A number of young Taiwanese politicians, frustrated by the slowness of their advancement through the party and government bureaucracies, decided to run for public office in opposition to the Guomindang. These candidates gained 38 percent of the popular vote, an astounding feat in a single-party state. There were riots in Chongli and Gaoxiang over alleged election fraud by the Guomindang.

Another election was scheduled to be held on 23 December 1978 for 38 seats (out of approximately 400) in the Legislature, and 56 seats (out of approximately 1,200) in the National Assembly. The campaign was lively and aggresssive on all sides but was suspended after the normalization announcement.

Since that time, the degree of conflict has increased substantially. A large segment of the opposition has followed a somewhat confrontationist policy, whereby it tries to challenge the authority of the Guomindang (GMD) through actions such as holding public rallies, often without obtaining a legal permit. They also organized several new publications, the most striking of which was *Formosa* (Meilidao) magazine, whose circulation rapidly grew to 100,000. The magazine also opened "branch business offices" throughout the island in a manner suggesting the beginnings of an opposition political party organization.

The government had been showing many signs of impatience and annoyance at the actions of the opposition. A clear warning was issued in April 1979 when Yu Teng-fa, a seventy-six-year-old opposition leader, was sentenced by a military court to eight years' imprisonment for a "subversive" article in *Asahi Shimbun* and for failing to report the activities of the PRC agents. (Yu has since been released for medical reasons.)

A major direct clash occurred on 10 December 1979 in Gaoxiung, when a rally organized by the opposition to commemorate International Human Rights Day developed into a riot in which a large number of policemen were injured. Two days later more than a hundred persons were arrested, including the majority of the leading opposition figures. Opposition publications were also suspended. Since then, eight of the most important opposition figures have been convicted of sedition by a military court and sentenced to twelve to fourteen years' imprisonment. Thirty-three others are being tried on rioting charges in civilian court, and another eight are charged with helping a fugitive "rebel" escape. Throughout these trials, the defendants have repeatedly alleged that their confessions were obtained through coercion.

Aside from the riot and trials themselves, confrontation has increased in other areas. Rhetoric has gotten angrier. Last

December, in a fit of anger after the arrests, a group of Taiwanese living in the United States—including many persons who earlier were considered moderates—issued a proclamation calling for an all-out attack on the GMD, "until that evil regime is completely wiped off the face of the earth." In Taiwan, government-influenced newspapers repeatedly lashed out at persons deviating from the GMD line, freely using terms such as "traitorous" and "seditious."

But it is not only a war of words. Several offices of the Taiwan government in the United States were vandalized; the home of a son of a conservative GMD leader was reportedly firebombed. In the saddest occurrence of all, on 28 February 1980, the twin seven-year-old daughters and mother of Lin Yixiung, one of the eight principal defendants in the sedition trials, were murdered in broad daylight in Taipei. No arrests have yet been made.

## CONCLUSION

Some observers have suggested that the GMD might have "set up" the opposition for a fall. While that may be untrue, the end result is clear. The conservative wing of the GMD, with President Jiang Jingguo's backing, has carried out a massive crackdown against the opposition. One casualty of the crackdown obviously is the opposition movement, which has had many of its leaders jailed. But a second casualty is the moderate wing of the GMD, which now is unable and afraid to take any political action. Moreover, while the arrests have not strictly followed mainlander-Taiwanese lines, relations between the two groups clearly suffered great damage.

At present I see a sharp polarization in Taiwan's politics. The GMD conservatives have strongly reasserted their power and their determination to resist change. Persons favoring gradual reform, whether from the moderate wing of the GMD or the opposition, now find their position undercut. These developments mean that more and more of the persons seeking to change the political arrangements in Taiwan will turn toward the possibility of independence. As discussions concerning independence become increasingly explicit, China will be unable to continue the line that the Taiwan masses favor reunification and that the opposition movement seeks only greater democracy on Taiwan. Instead of the optimum scenario, we might get the minimum: unrest on Taiwan; a call for independence by some Taiwanese, especially those in the United States and Japan; strong steps taken by China to combat independence, ranging from economic sanctions to military action; and uncertainty on the part of the United States on how to react.

What might happen as the political dynamic inside Taiwan develops further? Here I stress that I am speculating. At one extreme may be a continued crackdown on the opposition by conservative elements with the Guomindang. If this crackdown expands in scope or virulence, the image of "Free China" will begin to erode, and with this erosion will come a loss of American public and congressional support.

Toward the other end of the spectrum of possibilities is a takeover of power, gradual or sudden, by Taiwanese political leaders. These persons clearly desire more control over their own destiny, perhaps an independent state of Taiwan. At the same time, they are sophisticated politicians who know that independence is opposed both by the Guomindang, in part because their own legitimacy would be undercut, and by the PRC, because such action would violate the one-China principle.

So far, the Taiwanese have generally avoided the term "independence," preferring merely to look and act independent, without making a change in the juridical status of the island. I do not know what the chances are that independence will be formally declared at some point. But *if* it occurs, what will the American response be? The answer to this question is not at all clear. While the concept of self-determination may appear attractive, we have yet to enunciate a clear principle on how to regard self-determination in such diverse examples as Namibia, Quebec, Northern Ireland, East Timor, Puerto Rico, Kurdistan, Free Lebanon, or the PLO. Moreover, in our own history a Civil War was fought in part over the issue of whether one section of the country can split off to form a separate state. The Pledge of Allegiance states: "one Nation, . . . indivisible. . . ."

Considerations of power politics would also be important. For domestic political reasons of its own, I think the PRC leadership, pragmatic or radical, would inevitably react strongly to an effort by Taiwan to become independent. The United States would then be obligated to make an enormously difficult political choice between support for self-determination and a possible rupture of relations with the PRC.

I am not saying that these unhappy possibilities will in fact occur. There are other, less dramatic scenarios. Rather, my point is that developments are taking place on Taiwan that may substantially change its political situation. These changes, in turn, would greatly affect political relations between the United States and China. At the least, I believe we have to begin thinking about how to cope with possible future developments on Taiwan. Yet I feel that people both in and out of the government are not doing so. Once again, we may be caught unprepared as change occurs.

Finally, I want to comment on American moral obligations to Taiwan. More than thirty years ago, in a world that was very different, the United States provided massive military and other assistance to Taiwan, when such assistance was sorely needed. In subsequent years, the United States contributed greatly to the remarkable growth of that island.

At some point, the original American commitments to Taiwan for military protection and economic assistance must be regarded as having been fulfilled. Taiwan is not a fifty-first state that must be defended and assisted under any circumstances and for all time. In the course of helping to build a new society on Taiwan, however, I believe the United States has incurred new obligations to give that society an opportunity to survive and grow.

Taiwan is going through a transition from being the Republic of China representing all of China to some new and still undefined status. What that status should be must be decided by the people on Taiwan. They must consider the offers being tendered by the PRC. If they feel the offers to be unsatisfactory, they must seek better terms or search for new solutions.

I believe the responsibility of the United States is to give the people of Taiwan a fair opportunity to make decisions about their own future. The use of the de facto entity approach that I have urged provides the smoothest means for making this transition. It is time for Taiwan to take its own problems in hand. If it wishes to continue the fiction of being all of China, then it has had ample notice that it must stand alone and face the consequences. If it wishes to reunify with the PRC or adopt some other status, then it must begin the process.

## NOTES

1. For example, the following exchange took place at an 18 December 1978 press briefing:

> *Q*: If the PRC is the sole legal government of China, which includes Taiwan, how can the State Department regard the Government on Taiwan as anything but illegal?
>
> *Mr. Herbert Hansell* (Legal Advisor of the Department of State): We don't propose to regard a government on Taiwan as a legal governmental entity. We do intend to maintain relationships, people-to-people relationships on an unofficial basis.
>
> *Q*: In other words, they are an illegal government?
>
> *Mr. Hansell*: No, no. That is not what I said.
>
> *Q*: What are they? What do you call them?
>
> *Mr. Richard Holbrooke* (Assistant Secretary of State for Asian and Pacific Affairs): As of January 1, the United States recognizes Peking as the Government of China, the Government of Peking.
>
> *Q*: How do you define the government that is on Taiwan, is my question?
>
> *Mr. Roger Sullivan* (Deputy Assistant Secretary of State for Asian and Pacific Affairs): The government on Taiwan asks to be recognized as the sole legal government of China, and we are saying we don't recognize that claim.

*Q*: What do you recognize them as?

*Mr. Sullivan*: You cannot recognize a government in any claim except what it seeks to be recognized as.

*Q*: But what do you call them?

*Mr. Sullivan*: They are the authorities on Taiwan.

*Mr. Holbrooke*: They are the authorities on Taiwan, which is widely acknowledged.

2. "Memorandum on Relations with the People on Taiwan," *Federal Register* 44:3 (4 January 1979) 1075.

3. PL 96-8, 93 Stat. 14 (10 April 1979).

4. "Resolution on Representation of China," UN Doc. A/RES/2758 (XXVI); 65 Dept. St. Bull. 556 (1971). See also Jerome Cohen and Hungdah Chiu (eds.), *People's China and International Law* (Princeton, N.J.: Princeton University Press, 1974), 267–291.

5. See, for example, Jerome A. Cohen, "Normalizing Relations with the People's Republic of China," *American Bar Association Journal* 64 (July 1978); "Legal Implications of Recognition of the People's Republic of China," *Proceedings*, 62d Annual Meeting of the American Society of International Law (April 1978).

6. Similarly, Article 1 of the Convention on Rights and Duties of States, 49 Stat. 3097, T.S. 881 (1933) says:

> The state as a person of international law should possess the following qualifications: (a) a permanent population; (b) a defined territory; (c) government; and (d) capacity to enter into relations with other states.

7. For a more detailed explanation of this position, see Victor H. Li and John W. Lewis, "Resolving the China Dilemma: Advancing Normalization, Preserving Security," *International Security* 2:1 (Summer 1977); statement of Victor H. Li in Subcommittee on Asian and Pacific Affairs of the Subcommittee on International Relations, House of Representatives, *Normalization of Relations with the People's Republic of China: Practical Implications* (1977) 87.

8. "Statement of the Chinese Government," PR 21:51 (22 December 1978) 8f.

9. Senate Report No. 96-7 (Committee on Foreign Relations), 9.

10. For a historical review and legal analysis of Taiwan's "undetermined" status, see "Prepared Statement of Hungdah Chiu," *Normalization of Relations*, note 7, *supra*, 219–224.

11. John Glenn, "Sino-American Relations: A New Turn," committee print of a trip report to the Committee on Foreign Relations (1979) 3f.

12. The Senate Committee on Foreign Relations Report, note 9, *supra*, 27, also states that for purposes of Section 25 of the Federal Reserve Act, 12 U.S.C. 632, "a representative of [a] foreign state" includes the representative of the instrumentality to be established by Taiwan.

13. Senate Report, note 9, *supra*, 27.

14. House Report No. 96-26 (Committee on Foreign Affairs), 10.

15. See, generally, Marjorie Whiteman, *Digest of International Law* 2, 904–915.

16. See Jack Young, "U.S.-China Aviation Relations—A Case of Control, Conflict and Compromise," *Journey of Air Law* 3:4 (1978) 210–225.

17. "U.S. and China Sign Claims Settlement," *New York Times*, 3 March 1979. For a discussion of some problems that may arise out of this settlement, see Victor H. Li, "United States-China Relations after Normalization," in *Private Investors Abroad—Problems and Solutions in International Business in 1979* (New York: Matthew Bender, 1979). See generally, United States and China: Blocked Assets-Claims," 8 *Cornell Intern'l L.J.* 254 (1975); Office of Foreign Assets Control, 1970 Census of Blocked Chinese Assets in the United States.

18. Note 2, *supra*.

19. Senate Report No. 96-7, note 9, *supra*, 17.

20. Similarly, Article 6 of the Vienna Convention on the Law of Treaties says: "Every state possesses capacity to conclude treaties." However, the Convention does not define "state." See also Section 108 of the *Restatement*, which discusses the obligations of an unrecognized entity.

21. For a detailed discussion of how existing legislation would be affected if the United States withdraws de jure recognition, although the Taiwan authorities continue to maintain de facto control, see Victor H. Li, *De-recognizing Taiwan: The Legal Problems* (Carnegie Endowment for International Peace, 1977). See also Li, "The Law of Non-Recognition: The Case of Taiwan," *Northwestern J. Intern'l*

*L. and Bus*. 134 (1979); and "Prepared Statement of Victor H. Li," in Senate Committee on Foreign Relations, *Taiwan* (1979).

22. 50 U.S.C. 852, 22 U.S.C. 613. Private citizens of recognized and unrecognized countries are treated alike: 22 U.S.C. 611. See also 49 U.S.C. 781 (similar treatment for recognized and unrecognized countries for purposes of seizing contraband).

23. 12 U.S.C. 632. See also note 12, *supra*.

24. 71 Stat. 642, 643; 8 U.S.C. 1101 (a) (15) (A), (C). Special legislation was needed to extend diplomatic immunity to members of the PRC Liaison Office. 22 U.S.C. 288 (i).

25. 22 U.S.C. 2311, 2751.

26. 22 U.S.C. 2191.

27. 7 U.S.C. 1701. Up until the mid-1960s Taiwan had received considerable economic aid under this and related programs. Such aid has since ceased.

28. 22 U.S.C. 2175.

29. 22 U.S.C. 1922. Other examples are: 22 U.S.C. 2102 (health research and training); 22 U.S.C. 2219 (family planning); 50 U.S.C. App. 1878 (e) (loan of military vessels); 10 U.S.C. 7227, 31 U.S.C. 529 (j) (routine disbursement of funds and services to military forces of a friendly country); 39 U.S.C. 407 (postal agreements).

30. See also 7 U.S.C. 1703 (j) (sale of agricultural surplus); 16 U.S.C. 1052 (b) (5) (encourage use of the National Aquarium by nationals of states with which the United States maintains diplomatic relations). (Emphasis added.)

31. 12 U.S.C. 635 (b) (2).

32. 19 U.S.C. 2462.

33. 19 U.S.C. 1202 (e). See also the Foreign Assistance Act, 22 U.S.C. 2370 (b), (f) [for purposes of sec. (f), the PRC is specifically listed as a "Communist country"]; 7 U.S.C. 1703 (d) (purchase of surplus agricultural products).

34. The two differences between the "functional" immunity granted Taiwan and the diplomatic immunity accorded de jure recognized states and their representatives are that personnel of the Taiwan instrumentality would not receive immunity from criminal prosecution and civil liability for acts committed outside the performance of their duties, nor would they be entitled to diplomatic license plates. Senate Report No. 96-7, note 9 *supra*, 29f.

35. Senate Report No. 96-7, note 9, *supra*; House Report No. 96-26, note 14, *supra*; House Report No. 96-71 (Committee on Conference).

36. Taiwan Relations Act, Section 5; see also Senate Report No. 96-7, note 9, *supra*, 28.

37. Li, *De-recognizing Taiwan*, 31–35.

38. Treaties and International Agreement Series (TIAS) 3178.

39. United States statement, 15 December 1978. See also Senate Report 96-7, note 9, *supra*, 17–20; Committee on Foreign Relations, U.S. Senate, *Termination of Treaties: The Constitutional Allocation of Power* (GPO 32-770, 1979).

40. Despite Vance's implication that the PRC will not interfere with continued sale of defensive arms to Taiwan, it should be noted that Chairman Hua's objection to such sales was strongly stated. He was asked at his 15 December 1978 press conference:

> *Q*: Will the U.S. government be permitted to continue providing Taiwan with access to military equipment for defensive purposes?
>
> *Hua*: Paragraph two of the joint communiqué which I announced just now states that "The United States of America recognizes the government of the People's Republic of China as the sole legal government of China. Within this context, the people of the United States will maintain cultural, commercial and other unofficial relations with the people of Taiwan." In our discussions on the question of commercial relations, the two sides had differing views. During the negotiations, the U.S. side mentioned that after normalization it would continue to sell a limited amount of arms to Taiwan for defense purposes. We made it clear that we absolutely would not agree to this. In all discussions, the Chinese side repeatedly made clear its position on this question. We held that after the normalization continued sale of arms to Taiwan by the United States would not conform to the principles of normalization, would be detrimental to the peaceful liberation of Taiwan and would exercise an unfavorable influence on the peace and stability of the Asia-Pacific region. So our two sides had differences on this point. Nonetheless, we reached an agreement on the joint communiqué. PR 21:51 (22 December 1978) 10f.

41. On arms sales to Taiwan see, generally, Senate Report 96-7, note 3, *supra*, 17.

42. Taiwan Relations Act, Section 6-12.

43. See, generally, Victor H. Li (ed.), *The Future of Taiwan: A Difference of Opinion* (White Plains, N.Y., M. E. Sharpe, 1980).

# V. CONCLUSION

## Chapter 5

# TOWARD A NEW REALISM IN US-CHINA RELATIONS*

**JOHN BRYAN STARR**

Executive Director
Yale-China Association

More than two years have passed since President Carter's startling announcement on 15 December 1978 that full diplomatic relations between the United States and China would be established two weeks later. Many both in this country and in China were caught up in a kind of euphoria analogous in kind, if not in magnitude, to the euphoria that accompanied the visit of Richard Nixon to China in February 1971.

In this country the euphoria, fostered in some measure by the administration's efforts to build support for its initiative, affected particularly certain members of the business community, in whose heads visions of a vast new market were made to dance. In China, where the difficulties of meeting the ambitious goals initially set for the sweeping program of economic development known as the Four Modernizations were

* An earlier version of this essay appeared in the *Yale Alumni Magazine* (December 1979). This emended version is reprinted here with the permission of that magazine. Copyright © 1979 by Yale Alumni Publications, Inc.

becoming apparent, the euphoria took the form of overestimating the degree to which the United States could be counted upon to help resolve these difficulties.

A pendulum swing between euphoria and disenchantment—illusions giving way to disillusionment—has, in many respects, been a characteristic of American relations with China during the course of the last century. What is needed to avoid a repetition of this pattern in the current period is a greater degree of realism on both sides about the future of this relationship.

To a degree, the period following normalization was marked by the beginning of an infusion of such realism in the outlook of both Peking and Washington. More is needed, however, if we are to avoid fostering expectations that cannot be met and engendering the mutual disappointment and hostility that will stem from the failure to meet these unrealistic expectations.

On the Chinese side, as Lynn Feintech has pointed out in some detail, inflated developmental goals have been scaled down to correspond more closely with the potential for achievement, and an effort has been made to publicize the scaled-down goals among the Chinese population. More sober assessments of the role that Western firms will choose to play in China's economic modernization have taken the place of initially exaggerated expectations, and attention is being given to laying the legal groundwork prerequisite to encouraging foreign investment in China.

In this country, two mistaken assumptions about our new relationship with China have been called into question and abandoned during the course of the last two years. The first was the assumption that formal diplomatic relations would increase the influence Washington can exert on Chinese foreign policy. China's invasion of Vietnam, immediately following Vice Premier Deng Xiaoping's visit to Washington—during which American disapproval of the prospect of such a move was conveyed to him with varying degrees of vigor by administration and congressional leaders—suggested that American influence over policymaking in Peking would remain limited despite the new ties.

The second assumption—that American trade with China

would burgeon following normalization—has gradually given way to the realization that, while certain industries in this country will increase significantly their economic interaction with China, the "China market" is likely to remain a very limited one for the majority of American firms. While the Chinese remain vitally interested in importing advanced technology from the United States, they are equally concerned with finding ways of balancing their trade with this country to the availability and marketability of goods and services the sale of which will build their foreign exchange reserves.

As we move beyond this initial period of "normal" relations with China, it is my view that a realistic approach to the future of this relationship must be based on certain assumptions about and appraisals of Chinese political realities and American interests. I will state, and then expand upon, certain themes implicit in these assumptions and appraisals as I see them:

1. The legitimacy of the current leadership in China, and, by extension, the future stability of the Chinese political system, rests heavily on the achievement of the goals of its current program of economic development.
2. A politically stable China best serves American interests in Asia and elsewhere in the world.
3. American assistance in the achievement of China's developmental goals, if realistically undertaken based on a mutual understanding of the inevitable limitations on that assistance, can contribute to the achievement of political stability in China.

## LEGITIMACY AND STABILITY

Depending on where one cuts into the Chinese political system, the three decades since the founding of the People's Republic can give the impression either of great political stability or of great instability. If we consider local-level political leadership, particularly in many predominantly rural areas of China, the last thirty years have seen a remarkable degree of continuity of leadership. The same is true if we look at China's state organs (as compared with the party and the army) that, like bureaucracies elsewhere, have been characterized more by persistence in office than by dismissal from office. Nonetheless, if we concentrate our attention on the central leadership of the party—the locus, after all, of supreme political authority in China—the last thirty years have been marked by an unusually high degree of instability and change.

It is important to realize, however, that the discontinuities in the Chinese leadership during this period have had to do with means and not with ends. There is a high degree of consistency in the goals that China's leaders have pursued since the founding of the PRC. These goals include the achievement of national independence and international recognition, the increase of agricultural productivity to raise the standard of living of the Chinese people, and the industrial modernization of the Chinese economy.

The means to achieve these consistently held ends have varied considerably over time and among individual leaders. The initial choice of means involved a rather mechanical borrowing of the Soviet experience to achieve Chinese goals. When this choice began to prove dysfunctional in the mid-1950s, Mao Zedong and certain of his colleagues sought an indigenous solution to the problem. This took the form of the Great Leap Forward in 1958–59 and soon proved equally dysfunctional in its own way.

Opponents of the Great Leap policies used the early 1960s to implement their own, more measured approach to development—an approach that Mao believed would lead to the same bureaucratic ossification that he took to be the principal flaw in the Soviet system following Stalin's death. His alternative was the Great Proletarian Cultural Revolution, a conscious attempt to destabilize the Chinese political system and thereby to avoid a restratification of Chinese society that he thought would re-create, under socialist auspices, the evils of the society that the Chinese revolution had been undertaken to overthrow. The current development plan constitutes a return to earlier, non-Maoist means for the achievement of China's goals, modified to involve a greater reliance on "Western"—Japanese, European, and American—experience as a supplement to indigenous solutions.

Chinese with whom one speaks today are at pains to emphasize that the policies of the current leadership are very popular among the Chinese people and that the excesses of the "Gang of Four"—Mao's widow and her radical colleagues—were, conversely, highly unpopular. Although this is no doubt basically true, it is important to bear in mind that there are those in China whose interests, at least in the short term, are not served by the current policies and who may thus be assumed to be unenthusiastic about, if not opposed to, them.

Many lower- and middle-ranking leaders had their careers significantly advanced by the overturning that occurred during the Cultural Revolution. Today they find themselves, as a result of the substantial movement to "rehabilitate" victims of the Cultural Revolution, either displaced by, or obliged to work alongside, those whom they helped to overthrow a decade ago. Highly selective admissions policies at institutions of higher education benefit the bright and well prepared but work to the disadvantage of the less capable offspring of workers and peasants, who were the beneficiaries of now abandoned "affirmative action" admissions policies of the immediate post–Cultural Revolution period. Agricultural workers have come, or are likely soon to come, to the realization that they may be obliged, over the short term, to bear a disproportionate share of the human costs of the modernization program as the fruit of their less well-paid labor is made to support the further development of China's urban industrial infrastructure. Finally, many of those who see themselves as the victims of what has come to be called the "lost decade" of the Cultural Revolution are frustrated by the fact that the current development plan does not include provisions for helping them to compensate for the career opportunities lost to them by the interruption of their schooling and by their having been sent into the countryside as a part of the program to relocate urban youth in China's less developed rural sector.

The existence of disaffection and its manifestation in the form of less than enthusiastic support for current policies has the further deleterious effect, from the point of view of the current leadership, of engendering among supporters of the new course a certain reluctance to commit themselves wholeheartedly and publicly to it. Mindful of the consequences of such commitment in the past, these supporters are, on the one hand, eager to see that the new course is permanently maintained but, on the other hand, are apprehensive lest this effort fail.

Despite these signs of potential instability, it is important to realize that a very significant obstacle stands in the way of any attempt by the disaffected to make their opposition to current policies effectively felt. That obstacle is the lack of a sympathetic and powerful element in the central leadership. It is clear that it was only because Mao himself was prepared to act on behalf of similarly disaffected groups in 1966 that the Cultural Revolution got under way. No one approaching Mao's stature among China's current leaders shares his views regarding the desirability of destabilizing the political system to redress the grievances of the disadvantaged.

Therefore, the most that disaffected individuals can do to manifest their dissatisfaction—and it is not a wholly insignificant means of protest under current circumstances—is to fail to give their all to the accomplishment of the current developmental program, a program the accomplishment of which is predicated on the all-out efforts of every Chinese citizen. Such "passive resistance," if we may term it so, is a matter of considerable concern to Hua Guofeng, Deng Xiaoping, and their colleagues, since it is only by achieving the goals set for this program that they can succeed in legitimating their rule among their supporters as well as among their detractors and thereby insure a continuity of leadership and policy.

On balance, then, I would argue that the chances for political stability in China in the coming decade are very good, assuming the success of the Four Modernizations program.

## AMERICAN INTERESTS VIS-À-VIS CHINA

A realistic American policy toward China must be based on a careful assessment of American interests in Asia and the world. Such an assessment should begin, in my view, with the realization that whereas American and Chinese interests in Asia and beyond are, in many important respects, parallel, they are not identical—a point eloquently developed by Robert Scalapino. As a result, despite the very considerable improvement in US-China relations over the last decade, China is not now, nor is it likely to become, an ally of the United States.

Beyond this we might go on to say that it is in the American interest to have China neither allied with, nor actively hostile toward, the Soviet Union. Talk in Washington of "playing the China card" to influence relations with the Soviet Union has given way more recently to a realization that American interests in the triangular relationship can best be served by an evenhanded American treatment of the Soviet Union and China. As Scalapino argues, this principle, while sound in conception, in difficult to implement, given the very different levels of development and potential threats posed by the two socialist systems. A policy of evenhandedness must thus be applied by Washington with considerable skill and flexibility, and with the realization that a policy conceived of as evenhanded by its American authors may not necessarily appear evenhanded to Chinese or Soviet leaders.

Moreover, it is important to bear in mind the significance to the United States of our relationship with Japan. While rejecting the Chinese idea of a Pacific alliance of the United States, China, and Japan aimed against the Soviet Union and Vietnam, it is nonetheless clearly in the interest of this country to maintain a close and cooperative relationship with Japan as our respective ties with China are developing.

Finally, building on the lessons of the recent past, we must realize the limitations on the extent we can expect to influence foreign and domestic policy in China. Having done so, however, it is important that we continue to exercise all of the potential influence that lies within these limitations. China is interested in, and to a considerable extent reliant on, the economic and technological assistance of the United States and its Japanese and European allies to realize its modernizing goals. Within limits, then, Peking is likely to be responsive to American views on international issues in Asia.

While this responsiveness was not illustrated in China's efforts to "teach a lesson" to Vietnam in 1979, nonetheless the United States should clarify and impart its policies toward Southeast Asia to the Chinese leadership. Equally important, the United States and Japan must continue to make clear to China their interest in the peaceful evolution of the relationship between Peking and Taipei. China's current inability and its apparent lack of interest in resorting to force to resolve the Taiwan question are reinforced by its realization that Japan and the United States would be seriously alienated by any change in the current Chinese approach. As Victor Li has shown, the Taiwan question is a complex one. Nonetheless, it remains true that a peaceful resolution of this question is, after all, in China's best interest as well as that of Taiwan, the United States, and Japan.

Finally, while the results of the Carter administration's attempt to exert its leverage with other nations to enhance their observance of human rights in determining domestic policy were mixed at best, there are indications that the situation with regard to human rights in China has been improved, at least marginally, as a result of Washington's concern over the question. If this is an accurate assessment, then that concern should continue to be made manifest to the Chinese.

## AMERICA'S ROLE IN CHINA'S DEVELOPMENT

Many Americans in the last century believed that China would be won over to Christianity as the result of the work of American missionaries. Subsequently many held equally fervently to the idea that American democracy could be replicated in the Chinese polity through the work of American political emissaries. In both instances our expectations were unrealistically inflated, and the disappointment attendant on the failure to achieve these unrealistic expectations contributed to the virulence of the subsequent anti-China sentiments that characterized American policy in the period following the founding of the PRC thirty years ago.

We risk making a similar error in the economic, scientific,

and technological spheres in the decade ahead. The United States can contribute significantly to the development of the economy and of science and technology in China, but there are finite limits to the scope of this contribution—limits that have been well covered by Joyce Kallgren. Moreover, and perhaps more important, there is no reason to assume that an economically developed and technologically sophisticated China in the years ahead will replicate in all respects our own economy and our own scientific and technological establishment, or that the developmental experience will engender a political evolution similar to our own.

In addition, we need to be particularly attuned to the danger of re-creating within China an elite that, because of its ties to the West, becomes dissociated from its cultural and social ties to the rest of Chinese society. Such an elite would be particularly vulnerable to attack from those elements of the society—constituting the vast majority of the population, after all—who neither have, nor see themselves as standing to benefit from, economic and cultural relations with the outside world. A revival of xenophobia in China would serve neither Chinese nor American interests.

In developing a new relationship with China, Americans today, unlike those of preceding generations, have the advantage (though it does not necessarily always appear to us as advantageous) of being able to be self-critical. Having grown more aware of our own problems and shortcomings in recent years, we are less likely to present our experience as a panacea for other societies coping with the problems of modernization and more likely to be open to learning from others as well as teaching them. The phrase "critical assimilation of foreign experience" has been frequently seen in the Chinese press in recent months. It is a phrase that we, too, might profit by in our future dealings with China, realizing that the interaction, if it is to be successful over the long run, must be mutual.

To have reestablished relations with a quarter of the world's population is a significant first step for the American government and people to have taken. Only if we are clearheaded about the potential of this relationship, however, will we be able to move on and to avoid the pendulum swings of the past that made taking that first step so problematic. If we are realistic in our approach, we have the capability of contributing to the economic and social development of China in the years ahead and, in so doing, of enhancing the stability of its political system and thereby bettering the chances for a peaceful evolution of international relations in Asia.

# INDEX